Their Fair Share

T0353053

To Derek Roper, for his friendship and his support

Their Fair Share

Women, Power and Criticism
in the *Athenaeum*,
from Millicent Garett Fawcett to
Katherine Mansfield,
1870–1920

Marysa Demoor

Routledge
Taylor & Francis Group

LONDON AND NEW YORK

First published 2000 by Ashgate Publishing

2 Park Square, Milton Park, Abingdon, Oxfordshire OX14 4RN
52 Vanderbilt Avenue, New York, NY 10017

Routledge is an imprint of the Taylor & Francis Group, an informa business

First issued in paperback 2019

British Library Cataloguing-in-Publication Data
Demoor, Marysa
    Their fair share : women, power and criticism in the Athenaeum, from Millicent Garrett Fawcett to Katherine Mansfield. – (Nineteenth Century Series)
    1.   Athenaeum – History 2. English literature – 19th century – History and criticism
    2.   English literature – Women authors – History and criticism 4. Women and literature – Great Britain – History – 19th century
    I. Title
    820.9'9287'09034

US Library of Congress Cataloging-in-Publication Data
Library of Congress Card Number: 00-100170

ISBN 13: 978-0-7546-0118-0 (hbk)
ISBN 13: 978-0-367-88258-7 (pbk)

Contents

The Nineteenth Century General Editors' Preface

The aim of this series is to reflect, develop and extend the great burgeoning of interest in the nineteenth century that has been an inevitable feature of recent decades, as that former epoch has come more sharply into focus as a locus for our understanding not only of the past but of the contours of our modernity. Though it is dedicated principally to the publication of original monographs and symposia in literature, history, cultural analysis, and associated fields, there will be a salient role for reprints of significant text from, or about, the period. Our overarching policy is to address the spectrum of nineteenth-century studies without exception, achieving the widest scope in chronology, approach and range of concern. This, we believe, distinguishes our project from comparable ones, and means, for example, that in the relevant areas of scholarship we both recognize and cut innovatively across such parameters as those suggested by the designations 'Romantic' and 'Victorian'. We welcome new ideas, while valuing tradition. It is hoped that the world which predates yet so forcibly predicts and engages our own will emerge in parts, as a whole, and in the lively currents of debate and change that are so manifest an aspect of its intellectual, artistic and social landscape.

Vincent Newey
Joanne Shattock

University of Leicester

List of Figures

Preface

This book has been long in the making. Assembling the material was a process to which I could only return during quiet intervals. On those occasions I usually went to London, to work long hours in the City University Library and the British Library leaving my husband, Patrick, in charge of the house and the children. For him these were hard times indeed since he had to combine the duties of two parents with the responsibilities of a full-time job. But he never complained and I am deeply grateful to him for it.

My trips to London were always adventurous. Jetfoils broke down in the middle of the Channel, trains did not run because there were leaves on the rails, because the wrong kind of snow had been falling or because Britain had just braved the storm of the century (well, this happened at least a couple of times). But there were ample compensations, not only in the form of research results but also in the form of friendships. Sheila Munton, Pam Lighthill and Ralph Adams at the City University Library were always helpful, interested and encouraging. Any depressed researcher will feel reborn after talking to Sheila. The staff in the British Library too were at all times friendly and helpful in spite of the many difficulties they had to cope with during the move to the new St Pancras building. I owe thanks to all of them. Jenny Naipoule kindly and generously helped me with my research on the *Spectator* file although my queries came at a most inconvenient time for her. I am indebted to the library staffs of Cambridge University and the National Library of Scotland, to Robin Francis of the National Portrait Gallery and Miranda Taylor of the Punch Library. Thanks are due also to the editors and publishers of *Women's Writing* and *Nineteenth Century Prose* for allowing me to reproduce parts of my articles first published in those journals.

My colleagues, both in Belgium and abroad, had to put up with me and such divergent moods as euphoria and self-doubt. Jurgen Pieters, Erik Thoen and Geert Lernout probably bore the brunt of this. To Jurgen en Geert I am also grateful for reading part of this book and for telling me to get on with it. But it was probably Dame Gillian Beer who was the first to encourage me in my research. She, Linda K. Hughes, Rosemary VanArsdel, Laurel Brake and Janet Todd remained interested and supportive throughout. Laurel I should, in addition, like to thank for offering to read some of the work in spite of her many commitments.

The anonymous reader of the book made many helpful comments and I am thankful for those. I hope to have integrated them as he or she hoped I would. To Joanne Shattock, finally, I am deeply indebted for believing in this book.

Derek Roper read it all. He sent me his honest comments, seasoned with funny drawings and other jokes which turned his criticism into a most enjoyable experience.

'And some turn critics nature meant for fools'
(*Vernon Lee's Letters*, p. 53)

Chapter 1

Introduction

The 'Marked File'

In the course of my work as co-editor of the Athenaeum Indexing Project I spent hours in the company of the 'marked file', the editor's copy of the *Athenaeum* (1828–1921) which reveals the names of the anonymous reviewers of this Victorian weekly (see figure 1.1). From about 1830, the year Charles Wentworth Dilke assumed control over the paper's management, up to 1919, when the new editor, John Middleton Murry, introduced signed reviews, the successive editors (or their assistants) scribbled the name of every contributor in their copy of the weekly. Only a limited number of volumes during the early years of its existence, and some of the contributions published in the war years, were left unmarked.[1]

The pale green leather-bound volumes of this 'marked file' were carefully preserved first in the offices of *The New Statesman* and then in the Special Collections Room of the City University Library. One of my responsibilities in the late 1980s was to copy the names of the anonymous reviewers in long hand on index cards, so as to identify those writers by means of all the available reference works, biographical dictionaries, library catalogues, and so on.[2] The job was not always a very exciting one. Occasionally I came across the names of Victorians whose fame survived or even grew during the twentieth century. Overall, however, it appeared that the successive editors preferred to stick to a relatively small group of not always very well-known reviewers on whose competence and honesty they could rely. When reaching the 1870s, however, I noticed a significant growth in the number of reviews by women. Of course, the weekly had not been totally without its women contributors up to then; in fact, Geraldine Jewsbury (1812–1880) had been one of its most prolific reviewers in the 1850s and 1860s with some 2,300 book reviews to her 'marked name'.[3] Her subject matter and that of her female colleagues was mainly restricted to literature, local history and

---

[1] One will look in vain for the names of the contributors to the volumes covering 1828, 1829, 1830(II), 1832, 1835, 1836, 1837, 1838, 1844 and to many of the monthly issues in 1917 and 1918.

[2] Some of the results are now available on the City University internet website: web.soi.city.ac.uk/cisr/athenaeum.

[3] Monica Frykstedt, *Geraldine Jewsbury's 'Athenaeum' Reviews*, Uppsala: Uppsala University Press, 1986, p. 15.

social matters. Other women reviewers who contributed more than just the odd review for the weekly in those first decades were Hannah Lawrance, Lady Morgan and Jane Williams.[4] In the 1870s, however, and even more clearly in

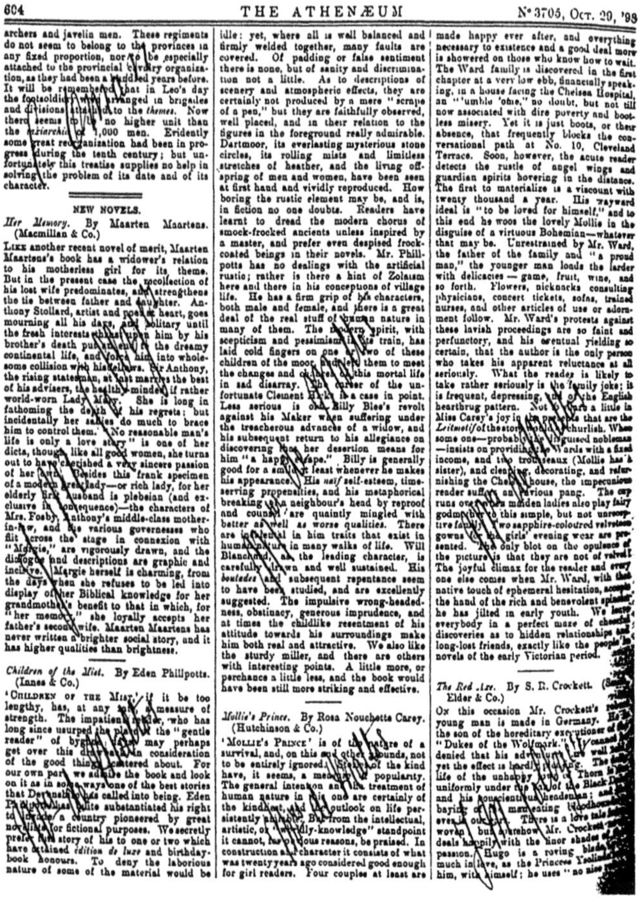

604 THE ATHENÆUM N° 3705, Oct. 29, '98

archers and javelin men. These regiments do not seem to belong to the provinces in any fixed proportion, nor to be especially attached to the provincial cavalry organization, as they had been a hundred years before. It will be remembered that in Leo's day the footsoldiers were arranged in brigades and divisions attached to the *themes*. Now there seems to be no higher unit than the *chiliarchia* of 1,000 men. Evidently some great reorganization had been in progress during the tenth century; but unfortunately this treatise supplies no help in solving the problem of its date and of its character.

NEW NOVELS.

Her Memory. By Maarten Maartens. (Macmillan & Co.)

Like another recent novel of merit, Maarten Maartens's book has a widower's relation to his motherless girl for its theme. But in the present case the recollection of his lost wife predominates, and strengthens the tie between father and daughter. Anthony Stollard, artist and poet at heart, goes mourning all his days, and solitary until the fresh interests thrust upon him by his brother's death put an end to the dreamy continental life, and force him into wholesome collision with his fellows. Sir Anthony, the rising statesman, at last marries the best of his advisers, the healthy-minded, if rather world-worn Lady Mary. She is long in fathoming the depth of his regrets; but incidentally her sallies do much to brace him to control them. "No reasonable man's life is only a love story" is one of her dicta, though, like all good women, she turns out to have cherished a very sincere passion of her own. Besides this frank specimen of a modern great lady—or rich lady, for her elderly first husband is plebeian (and exclusive in consequence)—the characters of Mrs. Fosby, Anthony's middle-class mother-in-law, and the various governesses who flit across the stage in connexion with "Margie," are vigorously drawn, and the dialogue and descriptions are graphic and incisive. Margie herself is charming, from the days when she refuses to be led into display of her Biblical knowledge for her grandmother's benefit to that in which, for "her memory," she loyally accepts her father's second wife. Maarten Maartens has never written a brighter social story, and it has higher qualities than brightness.

Children of the Mist. By Eden Phillpotts. (Innes & Co.)

'Children of the Mist,' if it be too lengthy, has, at any rate, a measure of strength. The impatient reader, who has long since usurped the place of the "gentle reader" of bygone days, may perhaps get over this drawback in consideration of the good things scattered about. For our own part we admire the book and look on it as in some ways one of the best stories that Devonshire has called into being. Eden Phillpotts has quite substantiated his right to invade a country pioneered by great novelists for fictional purposes. We secretly prefer this story of his to one or two which have attained *édition de luxe* and birthday-book honours. To deny the laborious nature of some of the material would be idle: yet, where all is well balanced and firmly welded together, many faults are covered. Of padding or false sentiment there is none, but of sanity and discrimination not a little. As to descriptions of scenery and atmospheric effects, they are certainly not produced by a mere "scrape of a pen," but they are faithfully observed, well placed, and in their relation to the figures in the foreground really admirable. Dartmoor, its everlasting mysterious stone circles, its rolling mists and limitless stretches of heather, and the living offspring of men and women, have been seen at first hand and vividly reproduced. How boring the rustic element may be, and is, in fiction no one doubts. Readers have learnt to dread the modern chorus of smock-frocked ancients unless inspired by a master, and prefer even despised frock-coated beings in their novels. Mr. Phillpotts has no dealings with the artificial rustic; rather is there a hint of Zolaism here and there in his conceptions of village life. He has a firm grip of his characters, both male and female, and there is a great deal of the real stuff of human nature in many of them. The modern spirit, with scepticism and pessimism in its train, has laid cold fingers on one or two of these children of the moor, and left them to meet the changes and chances of this mortal life in sad disarray. The career of the unfortunate Clement Hicks is a case in point. Less serious is old Billy Blee's revolt against his Maker when suffering under the treacherous advances of a widow, and his subsequent return to his allegiance on discovering that her desertion means for him "a happy escape." Billy is generally good for a smile at least whenever he makes his appearance. His *naïf* self-esteem, time-serving propensities, and his metaphorical breaking of a neighbour's head by reproof and counsel are quaintly mingled with better as well as worse qualities. There are in[illegible] in him traits that exist in human nature in many walks of life. Will Blanchard, as the leading character, is carefully drawn and well sustained. His *boutades* and subsequent repentance seem to have been studied, and are excellently suggested. The impulsive wrong-headedness, obstinacy, generous imprudence, and at times the childlike resentment of his attitude towards his surroundings make him both real and attractive. We also like the sturdy miller, and there are others with interesting points. A little more, or perchance a little less, and the book would have been still more striking and effective.

Mollie's Prince. By Rosa Nouchette Carey. (Hutchinson & Co.)

'Mollie's Prince' is of the nature of a survival, and, on this and other grounds, not to be entirely ignored. Stories of the kind have, it seems, a measure of popularity. The general intention and the treatment of human nature in this one are certainly of the kindliest, and the outlook on life persistently amiable. But from the intellectual, artistic, or "worldly-knowledge" standpoint it cannot, for obvious reasons, be praised. In construction and character it consists of what was twenty years ago considered good enough for girl readers. Four couples at least are made happy ever after, and everything necessary to existence and a good deal more is showered on those who know how to wait. The Ward family is discovered in the first chapter at a very low ebb, financially speaking, in a house facing the Chelsea Hospital, an "'umble 'ome," no doubt, but not till now associated with dire poverty and bootless misery. Yet it is just boots, or their absence, that frequently blocks the conversational path at No. 10, Cleveland Terrace. Soon, however, the acute reader detects the rustle of angel wings and guardian spirits hovering in the distance. The first to materialize is a viscount with twenty thousand a year. His wayward ideal is "to be loved for himself," and to this end he woos the lovely Mollie in the disguise of a virtuous Bohemian—whatever that may be. Unrestrained by Mr. Ward, the father of the family and "a proud man," the younger man loads the larder with delicacies — game, fruit, wine, and so forth. Flowers, nicknacks consulting physicians, concert tickets, sofas, trained nurses, and other articles of use or adornment follow. Mr. Ward's protests against these lavish proceedings are so faint and perfunctory, and his eventual yielding so certain, that the author is the only person who takes his apparent reluctance at all seriously. What the reader is likely to take rather seriously is the family joke; it is frequent, depressing, and of the English hearthrug pattern. Not to share a little in Miss Carey's joy in the presents that are the *Leitmotif* of the story would be churlish. When some one—probably the disguised nobleman—insists on providing the Wards with a fixed income, and two trousseaux (Mollie has a sister), and cleaning, decorating, and refurnishing the Chelsea house, the impecunious reader suffers an envious pang. The cup runs over when maiden ladies also play fairy godmother to this simple, but not unreceptive family. Two sapphire-coloured velveteen gowns for the girls' evening wear are presented. The only blot on the opulence of the picture is that they are not of velvet! The joyful climax for the reader and every one else comes when Mr. Ward, with that native touch of ephemeral hesitation, accepts the hand of the rich and benevolent spinster he has jilted in early youth. We leave everybody in a perfect maze of cheerful discoveries as to hidden relationships and long-lost friends, exactly like the people in novels of the early Victorian period.

The Red Axe. By S. R. Crockett. (Smith, Elder & Co.)

On this occasion Mr. Crockett's young man is made in Germany. He is the son of the hereditary executioner of the "Dukes of the Wolfmark." It cannot be denied that his adventures are well [illegible], yet the effect is hardly pleasing. The [illegible] life of the unhappy [illegible] Thorn is [illegible] uniformly under the [illegible] of the Black D[illegible] and his conscientious headsman; and [illegible] baying of the man-eating bloodhounds [illegible] even in our [illegible]. There is a love tale [illegible] woven, but somehow Mr. Crockett [illegible] deals happily with the finer shades of passion. Hugo is a roving blade, [illegible] much in love, as the Princess Ysolinde [illegible] him, with himself; he uses "no nice [illegible]

Figure 1.1 The 'marked file' of the *Athenaeum*, October 1898

[4] Early contributors of note are Sarah Austin, 1834–1856 (16 reviews); Elizabeth Barrett, 1842 (6 reviews); Mary Margaret Busk, 1833–1840 (27 reviews); Louisa Costello, 1841–1853 (21 reviews); Cornelia Augusta Hewitt Crosse, 1865 (2 reviews); Madame de Peyronnet, 1850–1852 (9 reviews); Florence Doran, 1865 (1 review); Maria Dover Walker Dilke, 1849 (1 review); Elizabeth Gaskell, 1851 (2 reviews); Anna Jameson, 1843 (1 review); Julia Kavanagh, 1847 (7 reviews); Hannah Lawrance, 1830–1858 (206 reviews); Eliza Linton, 1859 (1 review); Lady Morgan, 1833–1843 (122 reviews); Dinah Maria Mulock, 1848–1849 (16 reviews); Caroline Norton, 1853 (1 review); Jane Sinnett, 1840–1860 (9 reviews); Frances Trollope, 1855–1861 (4 reviews); Jane Williams, 1839 and 1860 (188 reviews); Eleanor Hervey (1 review).

the 1880s and 1890s, the 'marked file' shows a noticeable increase of reviews by women on a much broader variety of subjects.

My findings at the time intrigued me. The fact of women contributing to periodicals is not all that surprising.[5] Yet most research done so far has, of necessity, concentrated on the women's magazines and signed reviews. Indeed, it is almost impossible to investigate the degree to which the sphere of influence of women reviewers extended beyond subjects that were deemed proper for them. Most Victorian journals upheld the policy of anonymous reviewing. The unlocking of some treasures of those periodicals by the *Wellesley Index to Victorian Periodicals 1824–1900*, has so far failed to change the current assumptions about the gender of the typical Victorian reviewer. Besides, the above-mentioned women reviewers do not figure prominently in its columns: the prolific Geraldine Jewsbury, for instance, is listed in volumes II and III for one and three articles respectively.

I began my research for this book by compiling a list of all the contributions by women, arranging the reviews under the names of the reviewers so as to find out exactly how frequently they reviewed and which subjects were assigned to them. Apart from that I tried to identify those reviewers precisely and to reconstruct the lives behind the names for, in spite of the influence of the *Athenaeum*, its reviewers were not always as well known as a present-day researcher would want them to be.[6]

Curiously enough, even those women who eventually did achieve some fame, have been left unmentioned by Leslie Marchand in his seminal work on the journal. But then Marchand concentrated his research on the early period of the journal, up to 1846, when Charles Wentworth Dilke (1789–1864) was still its editor. The criticism published during Norman MacColl's (1843–1904) editorship and Dilke's grandson, Sir Charles Wentworth Dilke's (1843–1911) proprietorship, was only cursorily glanced at.[7] Since Marchand there have been several laudable attempts by different researchers at studying the *Athenaeum*, its critical views and its reviewers. One notable concerted effort was the special issue of the *Victorian Periodicals Review* in 1990, devoted to the weekly and presenting it from several angles.[8]

---

[5] The year 1870 is generally taken to be a landmark in women's histories, see for example Geneviève Fraisse and Michelle Perrot, eds, *A History of Women in the West. Emerging Feminism from Revolution to World War*, Cambridge, Mass.: Belknap Press, 1993, p. 441.

[6] Identifying those reviewers might seem an easy task once one has the surnames, but the reverse proved true in the case of some very common names. And then there is the fact that maiden names disappear upon marriage and cannot be traced in biographical dictionaries: some of those reviewers simply vanished into oblivion.

[7] Norman MacColl was succeeded by Vernon Rendall (1869–1960) in 1901. See Leslie A. Marchand, *The Athenaeum. A Mirror of Victorian Culture*, Chapel Hill:University of North Carolina Press, 1941.

[8] *Victorian Periodicals Review*, spring and winter 1990. Before that, however, Jeanne Fahnestock had published 'Authors of Book Reviews in the *Athenaeum*, 1830–1900', *Victorian Periodicals Newsletter*, 15 (March 1972), pp. 47–52.

So far, however, the gender issue has been left out of the picture and very little is known about the critical writings of the poet Augusta Webster or the art critic Emilia Strong.[9]   Hence, their part in the cultural discourse of the late nineteenth and early twentieth century has hitherto been disregarded.   Of course, as stated above, this is not the first book to concentrate on the phenomenon of the growing numbers of female professional writers at the end of the nineteenth century.[10] Women's informal networks have been touched upon in several recent studies. Martha Vicinus's *Independent Women. Work and Community for Single Women 1850–1920* (1985) is possibly the best known and certainly one of the most valuable analyses.[11] Yet women's part in the critical reception of the age has remained largely undisclosed because of that policy of anonymity mentioned earlier. Finding that more women wrote criticism than is generally surmised one automatically wants to find out whether their gender had indeed been obliterated in their writings, had become invisible to their readers. In other words, did these anonymous women reviewers who contributed to the *Athenaeum* disappear behind a male-encoded review? Or did they reveal their gender in the language they used, the views they defended, the subjects they broached or the kind of books they accepted to review?

Another line of my research has led me to (re)construct a paradigmatic woman reviewer of the *Athenaeum*. Who were the women chosen to assess new publications of their age, why were they chosen, and did they derive any benefit from this part of their professional activities?

Finally, I hoped to relate the woman reviewer of the *Athenaeum* to her colleagues writing for other journals such as the *Spectator*, to the early and mid-Victorian woman of letters and to the generation who took up the banner after the First World War.

Aims and Scope

Automatically, the above aims led me to concentrate on the life and writings of a few representative women reviewers. The women selected were chosen on

---

[9] So was, as a matter of fact, Arthur Symons's reviewing for the weekly, although his contributions have since been faithfully recorded by Karl Beckson, Ian Fletcher, Lawrence W. Markert and John Stokes, eds, in: *Arthur Symons: A Bibliography*, Greensboro, NC: ELT–Press, 1990.

[10] See among others Monica Frykstedt, *Geraldine Jewsbury's 'Athenaeum' Reviews* (1986); Margaret Beetham, *A Magazine of her Own? Domesticity and Desire in the Woman's Magazine, 1800–1914* (1996); Bonnie Andersen and Judith Zinsser, *A History of their Own*, vol. II (1988).

[11] Other relevant studies are: Philippa Levine, *Feminist Lives in Victorian England. Private Roles and Public Commitment* (1990); Ruth Brandon, *The New Women and Old Men. Love, Sex and the Woman Question* (1990); Barbara Caine, *Victorian Feminists* (1992).

the basis of the quality of their reviews or the quality of the works they had been assigned. There was a natural correlation in that important books were nearly invariably treated by important reviewers. To be allowed to open a new issue was an honour not normally granted to women contributors. But most of the reviewers dealt with in the following pages were occasionally responsible for the opening columns.

As might be expected, the 'soft subjects' were the first in which women were allowed to have their say: prose fiction, 'new novels', and the gossip column probably being the most readily accessible ones. Prose fiction, as has been indicated, was 'women's field' from the very beginning, with the Jewsbury sisters, Maria and Geraldine, writing many of the reviews in the first decades of the journal's existence. Women's proficiency in the field of poetry was not as easily recognised; poetry remained a male-encoded topic for a long time. Indeed, Laurel Brake feels confident enough to classify poetry in the Victorian age alongside politics, science, psychology, classics and drama as an area of knowledge 'associated with men.'[12] When women infiltrate this field one may interpret this in two ways: as women acquiring their fair share of the market, or as a feminisation (read 'devaluation') of poetry as genre. If poetry was, by the end of the century, almost entirely women's province, with quite successful writers like Augusta Webster, Mathilde Blind, Edith Nesbit and Rosamund Marriott Watson (alias 'Graham Thomson') articulating their opinions in the *Athenaeum*'s pages, other fields were clearly hard-won bastions which were soon recaptured by male colleagues. Millicent Garrett Fawcett was to author several reviews on political economy in the 1870s and early 1880s, yet she relinquished that position after the death of her husband and the subject became Reginald Palgrave's. Similarly, Jane Ellen Harrison was asked to write on the classics with a certain frequency around the turn of the century, but she never really turned the subject into her rightful column, and Ernest Gardner colonised the field in the years preceding the First World War.

In the course of my research I have tried not to be too much influenced by certain commonly-held preconceptions about reviewing in general and the *Athenaeum* in particular. In fact, I have had to adapt my own (and other people's) views of the 'fabric' of the *Athenaeum* to my findings, depending on the reviews I was looking at, the year I was dealing with. It soon dawned on me that it was very hard to make sweeping statements about such a thing as 'the' *Athenaeum*. This journal had been a living composition, and its components had been constantly changing. Its contributors grew older, changed their opinions and were eventually replaced by others. Controlling, regulating and influencing this 'living matter' were, on the one hand, the editor or the weekly's editorial management, and on the other hand, the reading public and the market mechanism associated with that. Pierre Bourdieu tries to frame the living matter when stating that it is 'impossible to understand how

---

[12] Laurel Brake, *Subjugated Knowledges. Journalism, Gender & Literature in the Nineteenth Century*, Basingstoke: Macmillan, 1994, p. 30.

dispositions come to be adjusted to positions (so that the journalist is adjusted to his newspaper and consequently to that paper's readership, and the readers are adjusted to the paper and so to the journalist) unless one is aware that the objective structures of the field of production give rise to categories of perception which structure the perception and appreciation of its products'.[13] He believes it is the 'place', 'the site' which is of importance. In our case, this signifies that the *Athenaeum* points to a certain readership because of the homology between what Bourdieu calls the 'field of production' and the 'field of consumption'. Yet the interaction between the parties involved is difficult to assess. It is obvious that authors anxiously awaited the reviews of their books in the *Athenaeum* and, indeed, after the event sometimes sent letters to the weekly in the hope of correcting the reviewer's judgement and swaying the public's opinion, but it is all but impossible to find out the extent to which reviews actually boosted or decreased book sales. Nor do reviews always anticipate the popular reception of a book, although Vernon Rendall, the editor of the *Athenaeum* in the first decade of the twentieth century, once offered this rather dejected view of the overall quality of literary reviews and the general public's alleged dependence on them:

> The public moves slowly, but surely; some day, perhaps, it will learn that advertisements and achievement are different things. At present it has, perhaps, got so far as to realise that most criticism is biased and comparatively worthless, thus rendering nugatory the efforts of the honourable minority to assist on the choice of books. (*Athenaeum*, 1 January 1910)

'Advertisements and achievement' are different things, yet they may at times point to overlaps in the field of cultural production. In the case of publications they may reach the same audience, for instance. So the textual content of the one item may give a clue as to the composition of the reading public of the other. Because advertisements seem to conjure up a more precise picture of the readership they want to influence, their relevance seems beyond doubt. Monica Fryckstedt has already pointed to the unique position of the *Athenaeum* as a research tool for those wishing to study the reading habits of the mid-Victorians. The weekly had become widely available to the middle classes when its price was reduced from 4d to 3d in 1861.[14] In her article Frykstedt concentrates on the book advertisements, supported by John Sutherland's claim that the weekly was 'the main vehicle for book advertising in the Victorian period'. Interestingly, looking at the subjects of the books advertised, the middle-class readership of the *Athenaeum* was not exclusively male: cookery books were advertised next to popular science and political history. But the point is made more forcefully when one looks at the job offers or

---

[13] Pierre Bourdieu, *The Field of Cultural Production. Essays on Art and Literature*, ed. Randal Johnson, Cambridge: Polity Press, 1993, p. 95.

[14] Frykstedt, *Geraldine Jewsbury's 'Athenaeum' Reviews*, p. 93.

advertisements of people looking for jobs. In every issue young women were offering their services as governesses, translators, typists or teachers. Special series of lectures, especially aimed at ladies, were announced. In the issue of 3 February 1872 Emily Faithfull announces the resumption of her classes in 'reading aloud, public speaking'. If, therefore, the criticism published in the *Athenaeum* seems male-dominated, its adverts indicate that its readership included middle-class women.

Laurel Brake has positioned her *Subjugated Knowledges* in the field which D.F. McKenzie has labelled the 'sociology of texts': 'historical, textual, *and* (but not only) literary, and drawing on contemporary theory'.[15] This book follows her example in that it wants to look at the historical circumstances in which a number of late-Victorian professional women writers published texts in one particular periodical. The practice to some extent ties in with what the New Historicists attempt to do, especially in the use of the anecdotal. And some of the theoretical thinking is borrowed from Pierre Bourdieu's writings about the field of cultural production, and the functions of artistic mediators.

Brake also pointed to the relationship of the periodical to 'authorship' as such: 'The nature of "authorship" in the period almost inevitably included periodical publication as one source of readers and income, and a determining format'. This calls into question the persistent idea that periodicals became important only to the authors of the modernist generation after 1918. Moreover, as will appear from the following chapters, the nature of authorship was no different for the women writing at the end of nineteenth century. Assignments for periodicals were inextricably bound up with their professionalism. Women authors saw the financial rewards of their creative writings supplemented by the fees they earned as regular contributors to well-paying periodicals. The professional positions of these women may be opposed to or (at least) juxtaposed with the romanticised representations of the unsuccessful female hack writer in the novels of the period. As Penny Boumelha has argued, 'with professionalisation comes a certain status of self-worth often new to women; on the other hand journalism places writing in the area of commerce, money, paid labour, and the ensuing argument'.[16]

This latter awareness will be explored in the following pages mainly in light of the reviews of a number of successful, often vigorously feminist women reviewers who may have had to weigh their convictions against their need for this job and the power it entailed. For, as Pierre Bourdieu rightly contended:

All critics declare not only their judgement of the work but also their claim to the right to talk about it and judge it. In short, they take part in a struggle for the monopoly of legitimate discourse about the work of art, and consequently in the production of the value of the work of art.[17]

---

[15] Brake, *Subjugated Knowledges*, p. xi.
[16] Penny Boumelha, 'The Woman of Genius and the Woman of Grub Street: Figures of the Female Writer in British *Fin-de-siècle* Fiction,' *ELT*, 40:2 (1997), p. 166.
[17] Bourdieu, *The Field of Cultural Production*, p. 36.

To anticipate to some extent my findings, it seems to me that female critics gained this powerful place in the legitimate discourse about the work of art or any other publication they had been assigned, at the expense of concealing or even losing their gender when they wrote reviews. Virginia Woolf experienced this conflict between her gender and the task of the reviewer when writing her very first review. She couched the experience in that powerful visual image of killing the 'Angel in the House'.

Chapter 2

The Woman of Letters in Transition, 1870–1910

I say all the fault's with God himself
who puts too many women in the world.
We ought to die off reasonably and leave
as many as the men want, none to waste.[1]

Recent feminist criticism has led to a number of revisionist studies of Victorian women as authors, readers, translators and editors, and to alternative analyses of women's periodicals; but the subject of 'the woman reviewer' is still relatively untrodden ground.[2] Seminal articles and books such as those by John Gross (*The Rise and Fall of the Man of Letters*), John Woolford ('Periodicals and the practice of literary criticism'), and Isobel Armstrong (*Victorian Scrutinies*) invariably assumed a male reviewer. Women's criticism was mentioned only sporadically and nearly always in studies covering the critical reception of canonical authors and their books as, for instance, in the prestigious Critical Heritage series. It was, therefore, always presented as a negligible part in the literary production of the Victorian age.[3] There were some notable exceptions to this general rule: Elaine Showalter and Kate Flint mention a small selection of women reviewers in their respective analyses,[4] Monica Frykstedt demonstrated the influence and ubiquity of Geraldine Jewsbury in the 'New Novels' column of the *Athenaeum*[5] and, fairly recently,

---

[1] Augusta Webster, 'A Castaway', *Portraits*, 1870; rptd. *Victorian Women Poets. An Anthology*, Angela Leighton and Margaret Reynolds, eds, Oxford: Blackwell, 1995, p. 440.
[2] For recent studies of the woman's magazine see Marjorie Ferguson, *Forever Feminine: Women's Magazines and the Cult of Femininity*, Aldershot: Gower, 1983; Ros Ballaster, et al., eds, *Women's Worlds: Ideology, Femininity and the Woman's Magazine*, London: Macmillan, 1991; and Margaret Beetham, *A Magazine of Her Own? Domesticity and Desire in the Woman's Magazine, 1800–1914* (1996).
[3] Ellen Miller Casey, in an interesting article on the reviews of women's novels in the *Athenaeum*, does not mention the relevance of the reviewer's gender either, even though Geraldine Jewsbury's considerable part in the 'novels of the week' section of the 1860s and 1870s was identified and discussed by Monica Frykstedt in 1986; see Casey, 'Edging Women Out', *Victorian Studies*, 39:2 (Winter 1996), pp. 151–71.
[4] Elaine Showalter, *A Literature of Their Own. From Charlotte Brontë to Doris Lessing*, London: Virago, 1979. p. 177; Kate Flint, *The Woman Reader 1837–1914*, Oxford: Oxford University Press, 1993, pp. 164–5.
[5] See Frykstedt, *Geraldine Jewsbury's 'Athenaeum' Reviews*, 1986.

both *Nineteenth Century Prose* and the *Victorian Periodicals Review* paid special attention to the involvement of women, among them women critics, with Victorian periodicals.[6]

In a statistical overview of women authors, as listed in the *Cambridge Bibliography of English Literature*, Nigel Cross concludes that a third of the professional women writers of the Victorian age were novelists, half were children's writers, 14 per cent were poets and only 3 per cent specialised in other types of literature. 'Men', Cross concludes, 'appear much more versatile – thanks to their university education'. Within the group of male writers he is also able to distinguish a group of 'prose writers', critics and essayists, in other words, the 'man of letters' type, which appears to be exclusively male.[7] Relying on one bibliographical source, the *CBEL*, which has since proved to be rather deficient with regard to the representation of professional women writers, Cross could only have reached the conclusion he did reach. 'Marked files' of Victorian weeklies associated with anonymous reviewing, such as the *Athenaeum* or the *Spectator*, suggest a different picture and clearly show the extent to which women were involved in the literary marketplace.

The *Spectator*'s 'marked file', like that of the *Athenaeum,* was carefully preserved. Yet its file only starts in the year 1880 although like the *Athenaeum*, the weekly had been launched as early as 1828. The file lists authors and titles of contributions with a view to paying those anonymous reviewers. It is organised quite differently from the *Athenaeum* file, however, since it consists of several exercise books in which current editors or their assistants recorded the facts and figures. The notes present a much better organised record than the 'marked file' of the *Athenaeum*, the names being written out in full in neat handwriting. Many *Spectator* contributors also contributed to the *Athenaeum*: John Dennis, Helen Zimmern, Malcolm MacColl and W.A.M. Rossetti are names we encounter in both files. Other contributors, however, reserved their writings for one of the two periodicals: R.H. Hutton, for instance, is associated manifestly and exclusively with the *Spectator*.[8]

An interesting aspect of the *Spectator* file is its specifying the exact fees long before the *Athenaeum*'s 'marked file' does. From 1897 on the *Spectator* has systematic monthly surveys of expenses per author, per subject, showing that male journalists earned as much as (and not more than) their female colleagues. The *Athenaeum* starts mentioning the fees, after the contributor's name (that is, scribbled through the column), in 1906. The *Spectator*'s monthly synopses also list the names according to the authors' prominence that month but, since that prominence depends largely on the contribution of leaders,

---

[6] See the issues of the *Victorian Periodicals Review* for summer 1996 and spring 1998 and the *Nineteenth Century Prose* issue of spring 1997.
[7] Nigel Cross, *The Common Writer. Life in Nineteenth-Century Grub Street*, Cambridge: Cambridge University Press, 1985, p. 167
[8] Hutton's life and writings are discussed in an introduction to a selection of his reviews edited by Robert Tener and Malcolm Woodfield; see Tener and Woodfield, eds, *A Victorian Spectator. Uncollected Writings of R.H. Hutton*, Bedminster: Bristol Press, 1989.

women hardly ever occupy one of those top positions. They would write the occasional sub-leader but their contributions were mainly reserved to the literature department (see figure 2.1).[9]

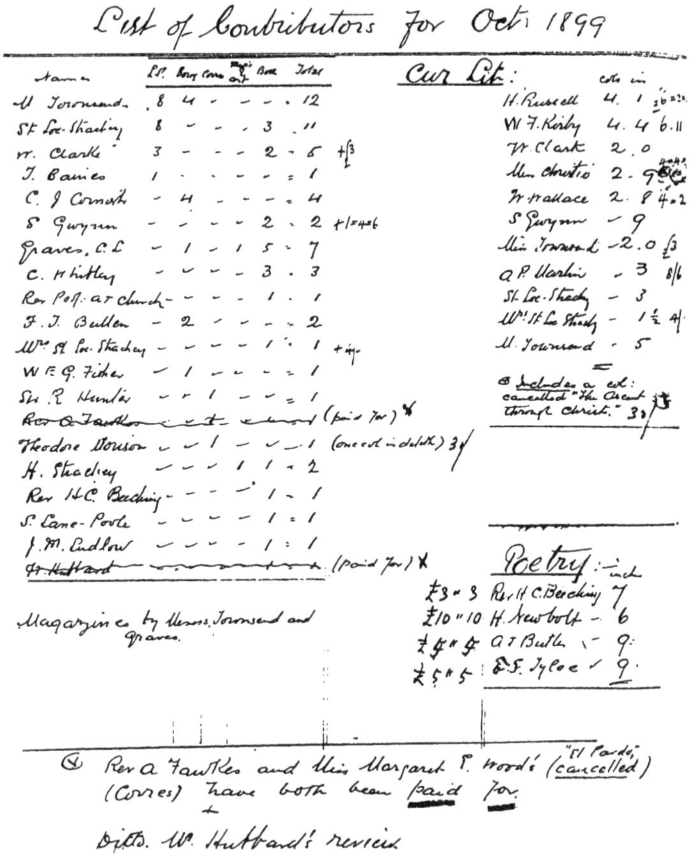
List of Contributors for Oct. 1899

Cur. Lit.

Poetry

Figure 2.1 The 'marked file' of the *Spectator*, October 1899

A fair remuneration contributed significantly to the professionalisation of the woman writer. Virginia Woolf's first attempt at writing was, as she confessed many years later, also a review. The money it yielded, enough to buy a Persian cat, encouraged her to write more : 'I grew ambitious'. Next she wanted to buy a car and therefore felt the need to write a novel.[10]

[9] Julia Wedgwood, Lucy Clifford and Miss Dillwyn, for instance, produced sub-leaders for the *Spectator* in 1880, see chapter 4.

[10] Virginia Woolf, 'Professions for Women', 1942; *Norton Anthology of Literature by Women*, Sandra Gilbert and Susan Gubar, eds, New York, London: Norton, 1996, p. 1345.

The Importance of Being Anonymous

One of the reasons for women's invisibility in periodicals such as the *Spectator* or the *Athenaeum* resulted from their own efforts to disguise their gender whenever they took to writing. The attitude ties in with the then widespread practice among women authors of choosing a male pseudonym. Elaine Showalter and others have discussed women's reasons for adopting pseudonyms when venturing into the male sphere of the printed text.[11] As a matter of fact, reviewers were invariably wary when new – seemingly male – authors appeared on the literary scene, especially when they seemed to be extremely well acquainted with a world generally associated with women.[12] Ellen Miller Casey has convicingly demonstrated the degree to which reviewers engaged in speculation about the novelists' gender.[13]

The situation was different with regard to periodical publications since reviews were usually anonymous whether written by men or women. Readers hardly ever speculated about the reviewers' gender. The person behind the review was inconsequential, his or her individuality had to disappear behind the ideological uniform of the periodical in question. In William Beech Thomas's history of the *Spectator*, Leigh Hunt is quoted as having said that 'the paper was so well edited and written that all the articles seemed to have emanated from the same pen'.[14] A reviewer invariably wrote from a powerful pulpit position, delivering the verdict on the book in question. The 'we' was right. Nicola Thompson has likened reviewers to 'a cultural police responsible for protecting public standards and taste'.[15] Their writings were aimed at a general reading public whom they hoped to guide, counsel and coerce.[16] In a recent article on the anonymity debate by Dallas Liddle, the influential position of this corporate body of 'gentlemen-journalists' writing from a shared *esprit de corps* is mentioned as the most convincing contemporary argument in favour of anonymous articles.[17] The anonymous persona behind the *Athenaeum* reviews, however, did not apply that uniform set of literary criteria which it was (and is) generally assumed to have used, as will be shown further on in this

---

[11] See Showalter, *A Literature*, p. 91; Sandra Gilbert and Susan Gubar, *The Madwoman in the Attic. The Woman Writer and the Nineteenth Century Literary Imagination*, New Haven and London: Yale University Press, 1979, 1984, p. 65; Julia Swindells, *Victorian Writing & Working Women*, Cambridge: Polity Press, 1985, p. 102.

[12] Nicola Thompson demonstrates in her study how Anthony Trollope's anonymous publications were ironically and erroneously attributed to a female hand (see Nicola Diane Thompson, *Reviewing Sex. Gender and the Reception of Victorian Novels*, Basingstoke: Macmillan, 1996, pp. 66ff.)

[13] Miller Casey, 'Edging Women Out', 1996, p. 54.

[14] William Beech Thomas, *The Story of the Spectator 1828–1928*, London: Methuen, 1928, p. 231.

[15] Thompson, *Reviewing Sex*, pp. 3–4.

[16] On readership see Thompson, *Reviewing Sex*, pp. 120ff.

[17] Dallas Liddle, 'Salesmen, Sportsmen, Mentors: Anonymity and Mid-Victorian Theories of Journalism', *Victorian Studies*, 41:1 (Autumn 1997), pp. 31–68, pp. 53ff.

study, or perhaps one should say there was no such single persona in the case of the *Athenaeum*.

It is not difficult to imagine the feeling of power which the simple act of reviewing imparted to women reviewers, although the pleasure was a secret one which had to be enjoyed in private. Indeed, Victorian commentators generally agreed that anonymity enhanced power rather than diminished it, and this was certainly much appreciated by the unknown author of an article. As Anthony Trollope put it, 'an ordinary reader would not care to have his books recommended to him by Jones; but the recommendation of the great unknown comes to him with all the weight of *The Times*, the *Spectator*, or the *Saturday[Review]*'.[18]

UNSIGNED MAGAZINE ARTICLES.

Keats-Jones. "I SAY, JUST LOOK WHAT SOME ANONYMOUS ASS IN *THE KNACKER* SAYS ABOUT THOSE SONNETS OF MINE, WHICH YOU TOLD ME YOU CONSIDERED AS GOOD AS WORDSWORTH'S!"
Shelley-Brown. "MY DEAR FELLOW, WE'RE IN THE SAME BOAT! YOU KNOW THAT LAST BOOK OF MINE THAT YOU SAID YOU LIKED SO MUCH! WELL, JUST SEE WHAT'S SAID OF IT IN *THE GADFLY!* I WONDER WHO THE FOOL IS!"
[*Keats-Jones is the Author of the "Gadfly" review of Brown's book, and Shelley-Brown writes all the literary notices in the "Knacker."*]

Figure 2.2   'Unsigned Magazine Articles', *Punch*, 21 December 1895.

---

[18] Anthony Trollope, *Autobiography*, Oxford: Blackwell, 1929, p. 192.

Anonymity of reviews was a policy which many editors preferred to maintain until after the First World War even though the success of periodicals publishing signed reviews, such as the *Fortnightly Review* and the *Cornhill Magazine*, was a powerful incentive to change the policy.[19] The *Times Literary Supplement*, on the other hand, was to hold on to the anonymity of its reviewers until well into the 1970s, and some of its erstwhile anonymous reviewers still maintain that that policy was, and is, preferable to today's signed reviews.[20] In the case of the *Athenaeum* it appears that the reviews-section is the one where identity is least easily disclosed. Authors of letters, conference reports and poems may be identified by way of initials or even the full names; the person behind a review, however, remained unidentified whether male or female. In her article on anonymity, Mary Ruth Hiller presents an overview of the chief publications on this particular tradition as well as enumerating the advantages and disadvantages of anonymity (see also the *Punch* illustration, figure 2.2). She does not introduce the aspect of gender, however, possibly because that had disappeared together with the reviewers' names and because in the late 1970s literary scholars, like Hiller, were only beginning to look at the apparent absence of the feminine.[21] Yet, the policy of anonymity undoubtedly had advantages for potential and actual women reviewers. In the second half of the century the attitude towards professional women writers had developed into an open hostility from writers and critics towards the so-called feminisation of culture. The critic Andrew Lang, for instance, sharply complained about the lack of fairness in 'the' woman critic even though his own wife, Leonora Blanche Lang (née Alleyne), was a frequent reviewer for periodicals such as the *Saturday Review* and the *Academy*.[22] Nor did he have any qualms about 'using' her as a sagacious reader of some of his friends' books. He would then faithfully pass on her comments, giving the impression that he underwrote her opinion.[23] Yet his

---

[19] Dallas Liddle pointedly remarked on this development that 'signed journals tended to succeed, anonymous ones to fail, and that was all publishers knew and all they needed to know'. Liddle, 'Salesmen', p. 62

[20] The controversy about anonymous versus signed articles continues to rage to this day in the pages of the *London Review of Books* (1 April and 15 April 1999).

[21] Hiller, 'The Identification of Authors: The Great Victorian Enigma', J. Don Vann and Rosemary T. VanArsdel, eds, *Victorian Periodicals. A Guide to Research*, New York: MLA, 1978, p. 125. Hiller mentions 'honesty' as a definite advantage and goes on to point out that: 'Many young writers were able to get articles published that would never have appeared had the authors been required to put their names to them. In addition, editors were able to exercise a useful flexibility. They could print several articles by the same author in a single issue if they so desired, and none would be the wiser. Also, they were freer to rewrite material to suit themselves, since the final product was not the author's responsibility'.

[22] She is said to have been the one behind the disparaging review of Thomas Hardy's *Tess* in the *Saturday Review* in 1891. For Lang's comments see Marysa Demoor, ed., *Friends over the Ocean. Andrew lang's Letters to his American Friends*, Gent: Universa, 1989, p. 101.

[23] See for example Andrew Lang's undated and unpublished letter to H. Rider Haggard: 'Eric has kept my wife company in a sleepless night with neuralgia, and she thinks him very good', or 'The critic on the hearth does not think the last fight good enough for you'. (Lockwood Memorial Library, State University of New York at Buffalo).

public attitude towards women and writing was generally dismissive and essentialist. Women were the Other species: they were good at languages,[24] they had no respect for manuscripts.[25]

Not surprisingly, therefore, women writers, when faced with such stereotypical attitudes, tried to conform to the critical double standard once they themselves wielded the anonymous pen. In *Edging Women Out*, Gaye Tuchman and Nina Fortin selected Harriet Martineau, Elizabeth Rigby and Geraldine Jewsbury as typical women reviewers in their efforts to conform 'to the expectations of the men who paid them for their reviews (and to the readers who identified criticism as a male activity)'.[26] Yet one needs to remember that these three women writers belong to an earlier generation than the one treated here: the circumstances for professional women writers had changed considerably after 1870. But Tuchman and Fortin do convincingly prove the extent to which the entire publishing establishment (financially) discriminated against women novelists in the second half of the nineteenth century, again demonstrating the need for women to hide their gender if they wanted to be given fair treatment. The same line of approach is taken by Susan Drain in her article on 'Journalism and Journalists' in *Victorian Britain: An Encyclopedia*, when she explicitly points to anonymity as the gateway to the world of journalism for 'unknowns' and women. Dallas Liddle, for his part, is wary of these kinds of interpretations. 'No Victorian editor or writer I have seen, regrettably, dares to argue publicly that increased access of women to the press is one of the advantages of anonymity'.[27] It is true that such public claims are difficult to find, certainly with respect to the periodical press, but there are quite a number of private admonitions by male writers to women writers to hide their gender if they want to be fully and impartially accepted as professional writers by both the reading public and the critics. The advice George Henry Lewes gave to his partner, George Eliot, is a case in point. But others shared Lewes's opinion. In a letter from Arnold Bennett, Victorian editor, author and journalist, to the writer Lucy Clifford one finds him advising Clifford to submit her new play under a male pseudonym. But, he adds, 'you had better let me invent it for you. The ablest Women are apt to give the show away at once when they choose a masculine pseudonym. Pardon me'.[28]

---

[24] Women 'are supposed to acquire a mastery of the Teutonic speech', Lang wrote in 'To Parents and Guardians', *Illustrated London News*, vol. CI, 20 August 1892, p. 288.

[25] He claimed that: 'Women burn and sell everything. If a woman has got the letters the game is up'. Unpublished and undated letter to Richard Garnett in the Humanities Research Center, University of Texas.

[26] Gaye Tuchman with Nina E. Fortin, *Edging Women Out. Victorian Novelists, Publishers and Social Change*, London: Routledge, 1989, p. 184.

[27] Liddle, 'Salesmen', p. 34.

[28] Undated and unpublished letter, May 1914, in the possession of Mrs Alice Dilke.

The Professionalisation of the Woman Writer

The victimisation of the feminine in society came to a head in the 1890s with 'decadence' almost becoming synonymous with 'the feminine'. The explosion of the Wilde scandal merely exacerbated the latent antagonism against assertive women and suspiciously feminine men. Homophobia and misogyny went hand in hand. 'Decadent tendencies', Ruth Robbins pointed out, threatened masculinity.[29] Already a decade earlier, one of Henry James's characters in the *Bostonians* (1886) felt so strongly as to repudiate that 'most damnable feminisation'. The words may well have been James's little act of revenge after his inordinately articulate acquaintance and colleague Vernon Lee had dedicated her first novel, the satirical *roman-à-clef, Miss Brown* (1884), to Henry James, thereby (nearly) entirely reducing him to a humiliating silence when he really would have wanted to speak his mind.[30] James, Ann Ardis claims, continued to denounce New Women such as Vernon Lee and the candour of their fiction both publicly, in his fiction, and privately, in his letters to fellow-writers.[31] Ardis refers to his caricature of George Egerton in 'The Death of a Lion', and his possibly more condemnatory letter to W.D. Howells; and she summarises James's point of view in this brilliant pseudo-Jamesian metaphor: 'the house of fiction has many windows; and, ... if certain windows are opened, or broken by an overly active female elbow, the health of all its occupants might be at risk'.[32] Nigel Cross, too, had noticed James's particularly unfair treatment of women novelists, noting that the characters who were novelists tended to be distinguished artists when male but merely 'prolific', 'precious', or 'popular' when female.[33] All in all, it seemed that the woman journalist, the woman of letters, like Vernon Lee, whose male pseudonym barely disguised her masculine ambitions, increasingly had to bear the brunt of a reactionary backlash. She had come to be associated with that creature which every conservative Victorian believed to be most objectionable: the New Woman. In an article on Henry James's *The Bostonians*, Sally Ledger points to the New Woman as a 'problem, a challenge to the apparently self-identical culture of Victorianism', because she was poised to enter the masculine space.[34] Both the New Woman and the Wildean decadents, Ledger

---

[29] Ruth Robbins, 'Vernon Lee: Decadent woman?' In John Stokes, ed., *Fin de Siècle/ Fin du Globe*, London: Macmillan, 1992, p. 145.

[30] See, for instance, his letters to Grace Norton and Thomas Sergeant Perry in Leon Edel, ed., *Henry James Letters*, Cambridge, Mass.: Harvard University Press, 1974–1984, vol. III, pp. 66–7.

[31] For recent analyses of the New Woman phenomenon I refer the reader to Ann Ardis, *New Women, New Novels. Feminism and Early Modernism,* New Brunswick and London: Rutgers University Press, 1990, and Sally Ledger's *The New Woman. Fiction and Feminism at the Fin de siècle*, Manchester and New York: Manchester University Press, 1997.

[32] Ardis, *New Women, New Novels*, p. 48.

[33] Cross, *The Common Writer*, p. 186.

[34] Ledger, *The New Woman*, p. 55.

argued, 'overtly challenged Victorian sexual codes'.[35] Margaret Beetham then sees a parallel between the New Woman and the New Journalism in the sense that both were 'manifestation of and symbol for a more general crisis.'[36] For Beetham, however, the 'economic and editorial power was still retained almost entirely by metropolitan, middle-class men and in this respect the New Journalism was the Old Journalism writ large'.[37]

One of the most precise and most revelatory instruments for gauging the reaction of the general British public to a new phenomenon such as the New Woman, and all her prefigurations before she was named and framed by Sara Grand and Ouida in 1894, comes in the form of the cartoons, jokes and comments of the reactionary weekly *Punch*. Here one finds a wealth of drawings which were all meant to put off all young women who wished to follow a less conventional course of life and, possibly, thought of a writing career (figure 2.2).

Very few of the women who actually did achieve a professional literary career succeeded in obtaining 'editorial power' and those who did were usually in charge of women's magazines. In his introduction to a special issue of the *Victorian Periodicals Review* on 'Nineteenth Century Women and Periodicals', D.J. Trela claims that 'women never became editors of "major" periodicals like the *Westminster, Quarterly*, or *Blackwood's*'.[38] Using the career of Margaret Oliphant as an example, he demonstrates how hard it was for professional women writers to obtain a secure position as editor. It should be said that their male colleagues, too, very much aspired to these jobs, and often did so in vain. Andrew Lang's complaints on that score are to be found in several letters to his friends: an editorship eluded him as well, in spite of his maleness and his manifest popularity.

The advent of the New Woman journalist, New Woman editor and New Woman novelist was presented as a real menace by the frequent articles on the subject in spite of the proportionally small number of women who eventually did make it (sometimes quite painstakingly) to one of those positions.[39] Emily Crawford felt the need to defend the profession of journalism for women in a paper she read at a conference in Lucerne: she thought women wrote well and had 'in a greater degree than men the faculty of throwing life into what emanates from their pen'.[40]

The regular reporter on press business for the *Athenaeum* in that period, G.B. Stuart, was equally enthusiastic. After the first international press

---

[35] Ledger, 'The New Woman, *The Bostonians* and the Gender of Modernity', *Essays from ESSE, Barcelona English Language and Literature Studies*, Marysa Demoor and Jane Moore, eds, 3:3 (1996), p. 95.

[36] Beetham, *A Magazine of Her Own*, p. 116.

[37] Ibid., p. 130.

[38] See his introduction to the special issue of *Victorian Periodicals Review*, Summer 1996, p. 90. He does not seem to have considered George Eliot's time as unpaid assistant editor of the *Westminster Review* as falling within the relevant category.

[39] David Rubinstein, in *Before the Suffragettes* (Hemel Hempstead: Harvester Weatsheaf, 1986), points out that many of these journalists earned no more than £200 (p. 85).

[40] 'Women as Journalists', *Review of Reviews*, August 1893, p. 289.

congress in 1894, she was eager to describe the event and the role of the British women journalists at the conference. Her own paper, 'Women in English Journalism', is said to have been the main topic of one entire afternoon.

> Miss Stuart and Miss Drew were the two women delegates of the British Institute of Journalists, and their presence in that body on a footing of absolute equality was the subject of much comment. Miss Stuart's paper, after dealing with the specific qualifications which women possess for journalism, touched on their increasing number and power during the last thirty years, and maintained that they had created, not usurped, their present position; and this drew some interesting remarks from M. de Zagoulaïeff (*Novoié Vrémia*), of St. Petersburg, as to the similar employment of ladies on the Russian press.[41]

OUR DECADENTS (FEMALE).

"Tell me, Monsieur Duboso. Of course you've read that shocking case of 'Smith *v.* Smith, Brown, Jones, Robinson, and Others'?"

"I confess I 'ave, Miss Vilkes. I am a Lawyer, you know."

"Well, now, what do you think of it as a Subject for dramatic treatment?"

"I—I—I do not know vat it may be as a Subject for dramatic treatment, Mademoiselle. I—I—I find it very—a—a—embarrassant as a Subject for conversation viz a Young Lady!".

Figure 2.3   'Our Decadents (Female)', *Punch*, 23 June 1894

The steady increase in the number of women journalists was made visible when Joseph S. Wood, a newspaper proprietor and the editor of *The Gentlewoman*, took the initiative to found a Society of Women Journalists in

---

[41] 'The Press congress at Antwerp', by G.B.S., *Athenaeum*, 21 July 1894, pp. 96–7.

1894.[42] It was to be an association 'for the benefit of women and managed by women'. This new professional body was welcomed by some of the women mentioned so far; it obviously indicated the need for some form of official network uniting those who lived by the pen.

The author and founder of the Society of Authors, Walter Besant (1836–1901), also observed the rise of the number of women writing and seemed, at first sight, to have no objections to this development. In *The Pen and the Book* (1899) Besant, quite surprisingly, displays that late-twentieth century politically-correct reflex of referring to both sexes when talking about the profession of the man of letters. Yet, as Beetham points out, Besant's dystopia, *The Revolt of Man* (1882), is directed against the threatening breed of new women.[43]

More encouraging was Rudolph de Corova's essay for *Cassell's Magazine*, full of admiration for women editors[44] and giving special prominence to Hulda Friedrichs because she was the first woman journalist to be engaged on exactly the same terms, both with regard to work and pay, as her male colleagues. But such a purely positive attitude was an exception.

The struggling bands of women writers must have been only too aware of the threat they posed for their male colleagues, especially as they could not ignore their growing numbers and the concomitant growing problems. There was hardly any room for all those aspiring journalists, translators and reviewers in petticoats. Only by dint of constant effort did some of them survive. The writer Lucy Clifford reported in one of her letters how Frances Low worked until the early hours of the morning ('her light was always burning') in order to support family members depending on her income.[45]

Curiously enough, Frances Low was one of several professional writers who thought it necessary to discourage young women from writing since they lacked the required basic skills.[46] Low wrote a manual, a textbook for aspiring women journalists, in which she set out to point to the deficiencies of the many

---

[42] There is some confusion as to the exact date. Rubinstein gives 1893 as the founding date, whereas a historical survey published on the occasion of the centenary of the society sets it a year later. Sally Mitchell in 'Careers for Girls: Writing Trash' gives still a later date, see *Victorian Periodicals Review*, 15:3 (Fall 1992), p. 109.

[43] Beetham, *A Magazine of Her Own*, pp.127–8.

[44] 'London Editors Who Are Women', *Review of Reviews*, May 1903, p. 485. The publications mentioned here are: the *Sunday Times*, edited by Mrs F.A. Beer; the *Westminster Budget*, by Hulda Friedrichs in conjunction with Mr F. Carruthers Gould; *Baby and Womanhood*, by Mrs Ada S. Ballin; the *Nursing Record*, by Mrs Bedford Fenwick; *Myra's Journal*, by Miss J. Heale; the *Lady*, by Miss Rita Shell; the *Ladies' Field*, by Mrs E. Macdonald; the *Green Sheaf*, by Miss Pamela Colman Smith; the *Onlooker*, by Mrs Harcourt Williamson; and the *Churchwoman*, in part by Miss Gertrude Ireland Blackburne.

[45] Unpublished letter preserved in the British Library (Add Ms 54 932, f. 152).

[46] Amelia Barr's earlier publication in the *North American Review* rather crudely states that women writers have done much to 'degrade the profession of journalism' because of their 'hasty', 'slipshod', and 'inaccurate' work. ('The Sins of Women Writers', *Review of Reviews*, July 1891, p. 179.)

young women who wanted to become professional writers.[47] There are, Low
claimed, not two sexes in Fleet Street, but two species: 'journalists' and
'women journalists', the one being about as far removed organically from the
other as a dog from a cat.[48] After this rather disheartening start she proceeds by
enumerating all the imperfections which characterise the second species.
Unlike Emily Crawford she believes women to be unreliable as a class, their
style deservedly accused of being slovenly. Women are inaccurate. Their
writing betrays a shrillness, a garrulousness which she has even detected in
books such as *Wuthering Heights, Aurora Leigh, Sonnets from the Portuguese*,
and, she adds, 'George Eliot, for all her spurious masculinity, is as the rest'.
All of these faults could, however, be remedied if the right training were
provided.

Then comes the practical advice. For those women living in London the
reading ticket to the British Museum is indispensable, although 'some time will
elapse before she is able to use handily the vast apparatus here placed at her
disposal, but she will find the officials benignantly omniscient, and always
ready to help the unskilled in research'. The next bit of advice concerns the
writer's relation to the editor. The advice is terse and clear: 'Don't write to an
editor'. Then follows a discussion of the range of periodicals which the
woman journalist should approach:

> most useful to the beginner is the 'popular weekly' class ... *Tit-Bits*,
> *Answers, Parson's Weekly*, Cassell's Saturday Journal ... Next to the
> popular penny weeklies ... I name the three 'Gazettes', the *Pall Mall*, the
> *Westminster*, and the *St. James* ... Monthly magazines divide themselves
> into three classes: – First, the purely popular, – *Strand, Ludgate,
> Pearson's, Windsor, Woman at Home, Lady's Realm* &c. Second, the
> high-class general *Blackwood's, Pall Mall, Macmillan's, Cornhill,
> Longman's*, etc. (p. 80)

There were, of course, also the specialised women's periodicals which
prospective journalists could try; or they could aim for the departments
reserved to women, the so-called 'Women's Sphere', in mainstream journals:
'fashion, cookery and domestic furniture, the toilet, and (less exclusively)
weddings and what is called society news'.

> It is unlikely that men will ever seriously compete with women in the
> business of supplying the stuff which women as a sex are supposed to
> read. My own belief is that men could deal very capably with these
> subjects ... but there happens to be a man's scope; men accept the
> superstition, and leave them alone ... Now almost all the work falling
> within this sphere is done badly.

---

[47] The book was published in 1904 but first appeared as a series of articles in the
Girl's Realm in 1903. Actually, the subject of women journalists crops up again and again in
the columns of women's and mainstream magazines.

[48] Frances Low, *Press Work for Women. A Textbook for the Young Woman Journalist*,
London: Upcott, 1904, p. 10.

'Reviewing', however, is totally beyond the grasp of the candidate woman journalist since this is an assignment sought after by 'University men of high distinction'. (p. 12) The tone of this exposé is discouraging but it seems unlikely to have influenced many of those for whom it was meant. The general tenor, however, merely echoes earlier remarks made by more authoritative writers, male as well as female. Alice Meynell, for instance, president of the Society of Women Journalists in 1898, stated that lack of training and the demands of women readers limited their work to fashion and society topics.[49]

Again, Arnold Bennett in his *Journalism for Women* (1898) accused the large majority of women journalists of an inability to spell, punctuate or write grammatical English. In truth, Frances Low seems to have borrowed Bennett's very own words with respect to the irresponsibility and unreliability of women journalists. He, too, blames the education of women. Bennett's information was probably believed to be entirely reliable, since he had run the woman's magazine *Woman*, first as an assistant editor and then as an editor, from 1894 to 1900.[50] The curious policy of this particular magazine, however, contradicts Low's rather self-assured claim that men, out of some superstition, would leave women's subjects alone. Indeed, it published essays by men using female pseudonyms which, again, might lead us to wonder whether the poor quality of some of these contributions was the work of women or a successful attempt of men to ape – or introduce – a 'woman's style'. Bennett, for one, used female pseudonyms whenever he 'engaged' himself as a contributor. He reviewed books under the name of 'Barbara', he (as well as the former editor, Fitzroy Gardner) used the name 'Marjorie' when writing on 'Town talk'; and the frivolous 'Sal Volatile' was the feminine guise under which he contributed short stories. Bennett's biographer, Reginald Pound, assumes that the editor was also 'Cecile' and 'Lady Vain', a fact which Pound derives, rather sadly, from 'a suspicious competence of style' in the writings by these contributors .[51]

Beetham is also intrigued by Bennett's gender-fluidity during his editorship of *Woman*, and his obvious conviction that his women contributors could not match his knowledgeability about feminine matters. She notes Bennett's attempt at presenting himself as the most advanced 'woman' on the staff who dared to reject corsets yet 'was made to understand that if my opinion got about ... the paper would be utterly ruined'. Thus, according to Beetham, Bennett was flaunting his intellectual superiority to women while simultaneously denying his own 'cultural power over the women contributors'.[52]

---

[49] See David Rubinstein, *Before the Suffragettes: Women's emancipation in the 1890s*, p. 86. There is a long chapter on Alice Meynell's work as a critic in Viola Meynell's biography of her mother.

[50] Beetham, *A Magazine of Her Own*, p. 178. Margaret Beetham has pointed out how Bennett consciously worked towards a feminisation of *Woman*, ibid., p. 188.

[51] Reginald Pound, *Arnold Bennett. A Biography*, Trowbridge and London: Redwood Press, 1952, p. 97.

[52] Beetham, *A Magazine of Her Own*, p. 189.

Late-Nineteenth Century Masculinities

'Manliness', 'masculinity' were the keys to success in the literary world in the 1880s and 1890s; 'femininity' had to be eschewed or discarded. In fiction, this meant the writer had to adopt a certain style. Arthur Quiller Couch, a child of his time, still strongly advocated the use of the masculine (or neuter) style many years later in *On the Art of Writing* (1923). [53] The male sentence was one which Virginia Woolf too seemed to distinguish from its Other, unmasculine, not neutral counterpart. [54] Some male critics went even further, urging novelists whom they befriended not to introduce any female characters into their fiction. Andrew Lang welcomed H. Rider Haggard's and R.L. Stevenson's stories in which the female element was conspicuously absent.

In real life, women's cultural advancement was resisted by literally keeping them out of the spaces traditionally reserved to men. Mrs Harry Cust, the wife of the *Pall Mall Gazette* editor and a woman quite capable of putting pen to paper, [55] remembered that her husband, 'was strongly averse to female influence in the office'. Her 'only contact with its various members was in occasional hospitality at our house. I did a certain amount of reviewing but (as Editor's wife) received no pay'. [56] Many staffs of periodicals met in all-male preserves. The role of the club in prolonging and, indeed, exacerbating the male prejudice against female colleagues has to my knowledge never been examined fully. Nigel Cross hints at its infinite beneficence when contrasting club life with the 'well-established ghetto for women writers': 'a cramped literary world where women wrote discreetly to each other courtesy of the General Post office while their male colleagues enjoyed the privileged freedoms of the Garrick Club'. [57] One of the most intrepid defendants of the Garrick, the journalist George Augustus Sala, described it as 'a weapon used by savages to keep the white woman at a distance'. [58] Nigel Cross succinctly sketched the reigning attitude towards the fair: 'Women were designed to be kissed or to serve mutton chops, but had no place in the club-room where the conversation was supposed to be both too clever and too coarse for them'. [59]

Club life was absolutely crucial for the male journalist. Morton Cohen has demonstrated the pivotal role of the Savile Club in the writing–publishing world by means of one long enumeration: 'Representing English publishing at the Savile were C.E. Appleton (*Academy*), Frederick Greenwood (*Pall Mall*

---

[53] Robbins, 'Vernon Lee', p. 146.

[54] Virginia Woolf, *A Room of One's Own*, London: The Hogarth Press, 1931, p. 115.

[55] She wrote, among others, *Gentlemen Errant. Being the Journeys and Adventures of Four Noblemen in Europe during the Fifteenth and Sixteenth Centuries*, London: Murray, 1909; and translated *Semantics, Studies in the Science of Meaning*, London: Heinemann, 1900.

[56] J.W. Robertson Scott, *The Life and Death of a Newspaper*, London: Methuen, 1952, p. 374.

[57] Cross, *The Common Writer*, p. 165.

[58] Ralph Nevill, *London Clubs. Their History and Treasures*, London: Chatto & Windus, 1911, p. 135.

[59] Cross, *The Common Writer*, p. 108.

Gazette), W.E. Henley (*Scots Observer*), R.H. Hutton (*Spectator*), Sidney
James Low (*St. James Gazette*), Norman MacColl (*Athenaeum*), William
Minto (*Examiner*), John Morley (*Fortnightly Review*), John Murray, Kegan
Paul, W.H. Pollock (*Saturday Review*). Owen Seaman (*Punch*), J.K. Stephen
(*Reflector*), Leslie Stephen (*Cornhill*), and H.E. Watts (*Melbourne Argus*)'.[60]
Clubs, quite naturally, led to literary friendships and collaborations. Bourdieu
clearly considered those, as well as the salons and the 'at homes', as 'private
tribunals' possessing the power of bestowing consecration on art and artists.
Members of clubs had acquired legitimate power,[61] and conferred power on
each other.

Women had no such exclusive meeting places, although some ladies'
clubs were established towards the end of the century.[62] They had their 'at
homes', 'house-warming parties' and other similar occasions which welcomed
mixed company and were often hosted by the woman of the house. 'Clubs
never played a major role in the lives of the women members', Martha Vicinus
claims, 'as they did for upper-class men or trade unionists'. She explains it as
women declaring themselves to be 'not clubbable', therefore preferring 'to
create homes rather than clubs'.[63] Vicinus gives a brief overview of the main
women's clubs, concluding that they did meet a need for some independent
working single women such as the scholar Jane Ellen Harrison and the novelist
Lucy Clifford. Harrison was a member of the Sesame Club where she was
especially spoiled by the porter, who was 'a kind of mother' to her and
generally dealt with most of her practical problems when she was in London.[64]
Lucy Clifford made use of the expensive Lyceum Club in order to wine and
dine her most cherished friends such as Henry James on his seventieth
birthday.[65] The part these networks played in promoting women's careers is
explored in the next chapter.

---

[60] Morton Cohen, ed., *Rudyard Kipling to Rider Haggard. The Record of a Friend-ship*, Rutherford: Fairleigh Dickinson University Press, 1965, p. 11.

[61] Bourdieu, *The Field of Cultural Production*, p. 51.

[62] Mrs Humphry, (alias 'Madge' of *Truth*) has some very interesting comments to make about club life for women. She herself was all for it, although she supposes Queen Victoria was not enthusiastic about those institutions: 'Her Majesty would incline to condemn them, knowing little of the domestic routine of the upper middle-classes, and still less about the lives of the educated women who support themselves by remunerative occupations such as lecturing, book reviewing, book producing, academic pursuits, journalism, dressmaking, and millinary. Such as these are often entirely dependent upon their club for companionship'. See Mrs Humphry, *Manners for Women*, London: Ward, n.d., p. 123.

[63] Martha Vicinus, *Independent Women. Work and Community for Single Women, 1850–1920*, London: Virago, p. 299.

[64] Ibid., p. 298.

[65] And there were the official bodies such as the Writers' Club established in 1892 and the Society of Women Journalists mentioned earlier.

Chapter 3

The *Athenaeum:* A New Team, A New Policy

... the Rossettis, Miss Blind, Miss Zimmern, Lang, Alma Tadema – you
see its always more or less the same creatures. [1]

The *Athenaeum* has its very own place in nineteenth-century culture. Indeed, it
is generally considered to be 'the single most important literary periodical of
Victorian times'.[2] Yet it constantly had to vie for its place in the literary market
because of the sheer number of quality periodicals at the time. Among the
best-known journals, one may mention such monthlies as *Blackwood's
Edinburgh Magazine* (1817–1980) and *Macmillan's Magazine* (1859–1907),
and such quarterlies as the *Quarterly*, the *Edinburgh* and the *Westminster
Review*. Nicola Thompson confidently concludes an overview of the numbers
of journals in the nineteenth century with the remark that there were more than
1,000 literary journals in the mid-Victorian age.[3] The survival of the
Athenaeum from the pre-Victorian age up to the dawn of modernism is nothing
short of a miracle.

Sir Charles Wentworth Dilke inherited the *Athenaeum* in 1869, after the
untimely and unexpected death of his father, the first baronet. He immediately
assumed control by dismissing the current editor, his former travelling
companion William Hepworth Dixon. The long-time staff member Dr John
Doran served as an interim editor until the young proprietor had found the right
man for the job.[4] In 1870, his friend and former fellow-student Norman
MacColl took the editor's chair.[5]

Dixon had seriously disappointed the young Dilke upon their return from
a joint trip to America. The older man was quick to publish his account of
their travels while knowing full well that Dilke himself intended to write on

---

[1] *Lee's Letters*, p. 75.
[2] Thompson, *Reviewing Sex*, p. 9.
[3] Ibid., p. 3.
[4] Dilke's letters in the British Library leave no doubt as to the circumstances. In a
letter of 15 June 1869 Dixon still pleaded for reconciliation but Dilke privately commented on
that letter: 'I dismissed him for writing books without leave & *such* books'. See British Library,
Add Ms 43,909, f. 117; see also ff. 118, 119 and Add Ms 38,794, f. 132. In Ella Hepworth
Dixon's autobiography, *As I Knew Them* (London: Hutchinson, 1930), we are presented with
the views of the Dixon family (pp. 26ff.).
[5] Leslie Marchand, *The Athenaeum*, p. 83.

this. True, Dilke's publication, *Greater Britain* (1868), was original enough to make its mark even though it was published later, but Dixon's book had taken the edge off Dilke's. When this situation repeated itself after they had, again together, visited Russia in 1869, Dilke retaliated by dismissing Dixon. It was an excellent opportunity to get rid of the man whose publications had considerably irritated him and whose editorship he thought to be damaging to the *Athenaeum*. Dilke did not even bother to publish his version of the Russian journey. Dr Doran's services, on the other hand, were rewarded when he was offered the position of editor of *Notes and Queries*,[6] the journal Dilke purchased in 1872.[7]

From the 1870s on, the 'marked file' shows a distinct new group of reviewers, often coming from among Dilke's or MacColl's circles of acquaintances. This does not mean that the critics were second-rate, or not up to their tasks, quite the contrary. The young Dilke and his editor obviously dared to select young, bright minds to comment on recent publications and in so doing, they injected this somewhat flagging weekly with a new life.

New faces, new names from the 1870s on were Robert Romer, J.R. Thursfield and his wife Emily, W. Walter Skeat, Sir Reginald Palgrave, Mathilde Blind, Elizabeth Christie, Margaret Hunt, Helen Zimmern, the blind economist Henry Fawcett and his wife Millicent. The last-mentioned contributor, Millicent Garrett Fawcett, must have been the youngest of the team when she joined the *Athenaeum* staff. These reviewers were soon to be joined by a selection of international contributors, for whenever either Dilke or the editor met exciting writers from abroad they would urge these new acquaintances to write for the *Athenaeum*. This would happen to Louise Chandler Moulton, Vernon Lee, Stéphane Mallarmé, Kate Field, Emile de Laveleye, Edmond About and many others who were asked to report on their home country for the *Athenaeum*. In the next paragraphs both the women contributors recruited by the MacColl–Dilke team and the internationalisation of the *Athenaeum* will be dealt with.

Women's World Behind the 'Athenaeum'

The notably growing number of contributions by women to the *Athenaeum* in the late 1880s and 1890s of the last century begs for some discussion of the professional situation of these contributors, especially as this aspect of their careers has never been revealed either by themselves or by scholars studying the period. The women involved did not all simply come straight from one of the newly-founded colleges for women, though these specialised women graduates would eventually come into their own and acquire positions within the pages of the *Athenaeum*. The usual practice seems to have been to invite

---

[6] The letter offering him the job is to be found in the British Library, Add Ms 43,909.
[7] See Stephen Gwynn and Gertrude Tuckwell, *The Life of the Rt. Hon. Sir Charles W. Dilke*, London: Murray, 1917, vol. I, p. 163.

them to contribute after direct recommendation by a common friend or a relative who was already a staff member. They may possibly also have been introduced to either Norman MacColl or Sir Charles Dilke as promising new writers at an, 'at home', organised by one of the many popular literary hostesses.[8] The influence of these hostesses is not to be underestimated. They were often writers or artists in their own right, they reciprocated the invitations by other society hostesses, they read each other's work, recommended each other's manuscripts to sympathetic editors, and supported literary fund applications and other claims for subsidies.

One of the most interesting witness accounts of the workings of such unofficial networks appears in the form of Violet Paget's letters to her mother. Paget, alias Vernon Lee, first came to London to stay at the house of the Robinsons in 1881. Lee's introduction to the literary circles in the capital had not only come through the good services of her talented and attractive friend Mary Robinson, her own first publication and the name of her brother, the poet Eugene Lee-Hamilton, had preceded her. In those early letters written home, the *Athenaeum* functions as some kind of invisible pivot around which much of the cultural life seem to revolve and which was used as a cementing factor between the many culturally aspiring. This is Lee's report of one of her first outings on her grand London tour:

> Sunday afternoon I to Mrs. Clifford ... I had a sort of feeling that I ought to attend to my more especial friends, the Clarks, the Cobdens, instead of interviewing celebrities ... Eugène must not be very angry that I would not be introduced to Mr. Browning, who was there, ménant train de grand génie. I thought it so derogatory to myself to be honoured in the sort of way that Agnes Clark was, by two minutes platitude. He is a rather common looking old creatures, by no means unlike Captain Huet. But we are going to see him at his house. Then Wm. Rossetti, the type of the stodgy interviewer, was introduced. This is what Mary calls so many people wanting to know me!!! Quite the nicest person is Mrs. Wm. Rossetti; I like her extremely. I also like Miss Zimmern, she who wrote books on Lessing & Schopenhauer, & Miss Mathilde Blind, the adopted daughter of Karl Blind. She is an ugly coarse, evidently amiable woman, extremely like Ouida. Mary says her poetry is just among the very best written at present. Young Sharp, with his pink fleshy, or rather meaty face & his prominent eyes, his whole linendraper's sleekness & prettiness, is quite repulsive to me, as I think he is to Mary. He looks the incarnation of underbredness. I quite understand his poems now. In conversation very dull. The wonderful Oscar Wilde was brought up – the

---

[8] Jerome K. Jerome had this to say about the institution : 'I fancy the At Home has died out. Anyhow one hopes so. It was a tiresome institution. Good women had a special afternoon: "At Home every Thursday". Sometimes it was every other Thursday, or every first Friday, or third Monday. One's brain used to reel, trying to remember them. Most often one turned up the wrong day'. See J.K. Jerome, *My Life and Times*, Bungay: Richard Clay, 1926, p. 3.

Posthlethwaite of Punch. I must send you a caricature of him. He talked
a sort of lyrico-sarcastic maudlin cultshah for half an hour. But I think
the creature is clever, & that a good half of his absurdities are mere
laughing at people. The English don't see that.[9]

After just a few weeks she had made the acquaintance of many of the reviewers
of the *Athenaeum*'s literature department: male critics such as Theodore Watts-
Dunton, Edmund Gosse and Andrew Lang, and the editor himself, Norman
MacColl; female writers such as Augusta Webster, Mathilde Blind, and Helen
Zimmern. Many of those were rewarded by being incisively sketched in Lee's
letters to her mother – immortalised, yet not always in a very flattering portrait.

Unfortunately there is, apart from Vernon Lee's letters, very little
information on such informal gatherings and the ways available to women
writers to be introduced to influential contributors or editors of periodicals . A
far more indirect indication of connections or relationships between writers
might be found in certain series of books or pamphlets. There is the Eminent
Women Series, for instance, for which Lee was asked to write the biography of
the *Countess of Albany* (1884).[10] Many of the authors contributing to that series
were *Athenaeum* reviewers as well. Seeing them appear within such a series
demonstrates that these people were in touch with one another, that they were
serious about earning a living by writing and about combining that with the
advantage of being the best-placed person to write about other women. Vernon
Lee's very matter-of-fact comment on the invitation to write on the Countess of
Albany also shows the financial reward carried a lot of weight: 'I have received
an offer to do a volume of *Css. Of Albany* uniform with Mary [Robinson]'s
Emily[Brontë] for £50 & have accepted'. [11] Such a series was obviously meant
to parallel the successful and prestigious English Men of Letters which John
Morley had edited, and the English Worthies edited by Andrew Lang. In both
these cases the men assigned for the job were close friends of the editor.[12]
Another noteworthy series of pamphlet-like publications dealt with the theme
of suffrage. It joined the efforts of, among others, Charlotte Stopes, Olive
Schreiner and Helen Zimmern's sister, Alice.[13]

---

[9] *Vernon Lee's Letters with a Preface by her executor*, ed. L. Cooper-Willis, privately printed, 1937, p. 64.
[10] Mathilde Blind wrote biographies of *George Eliot* (1883) and *Madame Roland*. Bertha Thomas did *George Sand* (1883), Helen Zimmern took care of *Maria Edgeworth* (1883), Julia Ward Howe of *Margaret Fuller* (1883). Mrs E.R. Pitman wrote on *Elizabeth Fry* (1884), and Mrs Kennard on *Rachel*, and *Mrs Siddons*. *Mary Wollstonecraft* (1885) was done by E. Robins Pennell, *Harriet Martineau* (1889) by Mrs Fenwick Miller, *Mary Lamb* by Anne Gilchrist. Mary Robinson was the author of both *Emily Brontë* (1883) and *Margaret of Angoulême, Queen of Navarre* (1887). *Susanna Wesley* and *Madame de Staël* were written by Mrs E. Clarke and Bella Duffy respectively. The general editor, John Ingram, chose to do *Elizabeth Barrett Browning* for the series.
[11] *Vernon Lee's Letters*, p. 141.
[12] Frans Korsten, 'De "English Men of Letters" serie. Een monument van laat-Victoriaanse literatuurkritiek', Nijmegen: Cicero, 1991.
[13] The pamphlets were bound together in a volume called 'Tracts on women's suffrage' in the British Library (0845.i.7) consisting of: E.P. Lawrence, 'The New Crusade'; Mrs James Ivory, 'Women's social and political union campaign', 1909; Philip Snowden, 'In

Many of the women writers listed above, however well-publicised at the time, have become mere entries in catalogues now. But it is clear that they had developed strategies, not unlike those of their male colleagues, to survive in the literary marketplace. Even so, there are signs that some of the single women writers, with possibly fewer social ties, ran into financial difficulties once their energy had been exhausted and they could no longer write as copiously as they had used to. In that situation they were sometimes forced to rely on their female colleagues in their effort to find some funding. The woman whose 'at homes' were graphically described in Vernon Lee's letters, Lucy Clifford, would quite spontaneously and fervently take up the cudgels on behalf of those whom she believed were worthwhile being published or those who urgently needed financial help. One of the former category was Mathilde Blind, as can be deduced from the letter which Clifford wrote to her own publisher, Frederick Macmillan, in the hope of convincing him to publish her first novel:

> This is about a novel which the author with becoming modesty will not speak to you about herself. She was in here last night & I promised to write to you. She is Mathilde Blind, she translated Strauss some years ago, wrote a poem which has been much praised & has always done a good deal of literary work. This is her first novel. It has been read by W. M. Rossetti, Dr Hueffer, Conway, Joseph Knight &c & they have all given it very great prominence.[14]

A sad example of the second category, the woman writer in need of help, is the case of Frances Low (born 1864), sister of the better-known Sidney Low, and the perfect example of the female drudge. When Low was looking for a well-paid, regular job after a spell of bad health Clifford again wrote to Macmillan for help. Low, according to Clifford, 'a handsome girl with a beautiful complexion and an ugly mouth', had been introduced to her as a promising young writer by Walter Besant. Since then Low had worked excessively hard, giving most of her money away to her siblings and those colleagues who found it hard to live by the pen. Clifford's letter to Macmillan illustrates the length to which Lucy Clifford would go in order to convince people that she was right.

> Frances Low came yest. – knew that I knew you – she is panting for work – begged me to speak to you, I had not *the heart* to spare you. She is a sister of Sidney Low – is very capable – very hard working. I happen to know that she Sidney Low, & another brother, have had to keep crowds of poor relations. She has had no life at all. Years ago was Librarian to People's Palace ... She has done everything, is hard working – cultured,

Defence of the Conciliation Bill'; Alice Zimmern, 'Demand and Achievement' (published by the National Union of Women's Suffrage Societies) February 1912; Mrs Henry Sidgwick, 'The Progress of the Women's Suffrage Movement', Cambridge 1913; Mrs Borrmann Wells, 'America and Woman suffrage'; Mrs Martel, 'The Women's Vote in Australia'; Henry W. Nevinson, 'Women's Vote and Men'; Teresa Billington-Greig, 'Suffragist tactics'; Laurence Housman, 'The Physical Force Fallacy'. Publication data are given only if available.
[14] Unpublished letter in the British Library, Add Ms 54 932, f. 167.

educated – sane in her views, anti-suffrage – well read in three languages.[15]

Later, when Frances Low's health had broken down completely, Clifford helped her obtain a grant from the Royal Literary Fund on two separate occasions.[16] Professional women writers, knowing the hazards of their profession, would pull together and support one another.   Interestingly, Clifford's reassurance in that letter saying that Low had 'sane, anti-suffrage' views sets her and Low apart from many of the *Athenaeum* women in the 1880s and 1890s. It would seem, in fact, that radical women had a better reciprocal support system. It would be going too far to say, however, that their solidarity was directed towards women only. Just as their own careers had at one time depended on male colleagues, they would step in for men as well if there was any need for it.[17] They saw no difference. Distress was ungendered. Frances Low eventually did write for the *Athenaeum*, but under a new editor whose sympathies were less with the suffragettes. [18]

And then there were the other networks. Those which seem only too natural: the mother introducing her daughter, the sister introducing the other sister, the husband introducing his wife. These, too, were at work behind the *Athenaeum*. Noteworthy family ties in the first decades of the weekly's existence are those of the Chorley brothers (Henry Fothergill[19] and John Rutter), the Cunninghams (father Allan and son Peter) and the earlier-mentioned Jewsbury sisters. These family connections were in some cases the sole reason for the choice of that particular reviewer: the wives of nearly all the consecutive editors, for instance, wrote for the *Athenaeum*.   The system, surprisingly, could lead to a particularly felicitous choice of reviewers. It seems quite unlikely, for instance, that the young Marie Stopes would have been chosen to review the latest publications on botany in the early decades of the twentieth century if it had not been for the fact that her mother was the weekly's faithful Shakespeare specialist.

The quite sudden upsurge in the number of contributions by women from 1885 onwards seems, because of the date and a recruiting system relying on (in)direct recommendation, to follow from the catastrophic scandal in which Sir Charles Dilke became involved annex happy marriage to the feminist

---

[15] Unpublished letter in the British Library, Add Ms 54 932, f.152.

[16] Letters to Royal Literary Fund, dated 4 October 1900 and 8 November 1913 (see British Library, Manuscripts Room, reel 105, file no. 2584). These applications would yield the sums of £75 and £150, respectively.

[17] Clifford supported anyone who needed her. She also recommended the work of Maurice Hewlitt to her friend Frederick Macmillan for instance; see Tuchman, *Edging Women Out*, p. 189; Charles Morgan, Charles, *The House of Macmillan, 1843–1943*, London: Macmillan, 1943, pp. 149–50.

[18] She wrote an article on the French literary world in the issue of 24 February 1912. More than half of that article is concerned with the image of the New Woman and the New Wife in France.

[19] A recent monograph by Robert Terrell Bledsoe discusses Henry Fothergill Chorley's career, see *Henry Fothergill Chorley. Victorian Journalist*, London: Ashgate, 1998.

Emilia Pattison. In what follows the place and influence of women's contributions will be gauged from 1871 on, when Sir Charles assumed control over the spiritless journal. Special attention will be paid to the new accents which Dilke introduced: his and MacColl's reliance on women competent in fields which were hitherto male encoded, culminating, in the 1880s and 1890s, in the considerable involvement of usually feminist women reviewers.

Internationalising and Modernising the 'Athenaeum'

The man who inherited the *Athenaeum* after the death of his father in 1869 has been thought of as a 'male feminist' *avant la lettre* as well as the man who squandered a brilliant political career as a result of his adulterous escapades.[20] Sir Charles Dilke (1843–1911) had everything with which to make a mark on Britain's political and intellectual life. He was intelligent, adventurous and courageous. He carefully planned his intellectual education. Thus, for instance, he visited several countries in Europe, scrupulously observing their ways of life, during his holidays as a student at Trinity College, Cambridge (1862-1866). He developed a taste for travel and set out to see more of the world after his studies. In June 1866 he embarked on a tour of the English-speaking countries (the United States, Canada, Australia, India and New Zealand) and cast his observations and thoughts on the British Empire into a book, *Greater Britain*, published in 1869. The book was highly praised and helped him secure the acquaintance of one of the politicians he admired most: John Stuart Mill. Mill's influence is crucial in the development of Dilke's political career, as he seems to have helped determine which subjects were to lie closest to Dilke's heart. As David Nicholls remarks: 'the two were to ... cooperate in the causes of free education, land reform and women's suffrage'.[21]

Dilke's political career effectively started when he was chosen as a representative for Chelsea in 1868. After that, his career quickly took off, reaching its zenith early in 1883 when he entered the Cabinet as the President of the Local Government Board. But success may have come too easily to him and he certainly cannot have suspected that it was to be as short-lived as it proved. In 1885, he was named as co-respondent in the divorce case of Crawford vs. Crawford, an event which signalled the end of his political ascent.

Charles Wentworth Dilke is generally seen as a radical liberal, and his progressive ideas were also to inform the policy with which he was to manage his most precious heirloom. The *Athenaeum* was precious to Dilke because he considered it one of his grandfather's most successful achievements, it was an honour for him to be able to continue the tradition. Dilke made no secret about the closeness which had existed between him and his grandfather. The energy

---

[20] See also below: chapters on Millicent Fawcett and Emilia Dilke.
[21] David Nicholls, *The Lost Prime Minister. A Life of Sir Charles Dilke*, London and Rio Grande: The Hambledon Press, 1995, p.31.

and care he was to bestow on the latter's brainchild were those of a respectful and grateful grandson. However, there was also an obvious parallel between the two men's convictions regarding the quality and the contents of the *Athenaeum*. Like the elder Dilke, Sir Charles believed the weekly had to serve as a window on the world, and present its readers with a kaleidoscope of foreign cultures. This policy was to be reintroduced as a salient characteristic of the weekly as soon as it came into Dilke's hands. Like his grandfather, too, Dilke wanted the best critics to air their views within the pages of his weekly and he knew that women could do the job as well, or even better than their male peers. But since he continued the anonymous tradition, the gender, indeed the identity, of all of his contributors remained a mystery.

Sir Charles Wentworth Dilke was involved with the weekly several years before he inherited its ownership. As a student he regularly contributed reviews and he commented on its reviews in many of his letters to his grandfather. As long as the latter lived, however, and even during his father's ownership, he had little influence on the current editor, William Hepworth Dixon. After his grandfather's death, in 1864, the journal had passed into the hands of Dilke's father, the first baronet, who had little interest in it. It was the journal's image constructed in this interim period, the 1860s, which prompted Gaye Tuchman to call its views 'utterly conventional.'[22] Hepworth Dixon's note on George Eliot, picked out by Elaine Showalter for its viciousness,[23] led Tuchman and Showalter to condemn the *Athenaeum* for wielding the double critical standard.[24] After a quasi-unanimous critical appraisal of Eliot's *Adam Bede* by the literary establishment and the subsequent revelation of the author's identity Dixon had, quite unforgivingly, returned to the book in the gossip section, dismissing its value offhandedly: 'It is time to end this pother about the authorship of 'Adam Bede'. The writer is in no sense a great unknown; the tale, if bright in parts, and such as a clever woman with an observant eye and unschooled moral nature might have written, has no great quality of any kind' (*Athenaeum*, 5 July 1859). This view was quite the reverse of the young Dilke's opinion of George Eliot's novel and he appears to have been incensed by the notice. In an unpublished letter to Dixon, dated 29 November 1866, he accuses the *Athenaeum* staff of a lack of professionalism. Dilke may not even have realised, at this stage, that the Eliot notice was Dixon's work:

> I am going to hunt up all the Athenaeum notices when I get home & see whether I think small beer or otherwise of y^r staff – so bid them tremble, as I am sure they highly value my good opinion. The only fact of w^h I am at this present very certain ... is that Miss Evans is not far from being the best *indirect describer* of character, & the wittiest observer of human nature that has lived in England since Shakespeare, & I think that there are touches in 'Amos Barton' (Sketches of Clerical life), & in the first

---

[22] Tuchman, *Edging Women Out*, p. 184.

[23] Showalter, *A Literature of Their Own*, p. 95.

[24] Tuchman, *Edging Women Out*, pp. 182ff.

few chapters of the 'Mill on the Floss' – quite worthy of Shakespeare himself.[25]

Dilke's letter must certainly have made Dixon 'tremble' after he had made this error of judgement in his future employer's eyes. His forced resignation in 1869 was almost predictable.[26] Yet except for this incident there seems to have been very little indication that the young proprietor, once he came into power, wanted his staff to express particular views in their columns. The result is, certainly at first, a varied reception of contemporary literature. The double critical standard with respect to the gender of the author under review occurs in certain reviews only. In other words, only some reviewers failed in that direction. And yet it is their biased attitude which has caught the eye of many recent scholars interested in periodicals, eventually overriding a more nuanced view of the journal's criticism.

Ellen Miller Casey, too, has reflected on this rather tenacious, one-sided view of the *Athenaeum* as a monolithic institution. In her article 'Edging women out?' with its title echoing Tuchman and Fortin's lengthy analysis, she claims that Tuchman and Fortin read the *Athenaeum* selectively because they failed to spot, amongst other things, those reviews which expressed admiration of Margaret Oliphant. The reviews chosen by Tuchman and Fortin were, in fact, written by another reviewer than those extracts (generally authored by J.M. Collyer) cited in praise of the same novelist in the 1890s. Such disagreements on the value of an author's work within periodical criticism should act as caveats for scholars (like the present author) attempting to generalise about review practices.

Returning to Dixon, however, and his time as the editor of the *Athenaeum* (1853–1869), the period of his editorship is now generally dismissed as the low-watermark of the run of the *Athenaeum*. In an analysis of the readership of the periodical press in the 1850s and 1860s, Alvar Ellegård points to the difficulties which several of the established periodicals underwent owing to the abolition of the compulsory newspaper stamp. This move quite naturally led to the establishment of a cheap daily press and the expansion of periodical publishing in general. The *Saturday Review*, for instance, a prestigious weekly which potentially threatened the position of the *Athenaeum*, was launched in 1856.[27] The *Newspaper Press Directory* for 1865 lists no fewer than 1,271 newspapers and 554 periodicals.[28] According to Ellegård it

---

[25] Unpublished letter in the British Library, Add Ms 38,794 f. 124.

[26] Dilke forbade Dixon to give an explanation for his departure in the columns of the *Athenaeum*: 'You are an editor & an editor resigning in the middle of y^r career, so anything said w^d leave the gap "What is to come after him". Nothing was said when my grandfather was followed by Hervey ; nothing when Hervey was followed by you, & the proprietors are of the opinion that they cannot have anything said now. I hope that on thinking the matter over you will see that we could not have come to any other decision.' (Unpublished letter 23 July 1869, British Library Add Ms 38,794 f. 132.)

[27] Alvar Ellegård, *The Readership of the Periodical Press in Mid-Victorian Britain*, Göteborg, Göteborgs univetsitets årsskrify, 1957, p. 3.

[28] Ibid., p. 5.

was something of a miracle that the *Athenaeum* even survived that period, as it was being conducted, as he has it, 'on rather unimaginative lines'.[29] Yet he had to admit that the paper occupied a special position, and that Britain's intelligentsia simply had to read it if they wanted to keep up with their own well-informed circle. True enough, many *Athenaeum* readers did not refrain from criticising the journal but, by the same token, admitted to reading it.[30] This attitude, an odd combination of respect and contempt, lingered on in some of its readers until the 1880s and 1890s. One of Andrew Lang's letters to Robert Louis Stevenson starts by referring to a gossip item in the *Athenaeum* which claims that Stevenson's return to Britain is imminent. Yet he immediately feels the need to make clear that he does not believe everything this weekly prints, for 'the truth', he writes, 'is not in it'.[31] Similarly, George Gissing followed the *Athenaeum* assiduously in those closing decades of the nineteenth century while pouring criticism on the weekly whenever he thought its views inept. He would recommend it to his brother Algernon alongside a selection of other essential journals for the aspiring novelist but,[32] at the same time, absolutely refused to accept some of the reviewers' verdicts.[33]

The international dimension supplied by the *Athenaeum*'s 'Notes from Abroad' (both from the European continent and from America) undoubtedly added to the weekly's prestige. These columns continued or returned to a policy initially introduced by the first Charles Dilke. According to Marchand the 'Foreign Correspondence' was a feature of the *Athenaeum* upon which the older Dilke 'particularly prided himself.'[34] Marchand relates how the column was written by members of the staff sent abroad for that purpose, such as Henry Chorley, George Darley and Sarah Austin, as well as by British expatriates such as Theodosia and Thomas Adolphus Trollope (son and daughter-in-law of that indefatigable traveller Frances Trollope). Indeed, twenty-seven of Theodosia Trollope's letters to the *Athenaeum* were collected and published in 1861 as *Some Aspects of the Italian Revolution*.[35]

---

[29] Ibid., p. 22.

[30] In this context Ellegård refers to a short passage in the *Printers' Register*, 6 September 1869 when it announced the founding of the *Academy* and *Nature*: 'At last ... some hope of the literary world being enfranchised from the thraldom it has long endured under the despotism of the *Athenaeum*.' (Ibid., p. 22)

[31] Marysa Demoor, ed, *Dear Stevenson. Letters from Andrew Lang to Robert Louis Stevenson with Five Letters from Stevenson to Lang*, Louvain: Peeters, 1990, p. 124.

[32] Paul F. Mattheisen, Arthur C. Young and Pierre Coustillas, eds, *The Collected letters of George Gissing*, 1863–1880, vol. I, Athens, Ohio: Ohio University Press, 1990, p. 141.

[33] On 29 June 1884, for instance, he reported on the *Athenaeum*'s review of *The Unclassed*: 'By the bye, don't think that notices like that in the Athenaeum will distress me one bit. I admired the cleverness of this one particular man. He is determined not to tempt one single reader to the book, & so, you will observe, does not give a hint of what it contains. He is, I am convinced, utterly wrong in what he says about the "style"'. (*Collected Letters*, vol. II, p. 233)

[34] Marchand, *The Athenaeum*, p. 47.

[35] See Lucy Poate Stebbins and Richard Poate Stebbins, *The Trollopes. The Chronicle of a Writing Family*, New York: Columbia University Press, 1945, pp. 181, 216.

Dixon had allowed this international aspect to go into decline, as did the rest of the journal during his term, and the young team in charge from the 1870s onwards opted for a return to it. They, too, were to secure correspondents from all over the world willing and competent enough to report on the cultural life of their respective home countries. Bourdieu's conviction that a successful cultural product such as this journal had to achieve a homology between the periodical and its readership, therefore implies that late-Victorian readers of the *Athenaeum* wanted their weekly to supply them with a briefing about the international cultural scene.[36] It is, perhaps, less predictable that women were going to be so prominently present in the weekly's re-adjustment to the international scene and the reading public. Both Dilke and MacColl played an important part in securing the right woman for the job though neither appear to have greatly encouraged signed contributions by women.

Signatures were there when the prestige of the weekly was involved and the resonance of a certain item depended on the contributor's eminence. Thus, early in 1871 Dilke wrote a letter to a Belgian professor of economics, Emile de Laveleye, outlining his plan of a completely new section within the journal, 'Continental literature', devoted to foreign publications. This was to be an annual feature, signed by scholars of distinction.

> Last year we had in the last number of the *Athenaeum* for the year a collection of articles on the literature of various countries during the year just finished. The idea was a success. This year we repeat it – leaving out England. Masson will do France, Vambéry – Hungary, Young Everett, America – in fact we hope to have *all* the articles done by first-rate men this year. *Most* of them were so done last year, but Belgium was not. Will you do Belgium ... we can only offer *5£*, for an article which may take *five* days – but I have some hope that a desire to see Belgium properly treated may possibly weigh with you in considering the matter.[37]

In this case Dilke's hope was justified. As mentioned above, De Laveleye accepted the assignment but he decided to share the responsibility and the workload with the young historian Paul Fredericq.

De Laveleye had been offered the job by Dilke because he was a man of sound judgement with an international reputation. Indeed, E.C. Coppens, Fredericq's biographer, stated that De Laveleye was considered to be an authority abroad long before acquiring fame at home.[38] One clearly had to be a 'famous' or 'eminent' scholar in order to be amongst the chosen few who were

---

[36] This *zeitgeist* was captured by Mark Pattison, when, in 1870, he observed with respect of the *Academy* that he wanted it to be 'a journal which should systematically survey the European literary and scientific movement as a whole, and pass judgement upon books ... from a cosmopolitan point of view', *Academy*, 2 (1870), p. 1.

[37] Unpublished Ms, 29 October 1870, Ghent University Library (Hs 3640).

[38] See E.C. Coppens, *Paul Fredericq*, Gent: Liberaal Archief, 1990, p. 52. With thanks to Luc François.

invited, year upon year, to comment on their national literatures for the
Athenaeum.[39]

Interestingly or disappointingly, no women were engaged to write these
signed annual surveys, but there were quite a number of women among the
foreign correspondents, notably those reporting on the United States.[40] And
those columns, starting with the words 'Notes from ...', were occasionally
signed. The management here seems to have opted for authors they had met
and appreciated for this job. The presence of women is noticeable. Totally
anonymous was the work done by those regular female contributors who were
asked to translate the essays and reviews by the foreign 'authorities'. Yet it was
a silent acknowledgement of women's language skills.

Notes from Abroad: Kate Field, Louise Chandler Moulton, Vernon Lee

One of Sir Charles's most important and most intimate confidantes in the early
1870s was the amiable, reliable but at the same time formidable American
journalist and author Kate Field. By the time he met 'Miss Field' she was
already a valuable friend of the Trollopes, George Eliot and the Brownings.
Anthony Trollope described her in his autobiography as his 'most chosen
friend', 'a ray of light' so that not 'to allude to her would amount almost to a
falsehood'.[41]

Kate Field was born in St Louis in 1838, but had crossed the ocean in
1859 to spend long periods in Europe with her uncle and aunt. Field acquired
fame as a journalist and as a critic of music, painting and drama. Her
Shakespeare criticism, especially, was admired. She returned to Europe after
the death of her mother in the early 1870s and acted as the Europe
correspondent of such papers as the *New York Herald* and the *New York
Tribune* for some time.[42] Once back in the United States she provided the
reverse service for the *Athenaeum*.

---

[39] From one of Sir Charles's letters to Joseph Reinach (1856–1921), a French
journalist and politician, it appears that, firstly, other periodicals wanted to emulate the
Athenaeum in featuring such international cultural reports. Therefore, the proprietor wanted to
preserve its hallmark of quality and authority. And, secondly, that the annual survey for the
Athenaeum had become a much coveted responsibility by foreign men of letters because of the
weekly's patent influence. I quote from Dilke's letter to Reinach which is an attempt to explain
why MacColl opted for Ferdinand Brunetière (1849–1906) and not the addressee: 'I think
MacColl told you that he wanted to get France done by one known in England as a professional
literary critic, and he has always said that you are known there as a statesman and not as a
literary critic ... Of course, all the other articles are done by mere critics, and, of course,
MacColl as an editor of 30 years standing looks on *us* as amateurs. I don't know Brunetière
and I don't know if he is likely to consent'. (7 October 1897, unpublished letter in the British
Library, Add Ms 43,884, f. 296.)

[40] The elder Dilke's attempt on this score had been less fruitful (compare Marchand,
The Athenaeum, p. 47)

[41] Anthony Trollope, *An Autobiography*, p. 225

[42] Lilian Whiting, *Kate Field. A Record*, London: Sampson Low, Marston & Co. Ltd,
1899, pp. 163, 277.

It is not clear when or where Sir Charles Dilke was first introduced to her. Field used to travel a lot on the European continent, but he may just as well have met her on his American journey in 1866–1867. She, at all events, was notified of his marriage the day it happened on 30 January 1872: 'A real marriage, in a real church, with a real parson, & the whole thing! Is it not dreadful',[43] he wrote to her.

They remained in touch, so much is obvious. She was in Britain in 1873, and wrote several letters to Dilke – apparently – complaining to him about the brevity and scarcity of his replies. His facetious solution to her 'problem', as suggested in his answer, was to forward her letters to his brother in Central Asia and tell him to answer them; 'he writes just like I do – as far as fist goes – & *likes* writing into the bargain'. Besides, he thought it absurd to write letters to someone who can read a daily paper; 'Daily papers killed letters – & very properly'.[44] But it is clear that Dilke was more quiet than usual in that period because of his wife's ill-health during her pregnancy.[45] Later that year she gave birth to a stillborn child and Dilke took her away for a holiday in the south of France. A letter from Monaco, addressed to Kate Field and beginning with 'My dear Cuffy', testifies to his change of mood.

In spite of the jocular tone of some of his letters to the American journalist, Sir Charles did take her entirely seriously when it came to reporting on his political exploits. Persistent rumours of his political ambitions angered him and led him to reassure her that he coveted no political office: 'I have made it absolutely impossible for a minister to so much as offer it to me. In the second place – when it still might have been offered to me I shld not have taken it. In the third place – putting morality & opinions wholly out of sight. *What* could make me want office?'[46] This letter was written in the midst of Dilke's campaign against the British monarchy. The series of public lectures was planned that year because of an apparent lapse in the public's affection for the Queen. In one of Field's letters home she paints a rather gloomy picture of the British monarchy's future:

> My friend Sir Charles Dilke has come out publicly as a republican. All the papers are howling, and some of his friends have cut him, but he has done a brave thing, and I honor him for it. He has merely anticipated events, and now becomes a leader. English monarchy is doomed within the next twenty years.[47]

Unfortunately for Dilke and his allies, the Prince of Wales's sudden illness and miraculous recovery entirely changed the public mood and provoked a storm of

---

[43] Unpublished letter in British Library, Add Ms 43,909, f. 250, 30 January 1872.
[44] See his unpublished letter kept in the British Library, Add Ms 43,909, f. 244.
[45] Neither Dilke nor his first biographers revealed the reason for Lady Dilke's ill-health.
[46] Unpublished letter in British Library, Add Ms 43,909, f. 225, 21 November 1871.
[47] Whiting, *Kate Field*, p. 281.

protest against Dilke and the growing republican movement,[48] so much so that
he even had to defend the right to hold on to his title which he had inherited
from his father.[49]   Even the trusted Kate Field tried him on this subject,
extracting this answer from him: 'it is affectation to pretend to drop a title wh
you have no legal power to lay aside & wh you'd not prevent your son
reviving'.[50]

Then the political storm around Dilke abated somewhat and he went on
to continue the political career he had started in such a remarkable fashion.
Kate Field, for her part, went back to America and turned her attention to its
literary or cultural production.   Under the initial 'D.'   she took care of the
'Notes from the United States' for the *Athenaeum* in 1874 and 1875.

Field's contributions reflected her own passing interests and convictions.
She would, for instance, digress on the position of the journalist in America.
Her view on the professional writer was confidently optimistic compared to the
rather distressing comments of some of her English colleagues.   She
acknowledges the importance of the daily press, noting with some satisfaction
that 'to-day's battles are fought with newspapers, not books'.   According to
her, journalism was at long last becoming a profession and it 'promises the
finest results in political and social influence'.[51] She also noted the publication
of books which had particularly attracted her attention, plays which she had
found particularly innovative.   In her note for 9 January 1875 she digressed on
Dr E.H. Clarke's *Building of the Brain*, dealing with the 'vexed discussion of
female education'. This Dr Clarke fully endorsed Field's own views on the
matter and was therefore quoted at length: 'from fourteen to nineteen the
utmost attention should be paid to girls' physical culture, after which should
come the severe mental training'.   Field also looked to a future ('one hundred
years hence') when these battles have been fought and 'their epoch' will be
looked upon as 'feminine struggling on the one side, and idiocy on the other'.
If her ideas about republicanism had sprung from her own education and
descent, her views on matrimony were positively unorthodox even in the
United States: 'I've had several escapes from matrimony, for which I thank
God ... I believe in love. I don't believe in being tied to a man whom I cease to
love. Therefore the less said about marriage the better'. [52] Kate Field did not
solely write about women's matters, or women authors.   She hailed W.D.
Howells's new novel, Bret Harte's new volume of poems and Mr Boucicault's
new play, but the penchant for women writers is distinct.   She does not quote
from Bret Harte's poetry because that will be known in Britain soon enough,

---

[48] See Roy Jenkins, *Sir Charles Dilke. A Victorian Tragedy*, London: Collins, 1958,
pp. 71ff.

[49] See his letter to Kate Field [1872] British Library, Add Ms 43,909 f. 325; and his
letters to and from J.G. Murdoch, 20–22 December 1871, British Library, Add Ms 43,909, ff.
230–234.

[50] Unpublished letter, [1872], British Library, Add Ms 43,909, f. 325.

[51] *Athenaeum*, 25 July 1874, p. 112.

[52] Whiting, *Kate Field*, p. 276.

but chooses a long poem by Nora Perry instead because she is as yet unknown in England.

Worth citing, too, is her note on the short stories of her colleague, Louise Chandler Moulton, the Boston literary correspondent of the *New York Tribune*. She takes this inconspicuous publication, entitled *Some Women's Hearts*, as an opportunity to urge Moulton not to be too lenient in her literary judgements. As the literary critic of the *New York Tribune* she occupies a position of power, and she should, therefore have the courage to speak the truth. She is simply too amiable and too generous, and yet American literature needs 'just criticism' (25 July 1874). This bit of criticism has, with hindsight, an ironic dimension to it since Louise Chandler Moulton was to replace Kate Field as the American correspondent for the *Athenaeum*. Or are we naïve to believe in coincidence here, and was Field instrumental in having Moulton as her successor?[53] The two certainly were close friends later on in that decade, with Moulton writing affectionate letters to Field when the latter was on the point of starting an actress's career: 'Dear Kate, I see your *debut*/ So go in and win, my dear. I shall await news eagerly./ Yours affectionately, L.C.M'. [54]

Shortly after that *Athenaeum* reference to Moulton, in 1874, Field stopped contributing to the London weekly. She did, however, remain an intimate friend of the Dilkes when Sir Charles remarried and went through a painful divorce scandal in 1886. His second wife Emilia Dilke sent her a progress report when Field wanted to publish an interview with Sir Charles in 1889.

> Affairs are now in so critical a state here with us that Charles does not think it wld be wise that an 'interview' shld appear even if 'managed' by your skilful pen on the actual lines & words of his speeches.
> The visit paid us by Mr Gladstone has been in the papers again. I believe things now are moving very rapidly in his favour & that he may ultimately obtain justice & I will if you like send you cuttings concerning ourselves & the movement in wh we are engaged. I enclose a few taken at random. It might however be a better plan if my Secretary Miss Abraham (who is also Treasurer of the Women's Trade Union League) sent you a London letter from time to time of gossip as to aspects of the Labour questions &c &c? The work of the Unions is 'catching on' & I am just going to the public for £4,000 to build a Women's Trade Hall &c & expect to get it. I wld offer to write you myself but I have not the time & you will find May Abraham an excellent substitute if you like to take her?[55]

---

[53] She was to try in at least one known instance to enlist one of her friends as a contributor, but Edwin P. Whipple declined: 'My dear Miss Field, – I must decline Sir Charles Dilkes invitation, none the less because my eyes are pleased at the renewed sight of your bold, clear, and strong handwriting ... ' (letter dated 19 November 1873; see Whiting, *Kate Field*, p. 299).

[54] Whiting, *Kate Field*, p. 325.

[55] See British Library Dilke papers – Ms 43, 908, ff. 180, letter of 6 December 1889 written by E.F.S. Dilke.

The contacts with Louise Chandler Moulton, the next American correspondent, were far less close. A likely explanation for her involvement with the *Athenaeum* is, as suggested above, that she was introduced by Kate Field. However, the new recruit's input was to be relatively limited.

Ellen Louise Chandler Moulton had already made quite a name for herself when she started to write for the British weekly. Born in 1835, she started her literary career at the age of fifteen with the publication of a miscellaneous collection entitled *This, That and the Other*. She married William Moulton, a Boston journalist, in 1855 and she had one daughter. But, as her biographer in the *Dictionary of American Biography* observes, 'though devoted to her only child, ... she was not domestic in her tastes'. In 1870 she obtained the prestigious post of Boston literary correspondent for the *New York Herald Tribune*, and from 1886 to 1892 she contributed a weekly letter to the *Boston Sunday Herald*. More relevant perhaps for this study is that, from 1876 onwards, she spent the summers and autumns in England. [56]

Chandler Moulton's contributions are few and easy to spot. She signed each one of her 'Notes from the United States' in the *Athenaeum* with her full name and was rewarded accordingly.[57] Longfellow himself wrote to her on two occasions to thank her for the appreciative reviews she had written first of Mrs Whitman, then of his own poetry.[58] After trying her hand at the notes from the United States in the late 1870s, Chandler Moulton contributed two poems to the *Athenaeum* : 'Hic Jacet' was published in 1881 and 'The Life-Mask of Keats' in 1892. The 'Notes from the United States' section disappeared after Moulton's stint. Its publication was apparently entirely dependent on whether or not there was a trustworthy correspondent.

Dilke's friendly relationship with the militant Kate Field and his evident wish for her to contribute to his journal was not a unique case. She was one of the many professional women of whose expertise he thought highly and who therefore ought to be given the opportunity to voice their opinions in the *Athenaeum*. His view was supported by the editor, Norman MacColl.

So far very little has been said about Norman MacColl's role in attracting new talents. Yet his efforts on behalf of the journal were as considerable as Sir Charles's, or perhaps even more impressive. About MacColl amazingly little

---

[56] She was certainly treated as American royalty when she came to London in the 1880s. A letter from Oswald Crawford, quoted in Lilian Whiting biography reads: 'We are going to give you Andrew Lang to take you in [at the dinner] on Friday, and on the other side you will have either James Bryce or Mr. Chapman, the enterprising young publisher mentioned by Dickens'. See Lilian Whiting, *Louise Chandler Moulton: Poet and Friend*, London: Hodder and Stoughton, 1910, p. 121.

[57] See the *Athenaeum* of 29 March 1879 (p. 409), 9 November 1878 (pp. 593–4), 21 December 1878 (pp. 804–5), 18 January 1879 (pp. 88–9), 1 March 1879 (pp. 288–9).

[58] Whiting, *Louise Chandler Moulton*, p. 103

is known. There is no biography, no autobiography.[59] From the writer Vernon
Lee's letters home it appears that MacColl was always on the lookout for
valuable contributors. Indeed, it was MacColl who attended the literary
gatherings, the 'at homes', the 'housewarming parties', not Dilke. Vernon Lee
too was one of a group of women reviewers MacColl encouraged. When they
first met she was known to him as a talented writer with a particular interest in
Italian history and literature.

Lee had adopted a male pseudonym in 1875 and, like George Eliot, she
stuck to it throughout her career without disguising her true gender. She chose
the name 'H.P. Vernon Lee' because it 'contained part of [her] brother's and
[her] father's and [her] own initials'. Besides, she first thought, 'it has the
advantage of leaving it undecided whether the writer be a man or a woman'.[60]
By the time she went to London she had already been invited by Angelo de
Gubernatis, editor of the *Rivista Europe*, to write a monthly contribution on
leading female novelists, and she had succeeded in having articles of hers
placed in *Fraser's Magazine*, the *Cornhill Magazine* and the *British Quarterly*.
Then, in 1880, her first book was published: *Studies of the Eighteenth Century
in Italy*. It was also at about this time that she met the poet Mary Robinson.[61]

The circumstances of Vernon Lee and Robinson's first meeting are rather
obscure. According to Lee's biographer they spent some time together in
Florence and Sienna in the autumn and winter of 1880.[62] The ambitious
expatriate gratefully accepted a later invitation from Mary Robinson to come
and stay with her parents in London. In those early years of the 1880s,
Robinson was to be Lee's friend and constant companion, until the former's
marriage to the French scholar James Darmesteter in 1888. Robinson was also
to introduce Vernon Lee into the fashionable milieux of the decade. The result
was, at first, an unmitigated success in spite of this expatriate's unorthodox
appearance and sharp tongue. Lee's letters home tell of the conquests she
made in literary London. Yet she was to go a bit too far when she wrote her
roman-à-clef, *Miss Brown*, in which she exposed and caricatured many of
those who had welcomed her into their midst. Henry James, to whom it was
dedicated, called it 'painfully disagreeable in tone'.[63] Norman MacColl met
Vernon Lee at one of Lucy Clifford's 'at homes' on 27 June 1881, to which
social occasion, Lee claims, he had been invited to meet her.[64] That first

---

[59] There is a painting of MacColl by Clegg Wilkinson. A photograph of this painting
can be seen in Christ's college, Cambridge and there is a good little sketch by Harry Furniss in
Punch (see figure 3.1)

[60] *Lee's Letters*, p. 49.

[61] The Robinsons ('Mr and Miss') were certainly in Italy in September 1880 according
to one of Robert Browning's letters to Mrs Thomas FitzGerald (see Edward C. McAleer, ed.,
Learned Lady. Letters from Robert Browning to Mrs. Thomas Fitzgerald 1876–1889, Cambridge,
Mass.: Harvard University Press, 1966, p. 97).

[62] Peter Gunn, *Vernon Lee. Violet Paget, 1856–1935*, London: Oxford University
Press, 1964, p. 76.

[63] Leon Edel, ed., *Henry James Letters*, Cambridge, Mass.: Harvard University Press,
1980, vol. III, p. 61.

[64] *Lee's Letters*, p. 66.

meeting left a favourable impression. MacColl is said to have been 'very civil & agreeable' to her. Her opinion of him was to fluctuate, though, as it did concerning so many of her acquaintances. A year later she calls him 'stupid', possibly because she was under the impression that he had no high opinion of her work. 'The R[obinson]s', however, had told her that 'it was poor[sic] stupidity of MacColl (he *is* very stupid) and that he has constantly spoken well of me'.[65] But she soon realises that like the Humphry Wards, Walter Pater, Leslie Stephen, Theodore Watts-Dunton and Mrs W. K. Clifford, he is one of the people who have 'taken her up' that first year of residence in London. Of those, it is only Lucy Clifford and her friends whose interest she wants to reciprocate: 'I see daily more and more that if any set claims me (and no set, in this exclusive London, particularly claims a person on the loose like me) it is the Clifford one'. And that excludes 'Watts, Marston, etc.'[66]

The *Athenaeum* editor, however, courageously invited this indomitable character for lunch in July 1883, an event which she proceeded to describe as a 'thin dull lunch in chilly half furnished rooms'.[67] And he repeated the feat in 1884, this time to the general satisfaction of his guest. More importantly, however, he wrote the positive review of Vernon Lee's controversial novel, *Miss Brown*, for the *Athenaeum*: 'The readers of Vernon Lee's former books will be quite prepared for the ability shown in "Miss Brown", but they will hardly have expected her to write such a good novel'. (*Athenaeum*, 6 December 1884) Unlike Henry James and many of Lee's former friends, MacColl likes the novel in spite of its merciless satire. He did have some reservations about the portrayal of the male protagonist: 'Walter Hamlin turns out to be an offence against the laws of dramatic propriety that the reader resents. Walter Hamlin himself is well portrayed, but it is a mistake to attribute wide popularity to his poetry'.[68]

MacColl did get something in return for his appreciation of her talents, albeit very little. When he invited Vernon Lee to review for the *Athenaeum* she was overworking and under strain, and partly for these reasons she alienated several of her friends by the severe criticisms she published.[69] Lee wrote four pieces for the *Athenaeum*. She started with one of those typical 'Notes from' contributions, a letter on 'Art in Italy' (4 November 1882). Shortly afterwards she was given a more prestigious assignment, the opportunity to review Mandell Creighton's *A History of the Papacy during the Period of the Reformation* (*Athenaeum*, 9 December 1882). Creighton was a distinguished historian who sometimes contributed to the *Athenaeum*. Behind the cloak of anonymity Lee denounces the book on three counts. First, she believes the subject to be excessively narrow: the history of the Papacy in the fifteenth and

---

[65] Ibid., p. 91.

[66] *Lee's Letters*, p.130.

[67] Ibid.

[68] Ironically enough, MacColl chose to snub Henry James in his anonymous review of *The Reverberator* (see *Athenaeum*, 16 June 1888).

[69] Gunn, *Vernon Lee*, p. 97.

sixteenth century cannot be presented without any attention to the religious and political movements of the time. This study, according to Lee, only 'laboriously and intelligently' compiles 'a vast digest of the documents and narratives made by the men who served the Curia in the fifteenth century'. Second, she regrets Creighton's 'antiquated' mode of writing, by which she seems to mean both his dry literary style and the aim of his writing. Third, she believes he should have sketched the intellectual climate, the 'mode of thinking and feeling in the late Middle Ages'. In short, it seems Mandell Creighton has 'deliberately [neglected] the study of social and intellectual conditions, [eschewed] all attempts at showing his readers the life of a specified time, and [limited] his history to the recital of bare facts'. The candid character of this review was, naturally, not exactly welcomed by the historian. Actually, his reaction is one of the few recorded responses to *Athenaeum* reviews. His wife, Louise Creighton, carefully reprinted a number of the letters discussing the publication of the first two volumes of the *History*. With respect to its reception she observed the book was very favourably noticed in 'the leading literary journals' of both Europe and America.[70] Yet she does not breathe a word about the *Athenaeum* review though Creighton himself was clearly upset at the time and confided this to a fellow-historian, Dr Hodgkin:

> I feel moved to write to you about my reviews. As to the 'Athenaeum', I think the editor might have sent my book to some one who knew something about anything. I never read so ignorant a review of any book. To his literary judgement I humbly bow; but his frank acknowledgement that he knows nothing about the subject is almost pathetic. I am quite sorry that the poor man should have had to cut the pages of so dull a book before he earned a guinea: it was hardly earned.[71]

It is quite impossible to trace the reviewer's confession that she knows nothing at all about the subject. If anything the review seems to hide a reader well-acquainted with this period in history. Creighton had certainly lost all the pretence of humility which he affects in his letters to his other (known) reviewer.

Whether Vernon Lee was right to dismiss this historical survey as a missed opportunity or not, her generally depreciative article brought MacColl little gratitude from the eminent ecclesiastical historian. A few months later, however, and despite this experience, MacColl asked Lee to judge another notable historical publication. Pasquale Villari – yet another *Athenaeum* correspondent – had published the third volume of his seminal work on Niccolo Machiavelli. Villari was a personal friend of Vernon Lee, one she and her mother had welcomed at their salon in Florence. Yet this did not keep Lee from savaging that book as well. This time, she regrets the author's efforts at embedding Machiavelli's life story in a general history of the Renaissance. The

---

[70] Louise Creighton, *Life and Letters of Mandell Creighton*, 2 vols., London: Longmans, 1904, vol. I, p. 226.
    [71] Creighton, *Mandell Creighton*, vol. I, p. 229.

result, she argues, is disastrous. He has digressed on literary and artistic matters instead of concentrating on political history, in a language which betrays his unfamiliarity with the subject: 'his account of Italian poetry is singularly weak and vague ..., and his chapter on art quite astonishingly poor, as is proved by the sudden attempt at effects of rhetoric'. She does pay tribute to Villari's unique knowledge of the character of Machiavelli but that praise does not counterbalance the disparaging start of her review. It is, then, from a position of unabashed (though anonymous) superiority that this young woman critic proceeds to lash out at the work of one belonging to her own circle.

Whether or not her criticisms were justified, the authors cannot have relished this harsh treatment, which cannot have made for easy relations between them and the editor of the journal to which they were valued contributors. So it is not surprising that Paget thereupon disappeared from the *Athenaeum* until 1887 when she made a brief reappearance under a 'Notes from Florence' contribution. After that she vanished from the *Athenaeum* scene altogether.

Even so, the reason why Lee's involvement with the *Athenaeum* stopped so entirely remains to be guessed at.   She had, one may add, not been particularly complimentary about the journal in her *roman-à-clef, Miss Brown*. So the decision for her contributions to be so few and far between was probably her own. MacColl at all events went to some length to encourage this young talented woman, even if she was *persona non grata*.

Gender and Translation: Helen Zimmern, Mary Robinson

The 'Notes from ...' section in the *Athenaeum* was not often anonymous. Authors were identified by their initials or in some cases even by their full names. A far less conspicuous contribution was that of the translator of articles sent in from abroad. MacColl himself translated quite a number of foreign contributions, but one is struck, when browsing through the 'marked file', by the frequent recurrence of women's names scribbled across those entries which have been translated. Even such a notable contributor as Geraldine Jewsbury was asked, at times, to translate from French. Other contributors combined occasional reviewing or reporting with a full-time job as translator. Sarah Austin (1793–1867), for instance, who considered herself first and foremost a translator,[72] contributed several reviews and letters from abroad in the period 1834–1856.

Gilbert and Gubar's thesis that Victorian women writers were still suffering from an extreme anxiety when indulging in the very male activity of generating texts,[73] cannot be applied to the act of translating, which had been

---

[72] Susan Stark, 'Women and Translation in the Nineteenth Century', *New Comparison*, no. 15 (Spring 1993), p. 37.
[73] Gilbert and Gubar, *Madwoman*, pp. 3ff.

accepted as a suitable female activity for a long time.[74] This part in the dissemination of texts perfectly symbolised woman's social position, the translation always being inferior *vis-à-vis* the superior original text. Paradoxically enough, this interpretation may well explain the scarcity of research on the subject even within feminist studies.[75]

It has now been recognised that the rigorous application to the text inherent in the translator's profession, provided a start or served as excellent practice for such important women writers as Harriet Martineau, Elizabeth Barrett Browning and George Eliot. Yet their fame was (and is) in no way based on those translations, however valuable those were. It should come as no surprise, therefore, that those women whose main or only achievement rested upon their translations never achieved any degree of eminence, with the sole exception perhaps of Constance Garnett, the assiduous translator of the Russian classics.[76]

Many of the women reviewers contributing to the *Athenaeum* were also experienced translators, translating being one of the few professional opportunities for women writers to add to their capricious earnings. It was quite natural, therefore, for them to be invited to discuss translated books as well as books originally written in English. In the context of this study, it seemed interesting to investigate whether these reviewers incorporated any of their views on translation (possibly derived from their practice) into their reviews. Theoretical reflections on translation or the skill of the translator were uncommon. Having those reflections articulated by women who are sometimes supposed to know more about the *métier* than others makes them doubly interesting. Some of the women reviewers, in fact, specialised in commenting on translations for the *Athenaeum*. Helen Zimmern (1846–1934) and Mary Robinson (1857–1944), for instance, were usually asked to discuss foreign publications (sometimes even when they were published in the original language). Others, such as Katharine de Mattos (1851–1939),[77] and Augusta Webster (1837–1894), were only sporadically assigned translations. The weight of their expertise lay elsewhere but they seem to have been keen to review the occasional translation. To be absolutely fair, however, the reviewing of translations was also taken on by such reputable critics as George Saintsbury and William E. Henley, who often pronounced judgement on the quality of the translation.

---

[74] Quite revealing in this respect is Tina Krontiris's study of women translators in the English Renaissance: *Oppositional Voices. Women as Writers and Translators of Literature in the English Renaissance*, London and New York: Routledge, 1992.

[75] The situation has changed considerably during the last few years with both the skill of the translator and translation theory being revalued in several very specialised publications (see for example Laurence Venuti, ed., *Rethinking Translation. Discourse, Subjectivity, Ideology*, London: Routledge, 1992; and Sherry Simon, *Gender in Translation. Cultural Identity and the Politics of Transmission*, London: Routledge, 1996).

[76] See Richard Garnett, *Constance Garnett. A Heroic Life*, London: Sinclair-Stevenson, 1991.

[77] De Mattos translated, it seems, only one book: *Saint Dominic* (1901).

Before discussing the regular women contributors it may be worth while to look at the reviews of a sporadic contributor, because hers is one of the better-known names of the late Victorian age.   In the early 1880s Mrs Humphry Ward (1851–1920) had started to contribute reviews to some newspapers and reviews. Her husband joined the staff of *The Times* in 1881 and that gave her first-hand experience of the work of a journalist. In her autobiography she recollects how, at one time, she and her husband shared the writing of the review of Morley's *Cobden* for it to be completed in time: 'We divided the sheets of the book, and we just finished in time to let my husband rush off to Printing House Square and correct the proofs as they went through press, for the morning issue'.[78] Later she was to write several articles for *The Times*, the *Pall Mall Gazette*, the *Saturday Review* and the *Quarterly*[79] as well as a few reviews for the *Athenaeum* and a number of shorter pieces for its gossip column. Ward was to achieve fame with the publication of her novel *Robert Elsmere* in 1888. Her only attempt at translation, however, was less of a success and the experiment was not to be repeated.[80] She had, in 1883, enthusiastically started the translation from the French of Henri Frédéric Amiel's *Journal Intime* (1885) but a discouraging review from the hand of her own uncle, Matthew Arnold, soon persuaded her that she had no talent in that direction. Besides, she had specialised in Spanish, not French. Her reviews in the *Athenaeum* reflect that expertise.

Ward's first reviews of translations appeared in April 1882, but she did not touch upon the merits or the difficulty of translation.[81] Her own translating skills only came to bear when she wanted to point out that the Spanish stories allegedly by Mrs Middlemore were in fact plagiarised. In this particular case she compared her own translation of Gustavo Becquer's tales with those produced by Mrs Middlemore's in her *Round a Posada Fire* and came to a rather damning verdict. [82] After that particular controversial contribution there were just a few more reviews by her hand but none as such were concerned with translation. Apparently, the whole episode had been distressing to all parties.

Mary Ward stopped contributing to the *Athenaeum* in 1886. By then she was occupied in writing *Robert Elsmere*[83] and could not spare the time for reviewing. Also, seeing that in 1885 the proprietor of the *Athenaeum*, Sir Charles, had married Emilia Frances Pattison (née Strong) who was known to be an advocate of women's rights, Ward may well have thought it better to leave the *Athenaeum* scene. She was after all going to move in the extreme

---

[78] Mary Ward, *A Writer's Recollections*, London: Collins, 1918, p. 189.
[79] John Sutherland, *Mrs Humphry Ward. Eminent Victorian Pre-eminent Edwardian*, Oxford: Clarendon Press, 1990, p. 90.
[80] Ibid, pp. 98–9.
[81] See *Athenaeum*, 22 April 1882: 'Juàn de Valdes *XVII Opuscules*', tr. John T. Betts; and 'Juan de Valdes *Three Opuscules*', tr. John T. Betts.
[82] 'Mrs Middlemore's Spanish stories', *Athenaeum*, 24 March 1883.
[83] Sutherland, *Mrs Humphry Ward*, pp. 106–22.

opposite direction, becoming the leader of the Women's National Anti-Suffrage League in 1908.[84]

Helen Zimmern (1846–1934) was one of those new contributors who seem to have come with the new editorial team. She soon distinguished herself as a frequent contributor in the mid-1870s, first writing gossip items, then moving on to reviewing. Vernon Lee, in her letters home, describes Zimmern as 'a pleasant, intelligent little black woman, quite capable of doing good work but who has to do hack reviewing to support her people'.[85] She is mentioned in *Who Was Who* (vol. III) but, unfortunately, not in the *Dictionary of National Biography* in spite of her ubiquity as a woman of letters. As a result, only a few facts of her life are known. She was born in Hamburg in 1846 and she probably accompanied her parents to Britain in 1848. She exchanged Britain for Italy in 1887 but continued to act as a foreign correspondent for several periodicals. She wrote for *Blackwood's Magazine*, the *Cornhill Magazine*, the *Fortnightly Review*, *Frazer's Magazine*, *Temple Bar* and the *National Review*.[86]

All this time she was also acting as a professional translator. She was fluent in Italian and German and translated such authors as Nietzsche, Lessing and Goldoni into English. The list of her translations is impressive.[87] She also regularly translated contributions sent in from abroad for a large number of British journals.[88]

Zimmern's obvious conviction that translation, as an aspect of the transmission of a literary work, deserves special attention in a review should therefore not come as a surprise. But such digressions on the quality of the translation were unusual in the *Athenaeum* reviews of the 1870s; remarks which paid attention to gender differences were even more scarce.

Zimmern quite often spends some of the space allotted to her review to the quality of the translation, whether that be positive or negative. In a contribution on the translation of *Ut Mine Stromtid* (1875), for instance, Zimmern praises the translator for having dared to render into English a work originally written in Low German: 'Not only has he produced a translation that is eminently readable, even to those who can peruse Fritz Reuter in the original, but he has thus proved how excellent the book is in itself' (*Athenaeum*, 14 December 1878). A good translation, according to Zimmern, is

---

[84] Ibid, p. 416.

[85] *Lee's letters*, p. 65.

[86] See *The Wellesley Index to Victorian Periodicals*.

[87] C. Benrath, *Bernardino Ochino of Siena*, 1876; *Heroic tales retold from Firdausi*, with a prefatory poem by E.W. Gosse, 1882; Paulina Elizabeth Ottilia Louisa [of Wied], *Pilgrim sorrow*, 1884; G.B. Basile, *The Pentamerone*, 1893; Edmondo de Amicis, *Holland*, tr. from the 13th ed., 1894; L. Lewes, *The Women of Shakespeare*, 1894; G. Ferruggia, *Woman's Folly*, 1895; *Selected Prose Works of G.E. Lessing*, tr. by E.C. Beasley and Helen Zimmern, 1900; R. de Cesare, *The Last Days of Papal Rome, 1850–1870*, Abridged and tr. H. Zimmern 1909; F.W. Nietzsche, *Beyond Good and Evil*, 1907; F.W. Nietzsche, *The Complete Works*, 1909–1913; Enrico Levi Catellani, *Italy and Austria at War*, 1918 (with Agnes McCaskill); Luigi Motta, *Flames on the Bosphorus*, 1920.

[88] See *Wellesley Index*, vol. II.

one that preserves or, indeed, enhances the literary quality of the original publication. The same philosophy inspired her into writing an unfavourable review of a new translation of Goethe's poetry.   She started her review with that rather worn cliché 'Traduttore, tradittore': 'Will certain people never comprehend that to translate a poet requires a poet ? ... anything more stale and prosaic than his [Mr Paul Dyrsen] renderings of the sublime melody and language of Goethe it has rarely been our misfortune to encounter'. The extract she adduces, 'Nur wer die Sehnsucht kennt' from *Wilhelm Meister*, quite convincingly illustrates her point:

> Who has a heavy heart
>   Knows my dejection !
> From every joy apart
>   Shorn of affection,
> My thoughts for ever start
>   In yon direction.
> Far's he who loves my heart
>   And imperfection.
> How deadly is the smart
>   Of this reflection !
> Who has a heavy heart
>   Knows my dejection !

The translator had hoped to achieve a translation in which the source culture, the source language, had disappeared so as to reveal the universally poetic nature of Goethe's work. Unfortunately, quite the reverse happened and it is the poetic quality which has, according to the reviewer, evaporated (*Athenaeum*, 9 March 1878).

Zimmern's reviews are interesting to read.   She has no qualms about condemning a translation outright. But she can couch the verdict in the most ironic phrases.   When she had to comment on the umpteenth translation of Goethe's *Faust* she feigned desperation:

> The persistency of the translating race is difficult for any but the translators to comprehend, since not one of them has ever attained to the excellence of the standard English version, Miss Swanwick's and Bayard Taylor's. Dr Webb ... is aware that forty translations of this poem already exist, but his knowledge has not deterred him from presenting us with the forty-first, doubtless honest in intention, but devoid of any poetical charm, of any grace or attraction.

She also criticised Dr Webb's knowledge of German. Webb had translated 'voller Mondenschein' as 'full moon' whereas it merely meant 'moonshine' when written in two words. Webb had, unfortunately, calculated the length of the play on this mistranslation.   His claim that English is more 'effective', more 'manageable' for the purpose of translation leads to more irritation on the part of the reviewer: 'unwieldy though the German language is in conversation and for every-day purposes, the genius of the language, its inflections, and its capability of variation have made it from all time the best vehicle for translation, and in translation the Germans have been pre-eminent'. It is such a pity, Zimmern concludes, that Webb has not given us the definitive translation of Goethe's famous play, it could have spared us the ordeal of having to read the next forty attempts (*Athenaeum*, 19 March 1881).

In these reviews of translations Zimmern adopts a neutral persona, never giving away her own gender. There is one occasion, however, where she comes perilously near betraying it, even giving the impression of being offended. In her review of S. Baring-Gould's translation of Frau von Hillern's *Ein Artz der Seele* she cannot help observing: 'It is remarkable that a woman should have written a tale that shows such extraordinary ignorance of her own sex, and, one would almost say, a positive bias against it'. (*Athenaeum*, 20 December 1879)

Zimmern is much more given to making remarks of that kind in those contributions dealing with historical, sociological or biographical studies. In a long review of a book entitled *German Home Life*, opening the 19 August 1876 issue of the weekly, she digresses at length about the unfortunate position of the German woman. This woman is from her birth to her death 'a slave', according to Zimmern:

> The subjection of women is certainly rampant in Germany above any other civilized European country, and an outcry raised there for women's rights would have some basis of actual grievance.

She talks about the non-existence of the unmarried German woman ('unmarried she is colourless'), while the married woman leads a totally useless life. To be sure, Zimmern herself has 'often been tempted to think that the German woman is furnished by nature with a supplementary brain, in which she stores her learning and accomplishments, and wherein they are hermetically sealed after she is "finished and confirmed", so little does she give evidences of culture in conversation or bearing'. German men and women have no opportunities to exchange thoughts, or ideas: throughout their lives there is a strict separation of the sexes. Her conclusion is anything but hopeful. She agrees with Heine that the 'husband has no wife, but a serving-maid, and he still goes on living his intellectually isolated life even in the midst of his family'. Zimmern's view of German men is therefore not a very lofty one. They are charged with 'arrogance', 'pedantry', 'prolixity', and 'silly importance'. In the last analysis the review gives the impression of having been written in a fury, the book being used as the reviewer's peg, allowing her to air some of her pent-up feelings against what she calls 'the most exasperating creation under the sun': the German.

In a review of Mrs Vaughan Jennings's *Rahel, her Life and Letters*, Helen Zimmern uncovers a bit more of her own background when she reveals a familiarity with the very restricted social life of the Jews in Germany. She points out to what extent it was an ignominy to be born Jewish at the end of the eighteenth century, and again women had had to bear the brunt of the situation: 'Women felt these restrictions socially: mixed marriages were impossible; the very notion raised repulsion, and some of Rahel's earliest troubles sprang from this source'. So it is the Jewish condition and woman's subservience which sets her to write in protest. When, therefore, she has the occasion to report on a performance of Wagner's *Der Ring des Nibelungen* at Bayreuth she explicitly has to distance herself from the composer's theory and (sometimes) his practice before she can enthuse about the performance she has just witnessed. (*Athenaeum*, 19 August 1876, 26 August 1876)

Ten years after Helen Zimmern's first contribution to the *Athenaeum* the editor, Norman MacColl, thought the time had come to start one of his reviews with a variant on Matthew Arnold's famous quotation: 'the present age [is] the age of criticism'. He declared 'the present age' to be 'an age of translation' (*Athenaeum*, 26 September 1885, p. 397) and went on to explain:

> never were so many translations issued as at the present moment. Only a few weeks ago we reviewed three translations of Homer; a little time before we noticed a translation of the Aeneid; and translations of Greek plays appear at intervals of a few months. And this activity is very far from being confined to classical authors. Dante, of course, attracts the greatest crowd of those who devote themselves to medieval and modern literature ...

'When it came to translations, women's work was ubiquitous', Dale Spender remarked in *Living by the Pen*,[89] but she does not elaborate that assertion. Similarly, Jacques Derrida admits women's part in translation is probably considerable, yet he has to use the conditional tense of the verb since there was and is little research to corroborate his viewpoint: 'statistics would show that women are often in the position of the translator'.[90] The notes and reviews in the *Athenaeum* certainly confirm the hypothesis. Looking at the names of translators usually – though by no means always – mentioned next to the authors, one notices the large proportion of women. A note in the gossip column illustrates this point even further:

> Miss Beetham-Edwards's novelette 'Exchange no Robbery' is being translated into German for immediate issue by the Baroness Stockhausen. 'Priest and Maiden' ... is to appear ... translated into Italian by Miss Mary Laing. A French translation of 'Kitty', by Madame P. Courdier, is in the press, and is to appear in volume form shortly. A French translation of 'Pearla' is also being prepared by Madame de Longeville, of Geneva. All this author's works are translated into Norwegian. (*Athenaeum*, 14 February 1885)

---

[89] Dale Spender, *Living by the Pen. Early British Women Writers*, New York and London: Teachers College Press, 1992, p.12.
[90] Jacques Derrida, *L'Oreille de l'autre*, Montmagny: VLB Editeur, 1984, p. 201; my translation.

The year in which the above passage was published, 1885, is the year in which the *Athenaeum*'s 'marked file' shows a significant growth in the number of reviews by women. This automatically produces an increased interest in the aspect of translation. Indeed, next to Zimmern there were, as mentioned above, several other authors within whose work translation figured prominently and who reviewed translations for the *Athenaeum*. Paradoxically, Helen Zimmern's own contributions declined from then on as in the mid-1880s she had decided to emigrate to Italy, but she continued to review for the *Athenaeum* until 1901 and the advent of Vernon Rendall, the editor who succeeded MacColl. Translating the German pieces was a task reassigned to her younger sister Alice Zimmern (1855–1939). In the second half of the 1880s, therefore, it becomes quite difficult to know which sister wrote the anonymous reviews marked only by 'Zimmern'. Alice Zimmern was nine years younger than her sister and a militant feminist. She only occasionally reviewed for the *Athenaeum* and, like her sister, she stopped contributing entirely at the turn of the century. Nor did she ever acquire her sister's prestige as a reviewer, since she was mainly dealing with the rather less grand column of the schoolbooks. Only in 1898 did she get the opportunity to review some books on women's education, the field within which she herself published.[91] Both sisters stopped contributing during the reign of Vernon Rendall, which leads one to assume that Norman MacColl was the necessary link between the weekly and their involvement.

Mary Robinson (1857–1944), another frequent reviewer of translations, started her *Athenaeum* career somewhat later than Helen Zimmern with two very short poems in 1880. She was then twenty-three and had launched herself on London's cultural scene two years previously with her volume of poems *A Handful of Honeysuckle* (1878). She was to remain a regular contributor of poems and reviews to the *Athenaeum* until January 1900:[92] again a date which seems to indicate the influence of the new editorial team. An illustration in *Punch* of 28 March 1885 featuring the round reading room in the British Museum shows Mary Robinson, the only identifiable female there, reading her own poetry right behind Norman MacColl (see figure 3.1).

There is no description of the young Mary Robinson in Vernon Lee's letters home for the simple reason that Robinson had met the Paget family in Italy in 1880, so the recipient, Mrs Paget, knew what this young woman looked like. Initially, Lee wrote many of the letters to her mother from 84 Gower Street, the Robinsons' family home at the time. Mary Robinson's father, an architect and an amateur art critic, then enjoyed the acquaintance of many of London's foremost artists.[93] The house was visited by such well-known writers

---

[91] She reviewed B.A. Hinsdale's *Horace Mann and the Common School Revival in the United States* (28 May 1898) and the Countess of Warwick's (ed), *Progress in Women's Education in the British Empire* (16 July 1898).

[92] Robinson wrote some twenty reviews in the *Athenaeum* and several signed poems.

[93] Sylvaine Marandon described him as an architect, while Peter Gunn calls him a banker. See Sylvaine Marandon, *L'Oeuvre Poétique de Mary Robinson*, Bordeaux: Pechade, 1967, p. 18, and Gunn, *Vernon Lee*, p. 76.

as Robert Browning, Thomas Hardy and Henry James. Mary and her younger sister Mabel were immersed in literature from their early childhood; their literary inclinations were stimulated to the full. If there is no full-scale description of the Robinson sisters in Vernon Lee's delightful letters home, one can amply compensate for that lack by reading her novel *Miss Brown*. Even allowing for some fictionalisation, it requires no real effort to draw a fine picture of the two sisters from its pages. The names of the characters, too, contain hints :

> Mary Leigh was ... a demi-semi-aesthete; she had studied art in an irregular, Irish sort of way, and she had a literary, romantic kind of imagination, which fitted her rather for an illustrator than a painter. She felt the incompleteness of her own endowment, in a gentle, half-humorous, half-sad way; and the incompleteness of her own life – for her ideal of happiness was to travel about, to live in Italy, and this she had cheerfully sacrificed to please her sister, whose only interests in life were school boards, and depauperisation, and (it must be admitted) a mild flirtation with young men of scientific and humanitarian tendencies.
> Between the sisters there was perfect love, but not perfect understanding; and Mary Leigh, who felt a little lonely, a little shut into herself by her younger sister, who was at once a philosopher and a baby in her eyes, vented her imaginative and artistic cravings in a passionate admiration for Hamlin's strange and beautiful ward or *fiancée* [Anne Brown][94]

The portrait of Mary Leigh, quite clearly, provides us with Vernon Lee's very personal, concise description of the young woman with whom she had fallen in love. Her allusion to the 'perfect love' between the two sisters, however, hides a more unfortunate turn of events since she and her 'attachment' to the one sister effected a breach between Mary and Mabel, culminating in 1882 by Vernon Lee and Mary Robinson being asked by Mrs Robinson to leave the house at 84 Gower Street.[95] The two thereafter lived, worked and travelled together for several years until Mary Robinson's surprise engagement to the French orientalist James Darmesteter in August 1888. [96]

Another certainty to be deduced from Vernon Lee's novel is the monopoly the *Athenaeum* enjoyed in the Robinsons' circle of friends and acquaintances. The central character in the passage below, Postlethwaite, is Lee's version of Oscar Wilde:[97]

> 'Who the deuce is that fellow?' asked Postlethwaite angrily of Mrs Spencer.[98]
> ... Do you know, Mr O'Reilly, who that big black man is, that has just come up to Miss Brown. Not one of *our* set, that's certain.'

---

[94] Vernon Lee, *Miss Brown*, London: Blackwood, 1884, vol. II, p. 3.
[95] *Lee's Letters*, p. 103.
[96] Ibid., p. 272.
[97] She borrowed the name from *Punch* (Ibid., p. 65).
[98] Postlethwaite, by the way, is described earlier as not a 'person to be ousted', being 'elephantine' with a 'flabby flat-cheeked face'.

'Oh Lord, no!' answered the little journalist. 'You don't read newspapers in your set do you?'

'We always read the "Athenaeum"', answered Mrs Spencer, seriously.

'Newspapers are Cimmerian inventions', said Postlethwaite. 'I'm a republican, red, incarnadine, a *démocrate* for Robespierre; but I never take up a paper, except to see which of my friends have left town'.

Thaddy O'Reilly laughed. 'Oh, well, you won't find Education Brown in the "Athenaeum", Mrs Spencer – a mere barbarian, Goth, Philistine, but well known in Philistia. He's a tremendous Radical, goes in for disestablishment, secular teaching; an awful fellow for obligatory education and paupers; he'll be in parliament some day soon, for he's backed by all the black trade'.

To that illustrious institution, then, Mary Robinson sent two poems in 1880, 'Unequal souls' and 'Lover's Silence'. A letter of hers sent from Italy, commenting on the drawings in the Uffizi gallery, was published in the gossip column in February 1882. But her career as a reviewer started five years later.

INTERIORS AND EXTERIORS. NO. 5.

VALUABLE COLLECTION IN THE READING-ROOM, BRITISH MUSEUM.

Figure 3.1   'Valuable Collection in the Reading-Room, British Museum',
Punch, 28 March 1885.

Robinson's fare consisted mainly of French and Italian history, and French and Italian literature, both in the original language and in translation. Her marriage to James Darmesteter (1849–1894) and, after his premature death, to the scientist Emile Ducleaux provided her with a deeper insight into French culture.[99] The marked file gives her name as 'Mme Darmesteter' after August 1888.

Her poetry reviews were very few in number, which is unfortunate as they show more of her poetic personality than the others, being written in a lyrical and emotive style. She welcomes a new edition of H. Cazalis's *Illusion*, for instance, decribing the poems admiringly as possessing a 'penetrating freshness, an unforgettable simplicity, in which there rang a tender echo of disenchantment, a dreamy note of Oriental sadness and resignation'. In such a review she can indulge in imagery and poetic language: 'The same toll rings with effective monotony from title-page to *finis*; one Dance of Death circles uninterruptedly from end to end – like the dim maze of skeletons and knights and ladies that at Rouen possess the four walls of the Court of St. Maclou'. (*Athenaeum*, 14 September 1889). 'Natural' and 'simple' are key-adjectives which for her stand for quality, for true poetry. Still, if the review betrays the reviewer's poetic nature and aesthetic bias it does nothing to shed light on that reviewer's gender. Nor does her gender appear in any of the reviews on historical studies.

As to her reviews of translations, Robinson's expertise was based on her translation of Euripides and her adaptations of Italian lyrics. Later she translated several of her own books into French, and French books into English. She was well equipped to discuss translations and did so with a certain gusto. R.H. Busk's translation of a number of Italian folk songs, for instance, was rigorously criticised by 'Miss Robinson'. In order to understand the problems of translation to the full, she argues here, one should first try to translate the original text oneself. Only then can one's criticism be taken seriously. Even so, she believes some of Busk's translations to be totally unacceptable, including lines such as: 'Would thou were sick within th' infirm'ry portal/ A suffering from malignant fevers three', and: 'In the midst of the ocean the Siren is warbling/ Lulling the mar'ner to treach'rous repose'. These 'ungainly' anapests could hardly be compared to the 'the dreamy iambs' of the Italian verse. The verdict leaves no doubt: R.H. Busk's idea was a good one; the selection is admirable (because not entirely her own), but the translations are clumsy. Busk has presented the reader with 'vulgar brass' in place of the pure gold of the original verse. The reviewer realises, however, that only a few hundred of British readers, that is, those who love the well-made poem, will be disappointed: 'the patient learning of Miss Busk and the solid value of her little book are manifest even through the travesty of her unhappy verse' (*Athenaeum*, 9 April 1887). Aesthetic considerations reign supreme.

---

[99] Marandon, *Mary Robinson*, pp. 47–54.

No need for comforting words in her review of Maude Valérie White's translation of Axel Munthe's Swedish travel story *Letters from a Mourning City* (*Athenaeum*, 7 May 1887, p. 602). The review ends with one long quotation followed by the reviewer's congratulations and expressions of thanks for such a natural translation. Apparently, little can be said about good translations. In those cases, it seems, even concerned reviewers like Robinson concentrated on what had been translated rather than on the translation.[100] Less successful ventures led to much longer digressions on the art, in an attempt to keep the translator from committing the same mistakes.

Mary Robinson never deviates from the gender-neutral position of the *Athenaeum* reviewer. She complains once, in a review of Marchesa Colombi's *In the Rice-fields and other Stories* (tr. Astor Willmott), that the 'incessant dwelling on the monotony of passive, uneducated, and unmarried women ends by becoming monotonous itself' (*Athenaeum*, 9 April 1887). But no other gender-related remarks pass her pen.

Only in some of the gossip items did her interest in women's matters appear.[101] She was, all too obviously, a woman with several faces, several guises perfectly adaptable to any situation. A postscript to one of Vernon Lee's letters to Eugene Lee-Hamilton, her brother, was composed by Mary Robinson while sitting on Vernon Lee's knees. The postscript contains Robinson's evaluation of one of Lee-Hamilton's books and ends somewhat abruptly because Lee's knees prove to be too hard a cushion: 'I am sitting on Vernon's pointed and slippery knees; it is an agony hard to be borne. Appreciate the friendship which – Ah. Ah, can't hold out any longer'.[102]

A few years later, a respectably-married woman, she is described by the French scholar André Chevrillon as the attractive Esmeralda to her adoring Quasimodo.

> I still remember the figure of the erudite orientalist ... His elbow leaning on the arm of the garden seat, his large head on a puny body supported by the hand, his eyes half-closed, he would remain motionless not attending to what we had to say. And when the clear and singing voice of his young wife was heard his eyes would find her and not leave her anymore. [103]

Or should we see her as yet another Dorothea Brooke, married to a man who could hardly understand let alone follow a spirited, imaginative and talented young woman?

---

[100] Raymond Van den Broeck, ed., *Literatuur van Elders. Over het vertalen en de studie van vertaalde literatuur in het Nederlands*, Leuven: Acco, 1988, p. 44.

[101] *Athenaeum*, 14 August 1886. And she wrote the obituaries of her brother-in-law Arsène Darmesteter (*Athenaeum*, 24 November 1888) of Siméon Luce (*Athenaeum*, 24 December 1892) and 'Reminiscences of M. Taine' (*Athenaeum*, 18 March 1893).

[102] *Lee's Letters*, p. 150.

[103] Marandon, *Mary Robinson*, p. 359.

In the last analysis, at the time of her first involvement with the *Athenaeum*, Robinson seems to fit into the pattern of the gifted woman writer who does not follow the prescribed path of the late-nineteenth century middle-class woman and who therefore seemed to the editor an excellent new recruit. Later, she was to refuse the spinsterhood which Vernon Lee and Kate Field willingly embraced, but she remained childless with enough spare time on her hands to continue her work. Like Vernon Lee, Kate Field and Helen Zimmern she represents a generation of women whose attitude towards writing can only be described as 'professional'. Their aim was to earn their own living by the pen. Mary Robinson could not have indicated the order of her priorities more clearly than in 1878, when she came of age: her parents then offered her the choice of either a coming-out ball or the publication of her first volume of poems. She chose the latter.

In the next chapter, three reviewers will be introduced who succeeded, perhaps more than the writers discussed so far, in changing women's social, legal and academic positions. They too, however, in spite of their obvious intellectual capacities, were helped along the way before they could help others. The opportunity to review for the *Athenaeum* undoubtedly gave them the self-confidence required to achieve their ambitions. But their contributions as reviewers remained, by and large, ungendered, neutral: illustrative of the age but, at the same time, lacking the critical bias towards women authors which one does find in the criticism of their male colleagues.

Chapter 4

Feminist Critics and the *Athenaeum*

Millicent Garrett Fawcett

The 'marked file' reveals few reviews written by women in the early 1870s. Geraldine Jewsbury's name was still a constant presence, but she was by then confined to the children's department. And yet, there were a few remarkable newcomers, remarkable because of their blatantly feminist inclinations: Helen Zimmern, Mathilde Blind and Millicent Garrett Fawcett.

Millicent Garrett Fawcett, political economist, feminist and puritan was certainly one of those women reviewers whose careers were especially promoted by Sir Charles Dilke. Millicent Garrett, born in 1847, was the seventh child and fifth daughter of Newson Garrett and Louisa Dunnell.[1] Three of the Garrett sisters – Milly herself; her oldest sister Elizabeth, the first British woman doctor; and Agnes, one of the first women decorators – were to contribute significantly to the women's movement in the latter half of the nineteenth century.[2]

Millicent Garrett's unusual adult life started when she was proposed to, at the age of nineteen, by the blind Professor of Political Economy at Cambridge, Henry Fawcett, then thirty-four years old. In spite of his blindness, Fawcett intended to live life to the full. Next to his academic career he intended to pursue a political career as well, and marriage to an intelligent and attractive young woman was only part of the whole 'normality' package.[3]

The marriage was to all appearances a happy one in spite of the age gap between the two partners. Millicent's intelligence, and her eagerness to learn, turned her into an ideal student and wife for Henry Fawcett. Reading his correspondence and books and helping him to write his own lectures and economical studies provided a firm basis for her own research and writings. Moreover, Harry was not one to curb his wife's personal aspirations. Hence, from 1871 on, she was replaced as his amanuensis by a paid secretary, which

---

[1] Louisa b. 1835, Elizabeth b. 1836, Newson b. 1839, Edmund b. 1840, Alice b. 1842, Agnes b. 1845, Millicent b. 1847, Sam b. 1850, Josephine b. 1853, George b. 1854.

[2] For interesting monographs of Millicent Garrett Fawcett, see David Rubinstein, *A Different World for Women. The Life of Millicent Garrett Fawcett*, New York and London: Harvester Wheatsheaf, 1991 and Barbara Caine, *Victorian Feminists*, Oxford: Oxford University Press, 1992.

[3] Rubinstein enumerates the series of women Henry Fawcett had proposed to before finally being accepted by Millicent.

left her more time for her household duties and her own writings. In fact, as her biographer David Rubinstein rightly contended, Millicent Fawcett soon proved to be much more than the eyes of her husband. Harry Fawcett had the advantage of age and he had enjoyed the right training when they were married in 1867, but she was possibly the more talented of the two. Again according to her biographer, it was Harry's active encouragement which set her to write her first article, 'The Education of women of the middle and upper classes' which appeared in *Macmillan's Magazine* for April 1868. She was then barely twenty-one years old. Never having had the educational opportunities which middle-class boys took for granted, and experiencing this as a serious disadvantage when it came to mixing in intellectual circles at Cambridge, she was to be a champion of equal educational opportunities for women for the rest of her life.

Her first book was the fruit of those early married years when, sitting by the side of her husband, she absorbed political economy with such an intensity and such an eagerness that she was able to select and reproduce the main lines in a introductory book on political economy. The success of Fawcett's *Political Economy for Beginners* (1870) is measured by the number of editions and translations published in her lifetime. Rubinstein mentions at least ten editions and translations into Italian, German, Arabic and several Indian languages, yet adds that the success of this early book was not to be repeated.

Another theme on which she freely expressed herself at the time, was the controversial issue of the free-school system. Her letter to *The Times*, published 14 December 1870, elicited heated responses from several fellow radicals among whom was the then rising politician and family friend Sir Charles Dilke. Though at odds with her views on free-schools, Sir Charles had been sufficiently impressed with her writings and temperament to want her to join the Political Economy Club.[4] He had hoped John Stuart Mill might have proposed her, as he considered himself too junior a member of the club, but Mill refused to do so and the plan failed.[5] She did become a conspicuous member of the Radical Club, a club consisting of twenty Members of Parliament and twenty 'non-members', five of whom were women. Noteworthy non-members were Helen Taylor (1831–1907), a feminist and the daughter of Harriet Taylor, and Emilia Strong Pattison (later Dilke).[6] Among the Dilke papers in the British Library there are several letters which testify to the closeness between Dilke and Millicent Fawcett. She wrote a lengthy report of the Club's meeting in February 1872 and sent him the members'

---

[4] Dilke had written her a long letter on the subject of education from Brussels (see British Library, unpublished letter 24 January 1871, Add Ms 43 907, f. 170ff).

[5] Rubinstein, *A Different World*, p. 31.

[6] In his memoir of Lady Dilke, Sir Charles recalls how she brought forward only one subject for discussion and that 'a special subject of her own': 'The conditions which should determine the wages of female labour'; see 'Memoir of fact and Letters chiefly before 1885', preserved at the British Library, Add Ms 43,946, p. 76.

subscriptions. He, in his turn, commissioned a portrait of the extraordinary Fawcetts to be painted by Ford Madox Brown.[7]

One of Dilke's reasons for suggesting Millicent Fawcett as a new member for the Political Economy Club in 1871 lay, as he had it, in her having written many articles both signed and anonymous.[8] As the owner of the *Athenaeum* he was in an excellent position to judge her anonymous contributions. It is quite remarkable that in spite of the detailed attention paid to Millicent Garrett Fawcett's long career as a leading suffragette, a public orator and a writer, in a range of recent publications there is hardly any mention of Millicent Fawcett's involvement as a reviewer for the *Athenaeum* or of her writings on political economy.[9] Yet the fact is not without any consequence. In a detailed analysis of the political economy column in the *Edinburgh Review*, Judith Newton stated quite unequivocally that the reviewers within the field of political economy in the 1830s were 'more authentically masculine' than other sub-groups of men, as theirs was a sphere which had not been invaded yet by women. She also points to the role of clubs in the construction of the professional male reviewer:

> Like other professional organizations, which proliferated in the 1830s and 1840s in Great Britain, scientific organizations such as the Royal Society, the Statistical Society, and the Political Economy Club, to which reviewers variously belonged, helped establish the social value of a specific form of expertise.[10]

'Those who most distinctly defined the outside to these insiders' clubs', she goes on to say, 'were women'. Dilke's efforts at trying to break down the exclusionary wall between the genders failed, but it did not keep him from pushing Fawcett's career, anonymously, through the pages of the *Athenaeum*.

Millicent Fawcett reviewed some twenty-eight books for the *Athenaeum*, all of which were concerned with political economy. Six of the reviews which I have counted as hers were attributed by an unknown editorial hand to a 'Fawcett'.[11] Because these were all about political economy, and because of the reference to an earlier review marked as 'Mrs Fawcett' as being by the same writer, I believe it justified to assume that those were hers as well.[12] Apart from those reviews, she used the *Athenaeum* to promote the imminent

---

[7] See unpublished letters at the British Library, Add Ms 43,909, ff. 184, 246, 254, 260.

[8] Mill Papers quoted in Rubinstein, *A Different World*, p. 30.

[9] Ibid., p. 31. There are no references to the *Athenaeum* in Millicent Garrett Fawcett's autobiography either.

[10] Judith Newton, *Starting Over. Feminism and the Politics of Cultural Critique*, Ann Arbor: University of Michigan Press, 1997, p. 109.

[11] One cannot possibly be sure as to who marked the names in the editor's copy.

[12] In a review of J.E. Cairnes's *Political Essays* the reviewer remarks: 'It is only a few weeks since we noticed a collection of essays on politico-economical subjects from the pen of Prof. Cairnes' (*Athenaeum*, 12 July 1873) which refers to Millicent Fawcett's notice of *Essays in Political Economy* (22 May 1873).

publication of a book by her husband and to publish the examination results at
Trinity College or other newsy items connected with her husband's activities.[13]

When Fawcett started to publish her articles and books, some female
economists had already made a name for themselves in the field. She could
follow the example of such popular writers as Harriet Martineau and Jane
Marcet.[14] By 1871, Barbara Caine asserts, Millicent Garrett Fawcett herself
was considered to be an authoritative political economist.[15] She was first asked
to review a series of works dealing with political economy for the *Athenaeum*
as early as 1870, when she was barely twenty-three. Her earliest contribution,
a review of T.E. Kebbel's *The Agricultural Labourer*, published 13 August
1870, shows her for the feminist she was: whenever possible, her interest
focuses on women and she expresses her view that women are exploited
economically as well as sexually. She was to retain this uncompromising
stance regarding man's sexual dissipations throughout her active life, a crusade
which was to isolate her several times, imperilling the other causes in which
she was involved.[16] In that review of *The Agricultural Labourer* she points to
the merits of the work under discussion, but then proceeds to attack Kebbel's
point that women should be withdrawn from field work because 'their
employment leads to immorality'. Female unchastity implies a corresponding
unchastity among men, she avers – it is therefore most unfair to blame only the
women. In a review published a month later, 3 September 1870, she again
mentions the woman question, this time in connection with the *American
System of Government*, a study by Ezra Seaman. The issue is raised at the very
end of the review in connection with Seaman's chapter on the women's rights
movement. But she has very little to comment, as Mr Seaman seems to give in
to the usual platitudes on the subject: 'women are cautioned that this movement
may probably diminish their chances of marriage and decrease the happiness of
married life'. After these two early contributions it took some time before she
was again to touch upon the economic position of women as a social group in
her *Athenaeum* reviews, but return to it she did.

There is, for instance, that contribution of a somewhat different calibre,
namely her coverage of the 'Economic Science and Statistics' section at the
annual Royal Society meeting in September 1875. It would be her first and last
report on that august body. She had obviously enjoyed the event but she was
not impressed with what had happened there. The papers discussed at length
were both by women. The issue addressed was the position of women on the
job market, an issue which had interested her since the mid-1860s. The first
paper contained a rather extravagant proposal by Mrs Crashaw to employ
ladies as domestic servants, apparently in an attempt to offer impecunuous

[13] *Athenaeum*, 6 January 1877, 24 October 1874, 4 April 1874.
[14] For a discussion of Marcet and Martineau's work see John Richard Shackleton, *Two
early female economists Jane Marcet and Harriet Martineau*, London: Polytechnic of Central
London, Faculty of Social Sciences and Business Studies, 1988.
[15] Caine, *Victorian Feminists*, p. 206.
[16] Ibid., p. 213.

middle-class women other outlets than teaching, governessing, nursing or sewing. Household work needs to be done by unskilled labour, Fawcett counters. Besides, she adds, nobody has ever suggested similar downgraded work for young gentlemen. The second paper, by a Miss Carpenter, advocated an extension of the power of school boards, enabling them to establish industrial day-schools where children would be fed as well as taught. In this scheme the public was meant to pay for the education of the child without inflicting the stigma of pauperism on the parents (*Athenaeum*, 4 September 1875). This modern idea could find no favour with Millicent Garrett Fawcett, as it would create confusion between 'the duties of school boards and Boards of Guardians'. Then, a year later, the *Athenaeum* published her review on *Domestic Economy of Girls* in which she could not suppress the sarcasm in her comment when reading that sick-nursing was 'indeed woman's work'. 'It is sufficient comment on this enthusiasm', she reflected, 'to remember that there are not, thank Heaven! enough sick people in the world to give work to all the women who need employment' (*Athenaeum*, 14 October 1876). Fawcett, according to Caine, wanted women to enjoy the same education as men, 'in order that they be equally equipped to deal with whatever situation they should face'.[17]

Fawcett's reviews were invariably informative, giving a good idea of the contents of the book under review. But she was not easy to please. She was sure to read the book from start to finish, giving the author a fair 'hearing', listing the good points, but also marking passages or chapters which could be improved. Though she obviously tried, on the whole, to make her reviews as objective as possible, she was tempted into giving Professor J.E. Cairnes,[18] a family friend, something of a preferential treatment. Five of the twenty-eight reviews she was to write for the *Athenaeum* discussed his work. He was merely given the most cautious of suggestions whenever she did not agree. Consider, for instance, the phrasing 'there is one point which, in our opinion, Prof. Cairnes does not place in a sufficiently clear light'. (*Athenaeum*, 12 July 1873). But then, Cairnes, whom she had called 'the ablest of living economists', in an earlier review (*Athenaeum*, 22 March 1873), was twenty-four years her senior and he was bound to know that she had written the review. Edmond About, on the other hand, though a foreign scholar of some renown (indeed, he was to author some of the 'Notes from Paris') was chidden because of his obscure and pompous language. Similarly, *Primitive Property*, the latest book by Belgian scholar Emile de Laveleye, yet another contributor to the *Athenaeum*, was dismissed because of its unrealistic praise of an 'agricultural communism' (16 March 1878). This review reveals Fawcett's reactionary attitude towards this kind of economic democratisation in spite of (or should one say alongside) feminist campaigns. Nor is she innovative in her views on foreign economies, since she shares the prevalent Victorian

---

[17] Caine, *Victorian Feminists*, p. 222.
[18] Cairnes was professor of Political Economy and Jurisprudence at Queen's College, Galway.

conviction that British economists as well as the British economy (including employers as well as employees) are superior to their Continental equivalents. In her review of Thomas Brassey's survey of *Foreign Work and English Wages considered with Reference to the Depression of Trade* she remarks with a touch of irony that Mr Brassey 'speaks well even of the weather'. Indeed, she agrees with Mr Brassey that 'the cost of labour is less in England, owing to the greater energy and efficiency of the English labourer', although much lower wages are paid elsewhere in Europe. Fawcett's last anonymous entry in the *Athenaeum* was a short gossip item in the issue of 28 November 1886.

Rubinstein's bibliography does not list Fawcett's reviews for the *Athenaeum*, but it appears that they were an important part of her writings on political economy.[19] Apart from those reviews there had been her *Political Economy for Beginners*, her far less successful *Tales in Political Economy* (1874), and the *Essays and Lectures on Social and Political Subjects* (1872) which she wrote together with her husband. The conclusion, inevitably, seems to be that the interest in economy kindled in the young Millicent Garrett Fawcett by her husband, had to make way for her commitment to the women's cause after his death in 1884, although she did lecture a few times on the topic in the late eighties.[20]

Barbara Caine has pointed out the degree to which Fawcett's puritanism ruled her life in respect of the Harry Cust case in 1894. Fawcett had taken it upon herself to have this Conservative candidate for North Manchester rejected on account of his 'liberal' premarital lifestyle. He had eventually married the woman whose reputation he had compromised but that, according to Fawcett, did not excuse his earlier misbehaviour.[21] Fawcett's puritanism, her struggle to protect women against man's exploitation, paradoxically, ties in with her feminism as well as her reactionary stance. She had shown this unrelenting attitude towards man's sexual presumptuousness when she proved a formidable obstacle in Sir Charles Dilke's attempt to regain his former political position a few years before the Cust case. Sir Charles's being selected for the post of alderman on the new London Council was prevented by means of a petition signed by 1,604 women, including four of the Garrett sisters.[22] Their formerly friendly relationship and his invaluable early support of her work could not compensate for the enormity of his crime towards women.

Caine points out that there are two strands in Fawcett's life: 'her work in the suffrage, education, and medical campaigns, all directed towards gaining legal and political equality for women ... and her discussions and campaigns directed towards purity, all of which centre on the sexual exploitation and

---

[19] Rubinstein observes he could not possibly list all of her articles and, therefore, only lists four (*A Different World*, p. 34). Yet the *Athenaeum* involvement does paint another picture of the place 'political economy' assumed in her career and her life.

[20] Rubinstein, *A Different World*, p. 106. This view is corroborated by Caine, *Victorian Feminists*, p. 207.

[21] Caine, *Victorian Feminists*, p. 213.

[22] Rubinstein, *A Different World*, pp. 89, 94.

victimization of women'.[23] 'The main problem' for Caine 'is how to bring these two sets of concerns together'.[24] But the link is there. Fawcett considered herself to be the protector of women's rights. These rights extended to the private sphere in the sense that she thought a man should always take the responsibility in cases of seduction and unwanted pregnancy. In light of her strong conviction that the sin should not be visited only on the women it was impossible for her to forgive an irresponsible philanderer like Harry Cust for having seduced a young belle. He had to serve as an example, just as Dilke had had to. Not letting them get away with this was the proof of consistent thinking and behaving. She resented hypocrisy and the 'boys will be boys' attitude. A man had to bear the consequences of his actions.

Fawcett's political involvement is another puzzling fact of her life since she found herself increasingly in conflict with the Liberal Unionists in the late 1880s and 1890s. David Rubinstein sees this as a consistent evolution towards a more conservative political attitude. On the basis of those early anonymous *Athenaeum* reviews, it seems that her politically reactionary inclination had been barely suppressed even in the 1870s. The fact is that she stopped contributing to the liberal *Athenaeum* in the second half of the 1880s, although the Dilke scandal will have played a major role in her decision to 'abstain'.[25]

The sudden death of Henry Fawcett in November 1884 may equally have contributed to the breach between Millicent and the politician who used to be a true friend and fellow militant. After her husband's death Millicent Fawcett almost immediately joined W.T. Stead's campaign against the sexual traffic in young girls. This decision only exacerbated her moral stance. Withdrawal from all collaboration with the *Athenaeum* was for her a logical step if one considers this merciless remark in a letter to a male acquaintance: 'many ladies feel very strongly against associating their names with that of Lady Dilke'. [26]

Millicent Garrett Fawcett continued her efforts on behalf of the women's movement, culminating in her militant advocacy of women's suffrage in the early decades of this century.[27] This aspect of her life has eclipsed her

---

[23] Caine, *Victorian Feminists*, p. 218.

[24] Ibid., p. 218.

[25] The *Athenaeum* paid tribute by means of these Miltonian lines by P.B. Marston:

> And he is gone now out of all men's sight
> Who sightless fought his way, nor failed one hour;
> Matched Fate with Will's indomitable power,
> Rose up from sickness and confronted Night.
> 'Others may flee', he said; 'I stay to fight'.
> Fighting, he saw his dread opponent cower.
> As human strength o'er his began to tower,
> While the blind Victor's brows were breathed with light …
> (*Athenaeum*, 15 November 1884)

[26] Quoted in Philippa Levine, *Feminist Lives in Victorian England. Private Roles and Public Commitment*, Cambridge: Blackwell, 1990, p. 100.

[27] Sutherland, *Before the Suffragettes*, p. 71.

other achievements. Her work for the *Athenaeum* or, should I say, the *Athenaeum*'s work for her, has never been fully considered.

Emilia Frances Strong Pattison

> Dear Friend, – Your kind letter from Stratford is indeed interesting. Ah, when shall I have an opportunity of seeing these, and so many other interesting places! But in a world where duty is *so much*, and so *always* with us, why should we regret the voids in our experience which, after all, life is filling in the experience of others? (From Mrs Casaubon to William Ladislaw, Esq.)[28]

A prominent feminist whose views on the Dilke scandal could not have been more unlike Fawcett's was Emilia Pattison. She, too, was a contributor to the *Athenaeum* at the time of the scandal but she refused to believe, or at least forgave and forgot (when she was allowed to) and became Dilke's second wife.

Emilia Frances Pattison (née Strong, 1840–1904) started to contribute to the *Athenaeum* in the second half of the 1870s. She had by then already made a name for herself both in real life and in fiction. Indeed, in her article 'Writing Inside the Kaleidoscope: Re-Representing Victorian Women Public Figures', Kali A.K. Israel focuses on Emilia Pattison to demonstrate the interaction between a Victorian woman's life and contemporary fiction because hers had been a life which shaped images as well as being shaped by images: 'Not only did she find images of which to make herself in literature and art, but she found herself made into images by others'.[29] What follows is yet another attempt at reconstructing an aspect of her life, using existing representations as well as some of her own writings.

The third daughter and fourth child of a retired Indian Army officer, Emilia Frances Strong became the wife of Mark Pattison, Rector of Lincoln College, Oxford, and twenty-seven years her senior, at the age of twenty-one. It was Emilia's deliberate choice, her way of giving sense to her life. Emilia, then known as Frances or Francesca to her friends, had by 1861 acquired a reputation as a brilliant and rebellious art student whose demand to be allowed to draw from the nude showed her unconventionality and her fighting spirit. She left South Kensington Art School in February 1861 with prizes in two subjects and with a study from the nude pronounced 'excellent' by the veteran painter William Mulready (1786–1863). But after this taste of the public sphere she had had to go back home, as there had been no prospects for her in the art world.

Emilia Strong had been a special child as well. She had stood apart on account of her intelligence, her mystic hallucinations and her unusual religious

---

[28] Andrew Lang, *Old Friends. Essays in Epistolary Parody*, London: Longman, 1892, p. 113.

[29] Kali Israel, 'Writing Inside the Kaleidoscope: Re-Representing Victorian Women Public Figures', *Gender & History*, 2:1 (Spring 1990), p. 45.

penances. Later, as an art student, she was still to punish herself by lying for hours on the bare floor in the form of the cross. Her marriage to Mark Pattison must have seemed an opportunity to live a valuable life in the service of others. Little did she know it was to be a kind of penance as well.

The Pattison marriage was to capture the fantasy of a number of contemporary novelists who used this somewhat unnatural union as the core of one of their fictional stories. Rhoda Broughton, a friend of the Pattisons, was to model her central characters in *Belinda* (1883) on the couple. Another young protégé, Mary Arnold (later to achieve fame as Mrs Humphry Ward) and W.H. Mallock caricatured the rector in *Robert Elsmere* (1888) and *The New Republic* (1876) respectively.[30] But it was George Eliot who was to confer immortality upon their marriage and their personalities by recreating this unhappy union in the characters of Edward Casaubon and Dorothea Brooke in *Middlemarch* (1872).[31] Dorothea's perception of Casaubon as 'a living Bossuet, whose work would reconcile complete knowledge with devoted piety' seems to fit Pattison like a glove.[32] And Emilia's unusually rigorous piety finds its counterpart in a Dorothea whose ambitions were comparable to Saint Theresa's.[33] 'It is impossible to compare the Prelude and several passages in the first book of "Middlemarch",,' Sir Charles was to observe, 'and not to see whence came George Eliot's knowledge of the religious ideal of her Dorothea Brooke'.[34]

The Pattison marriage was, it was rumoured, as unsuccessful as Dorothea's marriage to the fossilised Casaubon. The funniest piece of writing, commenting on two of the fictionalisations, came from the pen of Andrew Lang. In his *Old Friends*, a collection of essays in epistolary parody, Lang had the protagonists of *Middlemarch* and those of *Belinda* write confidential letters to one another ending with a letter from Dorothea to Belinda in which the one, quite exemplary, urges the other not to continue her clandestine relationship with Mr Rivers: 'when I saw you so lonely among all those learned men my heart went out to you, for I too know what the learned are, and how often, when we are young, we feel as if they were so cold, so remote. Ah, then there come *temptations*, but they must be conquered'.[35] Emilia Dilke, for her part, was never publicly to admit that she had made a mistake when marrying

---

[30] And then there were the many books and plays based on the Dilke scandal (see Israel, 'Writing inside the Kaleidoscope', pp. 42ff.)

[31] This is something of a controversial issue. In his edition of George Eliot's letters Haight adopts the sceptical point of view, arguing that the couple continued their friendly relations with the famous novelist even after the publication of *Middlemarch* (see Gordon Haight, ed., *The George Eliot Letters*, London: Oxford University Press, 1954, 9 vols, p. 39). Sir Charles Dilke, in 'Memoir of facts and letters before 1885', holds that 'it is impossible to compare the Prelude and several passages in the first book of "Middlemarch" with passages still existing in the diaries and manuscripts of Miss Strong penned before 1862, and not to see whence came George Eliot's knowledge of the religious ideal of her Dorothea Brooke'. (p. 23)

[32] George Eliot, *Middlemarch*, p. 47.

[33] Ibid., p. 112.

[34] Quoted from the manuscript of Dilke's 'Memoir of fact and Letters chiefly before 1885', preserved at the British Library, Add Ms 43,946, p. 23.

[35] Lang, *Old Friends*, p. 116.

Pattison. Moreover, she claimed never to have read Eliot's celebrated novel, arguing that judging by what 'I have heard from all, Mr Casaubon was much more to be pitied than Dorothea'.[36]

To all appearances, Mrs Pattison continued to respect and honour her husband until his death in 1884. The picture drawn in Betty Askwith's biography, however, is a different one. There was, in Askwith's words, 'a complete sexual incompatibility between husband and wife',[37] but there was also an incompatibility of character. Pattison had grown set in his ways and could, at the age of forty-eight, hardly be expected to change them, let alone admit his views were wrong. In a letter to Eleanor Smith, Emilia candidly admits Pattison had hoped to marry a woman who was merely 'a contented machine' describing marriage cynically as the 'peck, peck, peck of the cruel beak'.[38] Pattison's meanness was undoubtedly one of his most objectionable characteristics to his young wife.[39] But it was the physical revulsion which accounts for the final breach between the two spouses. Indeed, the rector's interpretation of his wife's frequent illnesses and subsequent absences as being psychosomatic may have been more perspicacious than Askwith, for one, assumes. Since divorce, at that time, was out of the question if one wanted to avoid scandal, each of the Pattisons went their own way, both finding new friends and both developing their skills and continuing their research. There is reason to believe that Emilia did come to terms with the situation a few years before the rector's death, nursing him during his last illness and publishing his memoirs after his death. In a letter written from Rector's Lodgings in February 1884 she was to state: 'If one life is to give way to the other I feel sure it should be mine; – his is worth much more – it represents much more, of much greater value to the world than mine. I think he is the only truly learned man I know'.[40]

But there was another 'learned man' whom she knew very well at the time and whose letters she carefully preserved. Her correspondence with Sir Charles Dilke is kept from the early 1870s onwards but it started much earlier than that. Their friendship pre-dated her marriage to Pattison. In 1859, when they were both still students, their paths crossed at the meetings of the Trap-bat Club in the garden of Gore House. Emilia Strong was nineteen at the time, that is, too old and too wise for the merely sixteen-year-old Charles. He himself rather fondly recalled years later that he 'loved to be patronized by her, regarding her with the awe of a hobbledehoy of sixteen or seventeen towards a beautiful girl of nineteen or twenty'.[41] A roughly scribbled remark in red pencil

---

[36] Dilke, 'Memoir', p. 119.

[37] Betty Askwith, *Lady Dilke. A Biography*, London: Chatto & Windus, 1969, p. 53.

[38] Levine, *Feminist Lives in Victorian England*, p. 44.

[39] After Pattison's death, in her life as Lady Dilke, Emilia Strong was to reveal her personal views on the material side of life by being responsible, for example, for the lavish hospitality of the Trade Union conferences (Rubinstein, *Before the Suffragettes*, p. 134) and making sure professional women were paid the wages they deserved (Ibid., p. 125).

[40] 'Memoir', p. 119.

[41] Gwynn and Tuckwell, *Sir Charles Dilke*, p. 17.

and in Sir Charles's handwriting prefaces the Dilke–Pattison collection now preserved in the British Library. It reads: 'I called her "Frank" from 1859 to 1876 or 1879 after which she dropped her "Frances"' (British Library Add MS 43.903 f. 1). There are indications that they had romantic meetings, in France, after the death of Dilke's first wife.

A letter from Sir Charles to Kate Field suggests that any proofs of this early infatuation were destroyed,[42] while the correspondence covering the period after the Dilke marriage in 1885 is extremely thin: since the two were always together, there was no need to write letters. The contrast with the middle years, when letters were exchanged almost daily, is a sharp one. In those days Sir Charles even complained when she remained silent for a few days. Theirs had obviously been a very intense relationship. Sir Charles looked to Emilia for understanding and appreciation. Every single one of his letters mentions with delight and pride the list of his engagements, the names of prominent politicians, aristocrats and artists. A letter of Thursday, 27 February, for instance, begins:

> Engagements.
> Tomorrow Friday dine with the Misses Lawrence (sisters to [Sir] Trevor Lawrence, & great Herbert Spencerists) Lady Waldegrave's evening. W. C. Cartwright's [dinner], Sat. Cambridge Ad [Eundem] dinner. Sunday Cambridge dine with Hopkins. Monday & Thursday House all night. Wednesday dine Lady Constance Shaw Lefevre, Mrs Brands evening. Thursday dine with Lady Stephen. Friday 7 March dine B W.E.Forster's. 8th Aston Clinton; & 9th [the rest of this page was cut][43]

Very few of her letters to him were preserved. There are her letters to Robert Browning, to Eugène Muntz, Edward Burne Jones and E.F. Watts, but her letters to her husband-to-be are scarce. Betty Askwith surmises that neither wanted to expose the closeness of their relationship long before the rector had breathed his last. The letters that did survive were dreadfully mutilated, but enough of the endearing little words remained for us to be able to guess at the intensity and intimacy of their attachment. Dilke had a passion for petnames. He would call himself 'Zz' (a shortening of the pet name Tsar) while addressing her as 'Hoya' or 'Tots'.[44] The result sounds rather ridiculous to the detached onlooker: 'Zz's crying today because he's had nothing from Tots for such a time. But he thinks it's all the fault of Xmas Day and Bank holiday. He posts this because otherwise [Tots] will be crying too'(29 December 1884).

The curious state of the manuscripts may be related to Dilke's involvement in the notorious divorce case of Crawford vs. Crawford. He, or his wife's niece Gertrude Tuckwell, quite drastically removed every scrap of

---

[42] Letter to Miss Field, 1 May 1873: 'I never wrote a love letter since I was nineteen, & I am happy in the belief that those I wrote before nineteen are all burnt' (British Library, Add Ms 43,909, f. 344).

[43] Unpublished letter kept in the British Library, Add Ms 43,903 f. 173.

[44] Askwith, *Lady Dilke*, p. 118.

paper that might incriminate him.[45] Of the Dilke–Pattison correspondence nearly all forms of address have been cut. Only very exceptionally do we find a letter still addressed to 'Darling' or 'Dearest, dear Love'. We do know, though, that one of the earliest letters of the collection bears upon the *Athenaeum*, Sir Charles's precious inheritance. It is a curiously interesting letter because it gives the uninformed reader the impression that Emilia had offered this male friend some assistance with his daily duties. 'I'll tell you one thing you c^d do that I should like', Sir Charles replies '[i]t is to read your Athenaeum for me. I.E. to suggest improvements in the conduct of this paper'.[46]

The above letter was written in August 1875, at a time when Emilia Pattison had already achieved a reputation as an art critic. She had been a regular art reviewer for the *Saturday Review*,[47] the *Portfolio*[48] and the *Academy* in the 1860s. She had also written occasional essays for the *Fortnightly Review*[49] and the *Contemporary Review*[50]. Moving upwards on the scale of prestige she exchanged the *Saturday Review* for a regular column on art in the *Westminster Review*.[51] Then, in 1873, she was appointed as the salaried art editor of the *Academy*. A letter from Charles Appleton, editor of the *Academy*, reads:

> If you will undertake the editing of the Art department, and give up the *Westminster*, the *Academy* will pay besides its own present rate (£ 1 a page-) the average sum you have received from the *Westminster* in addition.
>
> You shall have the £ 30.10 which we at present owe you for last year, so soon as I get any profit on my shares in the company. This I anticipate before long.
>
> You shall have all books & periodicals and the name control over the departments as the other editors – tho' I don't propose to burden you with Picture galleries, except of course in cases of emergency. [52]

---

[45] See also Nicholls, *The Lost Prime Minister*, p. ix.

[46] See his letter in the British Library, Add Ms 43.903, f. 21. She did read the *Athenaeum* attentively and suggested corrections to MacColl. In a letter of 20 February 1879, MacColl thanks her for pointing out the misspelling of the name of Max Schuster in the Dramatic Gossip section. See his letter in the British Library, Add Ms 43,908, f. 41.

[47] Askwith, *Lady Dilke*, p. 34.

[48] 'Memoir', p. 37.

[49] The information presented in this and the next note is based on the data collected in *The Wellesley Index to Victorian Periodicals 1824–1900* : 'Nicolas Poussin', 1872; 'France under Richelieu', 1885; 'France under Colbert', 1886; 'Royal Academy of Paiting and Sculpture in France', 1886; 'The Great Missionary Success', 1889; 'Benefit Societies and Trades unions for women', 1889; 'The coming elections in France', 1889; 'Art-teaching and technical schools', 1890; 'Trades Unionism among women', 1891; 'Women and the Royal Commission', 1891; 'Mulready', 1892; 'The Industrial Position of Women', 1893; 'Letter', 1887.

[50] 'On the French Renaissance', 1877; 'French Châteaux of the Renaissance', 1877 .

[51] See *Wellesley,*vol. III, p. 643.

[52] Unpublished letter, dated 20 October 1873 (British Library, Add Ms 43,908, ff. 13–14).

Consequently, she gave up her regular work for the *Westminster Review* but continued to write elsewhere. Appleton was obviously one of her most passionate admirers. In 1878 he praised her latest articles for him as 'some of the best things I have ever published in the *Academy*', adding that he – and others – were 'simply astounded at the scholarly & exact knowledge' with which her articles abounded.[53]   When she withdrew her participation in the *Academy* in 1883, the new editor, J.S. Cotton, greatly regretted her decision: 'Your *salon* was in my humble opinion not only the best thing done on the subject in England, but about the best bit of art criticism done anywhere'.[54] Emilia's energy was henceforth to be spent mainly on the *Athenaeum*, the journal owned by her prospective husband, and, after 1885, in trying to recover Dilke's good name. But her life's main work was to be the management and the expansion of the women's trade unions.

As early as November 1884, a mere three months after the death of Mark Pattison, we find another political friend, Joseph Chamberlain, congratulating the young widow on her approaching marriage: 'Dilke has told me his great secret, & I sympathized with him so warmly in his new prospects of happiness which are opening for him that I have asked leave to write to you & to offer my hearty congratulations'.[55]   Chamberlain was one of the select few who knew about this match long before it became common knowledge. This contradicts those printed sources which suggest that their marriage had been her attempt at redeeming the precarious situation in which Dilke found himself at the end of 1885.[56]   In August 1885 Donald Crawford had filed a petition against his wife, Virginia Crawford, for her alleged adultery with Sir Charles. The affair did not affect Dilke's forthcoming marriage but it did ruin his political career. Dilke was never to hold office again.

The historians who have explored the facts of the case have tried to exonerate Dilke. Like Nicholls, they have drawn up lists of arguments which lay the blame squarely on Virginia Crawford, the young woman at the centre of this mess.[57] Statements such as 'they have therefore been left wondering why she chose him as her victim' are hardly fair to Virginia Crawford. She was only twenty-two at the time and could certainly not destroy a powerful politician like Dilke single-handedly or without any grounds. Nor should we forget Dilke's carefully constructed image as a ladies' man and the fact that society condoned sexual affairs as long as they remained in the private domain. More importantly, and more distressingly, Dilke's political friends abandoned him even before the case had been heard. Then, as now, in Anglo-American countries it was best to discard a tarnished element from the government,

---

[53] Unpublished letter, 9 August 1878 (British Library, Add Ms 43,908, f. 37).

[54] Unpublished letter, 6 April 1883 (British Library, Add Ms 43,908, f. 90).

[55] Unpublished letter, 5 November 1884 (British Library, Add Ms 43,907, f. 226).

[56] See, for example, Ella Hepworth Dixon, *As I Knew Them*, p. 28.

[57] Nicholls, *A Life of Sir Charles Dilke*, p. 195ff.; Jenkins, *Sir Charles Dilke*; Askwith, *Lady Dilke*, pp. 151ff. Horstman does not explain why he thinks Dilke was innocent. But the mere fact that he erroneously calls the accuser 'Campbell' does not inspire confidence. (Allen Horstman, *Victorian Divorce*, London and Sydney: Croom Helm, 1985, p.140).

however valuable that element might have been. Emilia Pattison, however, far away in India in the early autumn of 1885, rose to the occasion and immediately cabled to *The Times* announcing their engagement. They were married at Chelsea Old Church on 3 October 1885 and, after a few weeks of drifting round the country, finally installed themselves at the Dilke family home, 76 Sloane Street, in November of that same year.

The early years of their marriage were certainly not idyllic, given the fierceness with which Dilke's political enemies tried to keep him out of public office. Askwith even thought it had been wrong for such a popular ladies' man as Dilke to get married at such a critical time in his career, because his many, often powerful, lady-friends could never forgive him that.[58]   One of the most tenacious foes, however, was certainly a man. The editor and journalist W.T. Stead launched a crusade against what he believed to be the depravity of such natures as Dilke's.[59]   Stead gloried in assuming the attitude of the martyr braving the world against all odds. Indeed, he had gone to prison for three months after his exposure of child prostitution in his 'Maiden Tribute of Modern Babylon' on a charge of buying a child prostitute without the parents' permission.[60]   Yet for all this puritanism it is not precisely known why Stead now turned to the Dilke case as if his life and his livelihood depended on it.[61] Stead's campaign started in March 1886 and all but succeeded in destroying Dilke's public life. Emilia Dilke's attempts at changing Stead's opinion of her husband can only have gratified him. His account of the interview he had with Lady Dilke and his description of her breaking down, sobbing and blaming herself because 'if she had only let him go on with his intrigues and life of pleasure, none of the trouble would have come upon him'[62] seems hard to credit.   The strength of her commitment, and the fervour with which she defended Dilke's innocence, serve to show a determination to restore her husband to his former position in society.

After her marriage Emilia Dilke wrote more frequently for the *Athenaeum*. According to the 'marked file', she wrote more than a hundred articles (reviews, notes and obituaries) on matters of art, from 1876 until her death in 1904. [63] Some of those were signed, yet these, too, escaped the notice

---

[58] Alice Comyns-Carr's *Reminiscences* give an idea of Dilke's charisma when she reflected : 'Charles Dilke was not an attractive man, but he must have had some winning qualities not apparent to the first-comer ... He was a great lady-killer in the 'eighties, and I remember that when I told Lady Lindsay I should like to meet him she whispered, "There's always a waiting list, you know, Feeble" - her doubtfully flattering name for me' (see Comyns-Carr, *Reminiscences*, London: Hutchinson, n.d., p. 9)

[59] See, for instance, the 'Character Sketch' in *Review of Reviews* of August 1892.

[60] Scott, *Life and Death of a Newspaper*, pp. 125 ff.

[61] He was to assume a much more lenient attitude with respect to the Parnell case a few years later (see *Review of Reviews*, 2 November 1891).

[62] See Scott, *Life and Death of a Newspaper*, p. 180.

[63] This, of course, is just a fraction of what appeared within the art section of the weekly at the time. The main exhibitions, certainly all national manifestations remained the monopoly of F.G. Stephens whose reactionary viewpoints left a bitter taste in the mouth of many a feminist critic looking to the *Athenaeum* for a contemporary appreciation of female artists at the end of the last century. Pamela Gerrish Nunn, for instance, found it hard to

of art historians. In her overview of Victorian women artists, Pamela Nunn is pleased to note the advent of women as critics of art exhibitions in the 1880 to 1900 period. She relies on an *Art Journal* article of July 1892 when listing Anna Jameson, Margaret Oliphant, Julia Cartwright and Helen Zimmern as writers on art, and Alice Meynell and Lady Colin Campbell as critics. Not a word about Emilia Dilke, whose art reviews had already been known for a couple of decades and whose books on French art were to sell in their thousands.[64]

Lady Dilke's enormous output as an art critic must be traced back to her first marriage. She admired Mark Pattison and was convinced of his intellectual superiority. Secure in the conviction that his scholarly views were well-founded, she was to follow his advice in the career she chose to make her own. In the memoir of his wife, Sir Charles Dilke was to recollect her words: 'It was put before me that if I wished to command respect I must make myself *the* authority on some subject which interested me'.[65] The advice came almost certainly from her first husband. Indeed, Sir Charles attributed the words to the rector in the margin of this memoir and, besides, the rector does not seem to have reserved such guidance to his own wife. Mary Ward recalled being urged to 'get to the bottom of something ... Choose a subject, and know *everything* about it' as a young woman in the privileged company of the rector.[66] The subject Emilia Dilke chose was eighteenth-century French art and she was to devote four volumes to it. But she also saw herself as a professional art reviewer providing herself with money and a certain degree of economic independence. 'When I began to write for money on reviews', she was to remember later, 'I used to be very sure that every word I put on paper represented exactly what I had it in my mind to say'.[67]

According to a recent analysis of Victorian art criticism by Elizabeth Prettejohn, the professional practice of art criticism became important only after the 1860s. She categorises art criticism into 'generalist' and 'specialist' with only the latter type being associated with professional art critics 'whose names and credentials were known in public'.[68] Lady Dilke's often lengthy

---

swallow Stephen's total disregard of the sculptor Mary Thornycroft when, upon the death of her husband Thomas Thornycroft, he described the latter as 'the well-known sculptor, and father of Mr Hamo Thornycroft'. See Nunn, *Victorian Women Artists*, London: Women's Press, 1987, p. 212.

[64] *French Painters of the 18th Century*, 1899, *French Architects and Sculptors of the 18th Century*, 1900; *French Furniture and Decoration of the 18th Century*, 1901; *French Engravers and Draughtsmen of the 18th Century*, 1902. Lady Dilke's life and work has recently attracted more interest. See among others Kali Israel, *Names and Stories: Emilia Dilke, Figuration, and Victorian Culture*, Oxford: Oxford University Press, 1998.

[65] 'Memoir', p. 36.

[66] John Sutherland, *Mrs Humphry Ward. Eminent Victorian, Pre-eminent Edwardian*, Oxford: Oxford University Press, 1990, p. 34.

[67] George Bainton, *The Art of Authorship. Literary Reminiscences, Methods of work, and advice to young beginners, Personally contributed by leading authors of the day*, London: Clarke, 1890, p. 329.

[68] Elizabeth Prettejohn, 'Aesthetic Value and the Professionalization of Victorian Art Criticism, 1837–78', *Journal of Victorian Culture*, 2:1 (Spring 1997), p. 79.

exposés undoubtedly fall within the second category but, as mentioned above, they largely remained anonymous as did those by the weekly's regular art critic, F.G. Stephens.

Emilia Dilke's first notes for the *Athenaeum*, published in the mid 1870s, were still signed 'E.F.S. Pattison'. Her first lengthy contribution appeared on 26 August 1876 and was a report on the collection of Monsieur Gambart at Nice.[69] The article is an excellent example of Emilia Dilke's professional approach to art and artists. It also presents us with her views on the implied reader of the *Athenaeum*. The ideal reader of her article and the one with whom she seems to identify is, like her, interested in the narrative of paintings as well as in the artists' technical excellencies. Her analysis of the paintings of Lawrence Alma Tadema in this collection, for instance, shows her as being familiar with the painter's work and assuming that her reader is as well – 'All these paintings are so well known and have been so recently exhibited that a minute déscription [sic] would be unnecessary'. She can, therefore, move on to the essence of what she wants to say. Most noteworthy is her conception of the paintings as texts, of the painter as a poet. Tadema, for instance, is said not to be 'a poet in the popular acceptation of the term': 'His work makes no appeal to the emotions'. And his oeuvre is pronounced to be Greek in its 'perfect sanity, in its intelligibility', his 'language is that of science rather than rhetoric'. In fact, the critic argues, Tadema addresses himself to those 'who have given themselves such a training as may enable them in some measure to appreciate his admirable technical skill in its infinitely subtle refinements of application'. She proceeds to illustrate this technical skill by commenting on the arrangement of colour in a painting like 'Poet reading Verses to his Mistress':

> The white draperies of the poet are carried along the line of napkins which rest upon it; but the blue and green robes of the reclining woman, playing, half pleased, half sullen, with her fan, float out from the grey-robed figures near her, and rest against the red and orange of the wall, throwing shooting colours, like a peacock's breast against the sun. In this way the ring of colour is broken. (26 August 1876)

In her lively description of Edouard Frère's paintings she focuses on the painter's excellence of arrangement and grouping and his special talent for painting children:

> In 'Saying Grace', for example, the most considerable work here in point of size, a large family of various ages are grouped round the table; the circle is varied, broken, and continued with great skill and charm; the general attitude of attention devoutly arrested is sufficiently indicated, but the picture owes its point and prettiness to the little

---

[69] She had gone to Nice in 1875 following the advice of the German doctor at Wildbad on account of her weak physical condition. It was the year which was to mark the complete and irrevocable rupture with her husband Mark Pattison; see Askwith, *Lady Dilke*, pp. 57ff.

touches of impatient movement which reveal a suppressed anxiety for dinner amongst the children. (26 August 1876)

In passing, she pays attention to some less well-represented painters of the Gambart collection, not missing the opportunity though to include a woman artist in her discussion. Rosa Bonheur's paintings on display at Nice receive generous praise. The study in oil of a badger, for instance, is said to be simply excellent:

> The painting of the loose fur, grey, tawny, black, and white the way in which the bony structure is felt, and the rendering of the muscular shapes, half obscured by the waves of soft hair floating over it, the gleaming of the mink skin showing through the shorter, more scanty growths of the coat on the upturned stomach, present all the best and most interesting qualities of Mdlle. Bonheur's painting. (26 August 1876)

There are, it is true, few occasions for her to write about women artists' work. So little was written about them and, she thought, few of the women painters achieved excellence. Many years later, in her review of Hofsteede de Groot's paper on Judith Leyster she observes that the author 'pays tribute to that rare thing, a really capable woman painter' (6 October 1894).

After that first *Athenaeum* appearance she was occasionally to take care of the section 'Notes from Paris' for some time, but she had to share that column with the French journalist Edmond About. The series *Jahrbuch der königlich Preussischen Kunstsammlungen*, on the other hand, was to remain her exclusive topic. These annual volumes were launched in 1880. Lady Dilke discussed them faithfully but certainly not uncritically in the *Athenaeum* columns up to her death in 1904. From those reviews one may easily reconstruct the general lines along which her art criticism was set forth. According to her, art criticism and art history had to tread a middle way between the academic exposé and the popularising story. The *Jahrbuch* does not always succeed in finding this path so that she has to warn again and again – and in almost exactly the same terms – that it treats of matters interesting to the specialist rather than the general public. Yet in her opinion all is well as long as the research uncovering details or discussing works of lesser value eventually leads to a more correct view of general movements: 'the ancient landmarks are now modified not by any grand discovery, but by the constant aggregation of infinite numbers of small facts', she writes in July 1886. One must, she stresses, at all times remember to look at the general picture. In her review of the *Jahrbuch* in 1887 she devotes much of the space allotted to her to a kind of manifesto of the art historian:

> The men who focus in themselves the spirit and character of a whole nation, and who, therefore, may claim to be studied for themselves, are very few; the greater number, even of brilliant workers, are but as details ... of a great whole, and the minute examination of their works and lives is profitable only when carried on in relation to the general bearing and

significance of national life. This is a truism of which we have all been
tempted to lose sight, we who have been born into this age of so-called
research; and the problem of art history which is constantly before us all
is, in its way, after all an old problem, familiar to workers in every
department of human knowledge – how to combine analysis with
synthesis, how to investigate details with due closeness of scrutiny, and
yet to lift our eyes to the light of general conceptions. (9 April 1887)

As an art critic, Emilia Dilke tries to follow her own advice: she likes to
display her knowledge of the art world, art terminology and the development of
art criticism, but she also digresses on the narrative of the paintings involved,
the way these works may be read by the general public. In a discussion of a
book on Hyppolyte Bellangé (9 April 1881) she discusses this military
painter's political ideas and the ways they affected the public: 'the historical
importance of [his] work lies in the fact that the fusion of democratic ideas
with Napoleonic traditions which made the Second Empire possible was
brought about to a great extent by [his] co-operation'. It remained the question
as to how low one allowed oneself to 'sink' towards the British public which,
according to Dilke, unlike the American or the Continental public, could only
appreciate literature of a gossiping kind: 'Authors are sometimes told that they
ought to be above such considerations, and one has often heard the same sort of
admonition addressed to artists by well-intentioned critics; but is there any
justification for such a doctrine?' (16 March 1889).

Apart from the *Jahrbuch*, Emilia Dilke generally reviewed books about
French art in all its forms: paintings, sculptures, furniture and 'cuisine'. She
wrote a couple of reviews of literary works, Zola's *Le Rêve* and Ohnet's
Monsieur Rameau. All of those reviews reveal a deep knowledge as well as a
passionate love of all things French. The combination is perhaps best illustrated
by the obviously spontaneous eruption of indignation in a review of James F.
Hunnewell's *The Historical Monuments of France*. The work leads her to
complain strongly about the tasteless restorations to which many French
monuments have been subjected. About the 'abominable vandalism', such as
that carried on in the Cathedral of St Mary at Oléron, she writes:

> This cathedral ... has a magnificent portal, the tympanum of which is
> filled in by three arcades, richly sculptured and in a perfect state of
> preservation. This splendid work has been recently covered by a coat of
> white and grey wash, whilst each head of man or beast has been
> decorated with a pair of glass eyes, such as we see in stuffed birds, or the
> lion skins ... (*Athenaeum*, 20 September 1884)

With her reviews of cookery books she does enter an area which is normally
associated with women. She was to discuss only very few cookery books but
British cooking, in general, was disappointing to her, therefore she probably
thought it her duty to savage the books when they seemed inadequate. The
wrong recipes of mayonnaise in two separate cookery books led her to the
following conclusion: 'they are the sort of mistakes of inaccuracy which cause
our own countrywomen to fail so egregiously in those very departments in

which French women excel' (*Athenaeum*, 19 November 1887). A work on *Dressed Vegetables* fared somewhat better, for 'it is in the cooking of vegetables that the English kitchen fails especially' (21 July 1888).

Finally, there is just one review which betrays her interest in the women's movement. Her review of Monsieur de Maulde la Clavière's *Les Femmes de la Renaissance*, published in November 1898, is quite noteworthy because of the easiness with which she uses words like 'feminism' and 'feminist' which after all were still relatively new:

> M. de Maulde la Clavière writes in great detail and with commendable erudition on the position of women and the feminist movement of the sixteenth century ... [drawing] many many inferences which have a direct application to the feminist movement of our day. (5 November 1898)[70]

All in all, however, it appears that her reviews (certainly the signed ones) contain unexpectedly few indications as to the gender of their author, let alone her commitment to the feminist cause. Her efforts to improve the position of women was something she reserved for a real world lying beyond art. Her feminist perspective had not yet been translated into a feminist theory on art or a consistent endeavour to place feminist accents in art reviews. Her feminist convictions were noticeable in the *Athenaeum*, but they were at work at another level of her involvement with the weekly, as I hope to demonstrate in the concluding chapter to this book.

Jane Ellen Harrison

> Beauty is truth, truth beauty, – that is all
> Ye know on earth and all ye need to know.[71]

Emilia Strong Pattison (later Dilke) and Millicent Garrett Fawcett were special contributors to the journal. They were special because the fields in which they were allowed to have their say were, as a rule, considered to be reserved to male intellects. They were special because they had had no academic training but came to acquire their unusual expertise and authority first by proxy: their husbands, Mark Pattison and Henry Fawcett, were academics who stimulated their wives, urging them to articulate their views on those subjects publicly as well as privately. Jane Ellen Harrison was different from these two colleagues in that she was not married and became a member of academia herself.

Harrison was an anthropologist and a classical scholar of the first rank, whose writings on Greek culture at the end of nineteenth and the beginning of the twentieth century are said to have turned classical studies upside down 'by

---

[70] On the introduction and uses of the term 'feminism' see Bonnie Anderson and Judith Zinsser, *A History of Their Own,* vol. II, London: Penguin, 1990, p. 492.

[71] John Keats, 'Ode on a Grecian Urn', 1819.

insisting that the rational religion of the gods was rooted in primitive chthonic cults'.[72] Influenced by the works of Friedrich Nietzsche and J.J. Bachofen, she was to rewrite the history of the ancient world in light of her appreciation of irrationality, intuition and a belief in the existence of matriarchy. She was one of those remarkable people whose work impressed friends and foes, feminists and anti-feminists alike. She was the 'J– H–' in Virginia Woolf's *A Room of One's Own*, described as 'a bent figure, formidable yet humble, with her great forehead and her shabby dress'.[73] Indeed, as K.J. Phillips has asserted in her article 'Jane Harrison and Modernism', it is Harrison's place in Woolf's *oeuvre* which seems to have caught most attention from later generations.[74] But Phillips does not refer to that most controversial author Camille Paglia, who acknowledged her debt to Harrison, in the construction of her own chtonian theory in *Sexual Personae*, while disagreeing with Harrison's vision of a peaceful matriarchy 'overthrown by warmongering men'.[75] Then, contemporaneously with Phillips, Jules Cashford and Anne Baring published an exhaustive analysis of the myth of the goddess in which they made ample use of Harrison's findings. And even more recently, Shelley Arlen published an eloquent defence of Harrison's position and theoretical assumptions in '"For Love of an Idea": Jane Ellen Harrison, heretic and humanist'.[76] Even so, in spite of this hesitant re-appraisal, mainly in the context of the influence which she exerted on other writers or scholars, Jane Harrison's work has hardly received its due. Her name is not listed in international reference works such as the *Fontana Dictionary of Modern Thinkers* (1983), and neither is it to be found in Duby and Perrot's *History of Women* or the *Macmillan Dictionary of Women's Biography* (1984). There is, fortunately, Sandra Peacock's excellent biography *Jane Ellen Harrison. The Mask and the Self*, published in 1988.[77]

Jane Ellen Harrison was born in 1850, the third child of Charles Harrison, a timber merchant, and his first wife, Elizabeth Hawksley. Her mother died a month after her birth and the widowed father was to marry the

---

[72] Vicinus, *Independent Women*, p. 152.

[73] Woolf, *A Room*, p. 26.

[74] K.J. Phillips, *Dying Gods in Twentieth Century Fiction*, Bucknell University Press, 1990, pp. 179–92. See e.g. Patricia Maika. *Virginia Woolf's Between the Acts and Jane Harrison's Con/spiracy*, UMI Research Press, 1987; Annabel Robinson, 'Something Odd at Work : The Influence of Jane Harrison on *A Room of One's Own*'. *Wascana Review*, XXII (1987), pp. 82– 88; Sandra D. Shattuck, 'The Stage of Scholarship: Crossing the Bridge from Harrison to Woolf'. *Virginia Woolf and Bloomsbury: A Centenary Celebration*, ed. Jane Marcus, Indiana University Press, 1987, pp. 278–98 and Martha Carpentier, *Ritual, Myth, and the Modernist Text: The Influence of Jane Ellen Harrison on Joyce, Eliot, and Woolf*, Amsterdam, The Netherlands: Gordon Breach Publishers, 1998.

[75] Camille Paglia, *Sexual Personae. Art and Decadence from Nefertiti to Emily Dickinson*, New York: Vintage, 1991, p. 42.

[76] *Women's History Review*, 5: 2 (1996), pp. 165–90.

[77] Much earlier, in 1959, Jessie Stewart published a tribute to Harrison in her *Jane Ellen Harrison. A Portrait from Letters* mainly based on Harrison's letters to Gilbert Murray. There is also a very personal, autobiographic account by Marianna Torgovnick relating her discovery of the work of Jane Harrison but she does not contribute substantial new insights in 'Discovering Jane Harrison', *Seeing Double: Revisioning Edwardian and Modernist Literature*, Carola M. Kaplan and Anne B. Simpson (eds), New York: St Martin's, 1996.

children's governess some years later. What followed is the stuff of fairy tales, with a daughter longing for the love of her father but being rebuffed and isolated by a cold and even malicious stepmother: 'Father and daughter still love each other, but the daughter wakes up to find herself wounded, inwardly desolate'.[78] Eventually the talented young woman was sent to Newnham College as one of the first students there. She sat for the classical tripos in March 1879, and, despite her high expectations, only obtained a second. 'Her standing upset her', Sandra Peacock writes, 'but it never stood in her way'.[79]

After a brief spell as a teacher at Notting Hill High School, Oxford, she went to London to study Greek art and achaeology under Sir Charles Newton at the British Museum. Jane Harrison arrived in London in 1880. She was to stay in the capital for seventeen years. The London period proved of immeasurable value to the progress of her work. For one thing she wholeheartedly embraced the aesthetic movement. Aestheticism stimulated new ways of looking at art while simultaneously challenging gendered Victorian values and traditions. For Harrison, experiencing all the problems of the single professional woman, aestheticism offered an escape. This philosophy behind her life and her work was to translate itself in the way she dressed (she is reported to have worn blue-green satin evening gowns with spangles) and the way she performed during her perambulating lectures round the Elgin Marbles and the Vase rooms.[80] One of her stock phrases, according to her early biographer Hope Mirrlees, was to call nearly every figure shown on her slides 'beautiful' even when the audience was clearly unimpressed.

More remarkable by all means was her habit of suddenly throwing back her head and bursting into a chorus of Euripides at the end of the lecture. Her later colleague, Francis Cornford, recalls how she once asked two friends to swing two bull-roarers at the back of a darkened lecture room in order to recreate the sound suggested by Aeschylos when he mentioned 'bull-voices roaring from somewhere'.[81] Such a passionate love for antique culture must needs have drawn great numbers of disciples. Harrison was herself remarkably apologetic about her lecturing days. In her autobiographical *Reminiscences of a Student's Life* she explains them purely in terms of financial necessity:

> Being one of a family of twelve, my fortune was slender, and social life is costly. I regret those lecturing years. I was voluble and had instant success, but it was mentally demoralising and very exhausting. Though I was almost fatally fluent, I could never face a big audience without a sinking in the pit of what is now called the *solar plexus*. Moreover, I was lecturing on art, a subject for which I had no natural gifts. My reactions to art are, I think always second-hand; hence, about art, I am docile and

---

[78] Harrison, *Alpha and Omega*, pp. 95–6.
[79] Sandra J. Peacock, *Jane Ellen Harrison. The Mask and the Self*, New Haven and London: Yale University Press, 1988, p. 54.
[80] Jessie Stewart, *Jane Ellen Harrison. A Portrait from Letters*, London: The Merlin Press, 1959, p. 10.
[81] See F.M. Cornford's entry on Jane Ellen Harrison in *Dictionary of National Biography*.

open to persuasion. In literature I am absolutely sure of my own tastes, and a whole Bench of Bishops could not alter my convictions. Happily, however, bit by bit, art and archaelogy led to mythology, mythology merged in religion; there I was at home. All through my London life I worked hard – [82]

The change of course in her research occurred in the mid-1880s after her treasured friend D.S. Maccoll had condemned the aestheticism in her work. She now turned towards the study of mythology and religion and, primarily, the study of ritual. Eventually, however, she was to link ritual with art through desire, through the collective (not the personal) emotion:

At the bottom of art, as its motive power and its mainspring, lies, not the wish to copy Nature or even improve on her ... but rather an impulse shared by art with ritual, the desire, that is, to utter, to give out a strongly felt emotion or desire by representing, by making or doing or enriching the object or act desired ... This common *emotional* factor it is that makes art and ritual in their beginnings well-nigh indistinguishable.[83]

Harrison's stay in London also meant meeting the cultural élite of the time. Unlike most other single women professionals who had flocked to the capital and who opted for rooms in a home or ladies' residential chambers, she had chosen to share a house with another woman, Get Wilson. Little is known about Get Wilson except that she worked at 'procuring trained nurses for the workhouse infirmaries'.[84] Sandra J. Peacock calls the friendship between the two women mysterious and hints at the possibility of a lesbian relationship, though she never actually uses the word. But she does not suggest that lesbianism may have been the reason why Harrison refused even attractive marriage proposals. The men in Harrison's life function as painful intermezzos. She seems to have been both attracted and repelled by male sexuality, encouraging certain men's advances by flirtatious behaviour but then rejecting the possibility of a long-term relationship. 'All my life long I have been in love', she is reported to have said.[85] Like several of the women writers discussed in these pages, however, she may deliberately have denied herself the prospect of marriage because she felt it would stifle her career. Peacock believes Harrison deliberately wanted to safeguard her hard-won independence both in the public and in the private sphere. It is nevertheless clear that each separation left her wounded and more lonely than before.

The *Reminiscences* show how Harrison was always consciously expanding her intellectual horizon, taking every opportunity of going abroad to meet the best scholars in the field:

---

[82] J. E. Harrison, *Reminiscences of a Student's Life*, London: The Hogarth Press, 1925, p. 63.

[83] *Ancient Art and Ritual*, New York: Holt, 1913, p. 26.

[84] Peacock, *Jane Ellen Harrison*, p. 64.

[85] Phillips, *Dying Gods*, p. 475.

My London life was happily broken by much going abroad. All my archaeology was taught me by Germans. The great Ernst Curtius, of European fame, took me round the museums of Berlin. Heinrich Brunn came to see me in my Lodgings at Munich, where I was thriftily living on four marks a day. I remember his first visit ...

At Athens I met Samuel Butler. We were in the same hotel; he saw me dining alone and kindly crossed over to ask if he might join me. Of course I was delighted and looked forward to pleasant talks, but, alas! he wanted me only as a safety valve for his theory on the woman-authorship of the Odyssey, and the buzzing of that crazy bee drowned all rational conversation ... (p. 70)

Crete I visited again and again, and to Crete I owe the impulse to my two most serious books ... (p. 71)

The building that figured most prominently in her London life, however, was the London Library, which, like the British Museum, was of crucial importance to many women writers at the time: '...When I first came to London I became a life member of the London Library. London life was costly, but I felt that, if the worst came to the worst, with a constant supply of books and a small dole for tobacco, I could cheerfully face the Workhouse'.

In 1898 Newnham offered Jane Harrison its first research fellowship. This brought the London period to an end. Harrison stayed on in Cambridge even when the five years of the fellowship had elapsed and she had to make do with two-thirds of her income.[86] Newnham was to be her home for twenty-five years, providing her with the company of supportive friends and adoring students. It was to prove a most congenial environment for new ideas as well as for her more mature work.

In the early years of this century Jane Harrison found herself at the centre of the Cambridge ritualist circle with Gilbert Murray, Francis Cornford and A.B. Cook as her fellow-thinkers: their label – 'ritualist' – derived from the fact that they saw ritual as having primacy over myth. Her importance for the group has always been acknowledged by its supporters. Robert Ackerman claimed Jane Harrison 'was the center of the group because she always seems to have had a broader conception of their common subject matter than any of the others'.[87] Her research and newly acquired insights culminated in the first major work of this period, the *Prolegomena to the Study of Greek Religion* published in 1903. Her second most significant book, *Themis, a Study of the Social Origins of Religion* (1912), went even further in its exploration of primitive religions, under the influence of the work of Henri Bergson and Emile Durkheim.

Harrison began writing for the *Athenaeum* in 1893, when she was still residing in London. She was a frequent visitor of the ladies' clubs and may therefore have easily met the other *Athenaeum* regulars. Nevertheless I have found no proofs of any direct contact with the *Athenaeum* management. There is unfortunately no description of her in Vernon Lee's letters, but she is

---

[86] Peacock, *Jane Ellen Harrison*, p. 91.
[87] Ibid., p. 128.

mentioned as attending a 'tremendous' party at Mrs Hancock's, Mathilde Blind's 'aesthetic' sister.[88] She became a regular but not a prolific reviewer of the weekly. In the period 1893–1901 she reviewed some twenty-three books. Then, after a long silence, there were two more contributions: one in 1907 and one in 1910.

Harrison was an excellent contributor, fitting the pattern which the editor, or the proprietor (or perhaps his wife) deemed the best choice for the journal. Not only was she highly intelligent and ambitious, she was also to become a supporter of the women's cause: her first pronouncements on women's position in contemporary society are to be traced in an interview for the *Pall Mall Gazette* in 1891.[89] Later she was to side with the suffragists' cause in an open letter, although she admitted to have reached the conclusion that woman's suffrage was the best way forward only after some rational deliberation. '*Homo sum*' may well have sounded all the more forceful because of that initial hesitation. It was an exemplary text to be used in the fight for the vote:

> embarrassing though I should find the possession of a vote, I strongly feel that it is a gift which ought to be given, a gift which I must nerve myself to receive ... (p. 80)
> ... *Homo sum; humani nihil (ne suffragium quidem) a me alienum puto.* (=not even a vote) ... The danger, never serious, of any tendency to 'ape the man' is over and past. The most militant of Suffragists never now aims at being masculine ... Woman, not man, now insists over-loudly on her own womanhood, and in this hubbub of man and woman the still small voice of humanity is apt to be unheard ... (pp. 85–6)
> ... An eminent novelist has recently told us that women are to have higher higher education, but not political power, not the Parliamentary vote. Women are 'unfit to govern'. ... Have Mrs Humphry Ward and Lord Curzon, in their busy and beneficent lives, found time to read M. Henri Bergson's *L'Evolution Créatrice*? Long ago Socrates told us that we only know in order that we may act. M. Bergson has shown us *how* this is, and *why* ... Mrs Humphry Ward and Lord Curzon are half a century too late. They may entrench themselves on their castle of sand, but the tide has turned, and the sea is upon them ... Women *qua* women remain, for the better continuance of life, subject to men. Women as human beings demand to live as well as to continue life. To live effectively they must learn to know the world through and through, in order that, side by side with men, they may fashion life to their common good.
> I am dear Anti-suffragist,
> Sincerely yours,
> An Anthropologist [90]

The reviews she contributed to the *Athenaeum* were quite long and detailed discussions. She knew how to praise while always maintaining a critical stance and her views clearly reflect her own current opinions. Her

---

[88] *Lee's Letters*, p. 207.
[89] See Peacock, *Jane Ellen Harrison*, p. 51.
[90] Harrison, 'Homo sum', *Alpha and Omega*, London: Sidgwick, 1915, pp. 113–15.

interest in early earth-goddesses and her search for the evidence of matriarchy is reflected in her very first review to the weekly. She produced a long and detailed discussion of Charles Waldstein's report of his *Excavations of the American School of Athens at the Heraion of Argos, 1892* in which she admits her special interest in the goddess Hera. At one point she observes: 'He [Waldstein] touches on none of those tempting questions as to the origin of the worship of Hera, the primitive tribe she belonged to, her first husband, her later annexation'. She then focuses on one find in particular which appears to her to be the head of Hera. Harrison finds such perfection in this head that, she writes, it 'makes the spectator go away quietly, and the reviewer keep silence even from good words' (*Athenaeum*, 1 July 1893). Her own more lengthy notes and considerations on the goddess Hera are developed in her *Prolegomena to the Study of Greek Religion*. A year later she revealed another of her preoccupations in a review of Maria M. Evans's book on Greek dress. Dress, for her, was a deeply historical matter which might help date statues and/or provide the right clothing for a Greek play (*Athenaeum*, 22 September 1894).

Her review of Percy Gardner's *Sculptured Tombs of Hellas*, published in February 1897, is perhaps even more revelatory as to her own convictions. 'Cults', she starts by saying 'are more venerable and more conservative than doctrine' (20 February 1897). 'Ritual, burial customs, funeral monuments', are therefore of crucial value if one wants to learn about the beliefs of a people. So far the author under discussion follows her own convictions and she has no difficulty in praising him. When Gardner starts to acclaim art unreservedly, however, she chooses to disagree. She dismisses his enthusiasm over the Sidon sarcophagi as 'excessive':

> His critical faculty seems overpowered by the *tour de force* accomplished by the artist, who has produced 'eighteen figures of women, all young and of the same type, all standing in poses both in themselves elegant yet suggestive of grief'. Yes, that is just what they are, 'all elegant yet suggestive of grief' (why 'yet'?); but to us they are rather tiresome *clichés*. (*Athenaeum*, 20 February 1897)

She warns against the indiscriminate praise of Greek art: 'every Greek stonemason is not an artist'. Again, her review of W. Warde Fowler gives much away of her own research and interests at this stage:

> It is a hopeful sign in modern scholarship that interest in Roman as well as Greek ritual and mythology is beginning to awaken. Greek mythology has swayed the minds of past generations with a prestige due rather to its beauty than to its scientific value. (*Athenaeum*, 5 May 1900)

Harrison welcomes Fowler's study because it should help Greek scholars understand Greek ritual. She was convinced that the two classical cultures shared the same cultural basis; according to her, 'Greek religious conceptions became overlaid and overgrown with a boskage of poetical mythology; Roman remained a stark ritual formality.'

In spite of her personal ambition to find the perfect balance between creative intuition (which she thought to be essentially feminine) and scientific rationale (according to her, essentially masculine), she wants reproductions of archaeological finds to be as objective as possible. Her review of two books with reproductions of Greek vases is a case in point: she praises the scholarly manner in which A.S. Murray and A.H. Smith have presented the collection held in the British Museum while the artistic reproductions of Henry Wallis are admired but said to be less accurate (*Athenaeum*, 24 July 1897). As one who uses such books she wants it left to her to interpret the archaeological finds, an artist's drawings deprive her, to some extent, of that freedom.

After 1901 she stopped her regular contributions to the *Athenaeum*. Again, the date seems to indicate the new editor had a hand in the disappearance of a woman reviewer's name from the 'marked file'. But she was asked again. Her July 1907 review probably contains the harshest criticism of a colleague's work. The third and fourth volumes of Lewis Richard Farnell's *The Cults of the Greek States*, she argues, do not fulfil the promise of the earlier two volumes. To start with he does not seem to be in touch with recent publications. More seriously defective, however, is his method, which she pronounces to be positively 'obstructive'. Firstly, Farnell has separated ritual and mythology and, secondly, he has classified his facts under the head of the various Olympian gods. This rigidity leads him to a blatant obfuscation of facts. She then illustrates her charge with several examples obviously dear to her, such as his treatment of the horse-headed Demeter. 'Now any well-furnished mythologist', Harrison begins, 'surveying this story of the horse Areion born from Demeter-Erinys, will instantly recall another horse, Pegasus, born of Medusa'. But Farnell dares to reject the possibility of an 'equine Medusa', forgetting about 'the fine archaic *pithos* now in the Louvre, where Medusa is figured with a horse-body'. He thus immediately and unequivocally receives the scorn of this reviewer. Her conclusion cannot be clearer. Farnell dismissed the truly innovative scholars, men such as James George Frazer and A.B. Cook, yet he would have done well to follow their example. Farnell lacks the prized 'constructive imagination', and what is worse 'we are left lamenting that so much industry and patience, such genuine enthusiasm, competent scholarship, and wide reading should result in a book which is so congested, so indigestible' (*Athenaeum*, 20 July 1907).

Harrison's convictions, by that time well–known, are freely expressed in this review. There is the possibility therefore that the informed reader (and the author under review) could guess who the reviewer was, in spite of the neutral, ungendered 'we'. Her criticism of Farnell was countered even before it had been expressed in the *Athenaeum*, by Percy Gardner, himself one of her earlier victims. Possibly, therefore, she had already expressed those views elsewhere.[91] Besides, insiders knew that Farnell had rejected Harrison's research objectives in the first volume of his study of the cults of the Greek

---

[91] Percy Gardner, Letter, *Cambridge Review*, 13 June 1907, p. 482. See also Shelley Arlen, '"For Love of an Idea": Jane Ellen Harrison, heretic and humanist', p. 9.

states, published as early as 1896.[92] The battle field was an extremely complex one with, it appears, several blows and counter-blows. Harrison can hardly be depicted as a passive victim in this but her opponents were certainly fierce and unrelenting. Eventually she was to sustain two more slashing reviews from the pen of Farnell, in the *Hibbert Journal* and the *Oxford Magazine*, when her own book *Themis* appeared in 1912. She was mortified, though she affected indifference: 'I don't mind what he says of me a bit ... a good deal of the book he simply doesn't understand & never will – & nearly all of it he temperamentally hates which is what one would expect'.[93] Harrison was unfortunate in the reviewers of her main publications, all published in the first decades of the twentieth century. Upon the appearance of the *Prolegomena* (1903), the *Athenaeum*'s editor, Vernon Rendall, had assigned her book for criticism to Ernest Gardner, the man who had been her rival and the more successful candidate for the Yates Professorship of Archaeology at University College, London in 1896. His judgement was restrained but obviously contemptuous. One may compare his remarks to the one appreciative review, published at the beginning of Harrison's career, when MacColl had asked Andrew Lang to discuss her *Myths of the Odyssey* in 1882. Harrison had dreaded the reception of this first book at the time because the publisher had revealed her gender by giving her full name and she had wanted to keep it a secret.[94] But Lang, in an anonymous review calls the book 'ingenious' and 'commendable' adding that he is not 'acquainted with any book produced by any man at either university which does so much for the popular knowledge of ancient art as this work by a student from one of the Cambridge colleges for women' (*Athenaeum*, 21 January 1882).

Harrison's anxiousness to preserve her anonymity when she published her first book is somewhat surprising, because she thought the gender of the author mattered a great deal.[95] She believed women's nature was different, that women's emotional life was richer and more accessible while men had the advantage of 'pure thought' and insulation. She saw collaboration between a man and a woman ideally as a spawning of ideas by the woman (*in casu*, herself) which are then brought to birth with the help of a male companion: 'I never looked to man to supply me with ideas ... The moment, as far as I can formulate the need, is when you want to disentangle [the ideas] from yourself and your emotions'.[96]

[92] Lewis R. Farnell, *The Cult of the Greek States*, vol. I, Oxford: Clarendon, 1896, pp. 199–206.

[93] Peacock, *Jane Ellen Harrison*, p. 214.

[94] Ibid., p. 58.

[95] After the publication of *Myths of the Odyssey* and the mentioning of her gender she wrote, in a letter to Mrs Malleson that she was 'very cross with Mr Rivington for exposing the fact that I belong to the frail gender. I specially desired to stand or fall irrespective of that'. (Peacock, *Harrison*, p. 58)

[96] Vicinus, *Independent Women*, p. 153.

Under Rendall, in the first decade of the new century, it was Gardner who became the regular *Athenaeum* reviewer of works on archaeology. Consequently, another expert had to be found when he himself published a new book in 1910. It fell to Jane Harrison's lot to review it. The book, *Six Greek Sculptors*, was meant to be a popular introduction to Greek art. A much needed publication, Harrison thought, laudable but, unfortunately, deficient in several respects. Thus Professor Gardner attributes Victorian ideas of propriety to the artists of antiquity in an attempt to explain their less successful renderings of the female form. His selection of topics, too, is flawed, since he omits for instance the Venus of Milo. And she accuses him of laxity in his use of sources and authorities. Her eventual recommendation of the book to amateurs as well as students is therefore not very convincing and it probably was not meant to be.[97] After this she stopped reviewing for the *Athenaeum*.

Shortly after the publication of *Themis* Harrison was faced with the consequences of the First World War and the impossibility of travelling to Greece. This, in effect, forced her to concentrate on other civilisations. Harrison is said to have begun to study Russian in Paris in 1915 and she started to lecture on the subject in 1917. Most suprisingly of all, however, was her decision, at the age of seventy-two, to exchange Cambridge for Paris and, much later, London. A college, she explained in a letter to Miss Conway, 'is best taught by the young'. And so, a voice had told her to 'go'. But also she had wanted 'to see things move freely & more widely & above all to get the new focus of another civilisation'. In the same letter she tries to capture the spirit of Cambridge in the 1880s and 1890s when she was there, in just a few lines:

> Cambridge [was] on the eve of a great awakening. Classics were turning in their sleep. Old men began to see visions young men to dream dreams. Henry Sidgwick and his band of friends had opened to women the gates of learning – gates still ajar. It was good to be young when Robertson Smith, exiled for heresy, saw the Star in the East & led us to the Bethlehem of a newly understood faith. It was good to catch the first glimpse of the Golden Bough lighting the dark world of Savage superstitions. Who could grow old while Schliemann was digging up Troy? Who could stagnate into middle age when Arthur Evans set sail to his new Atlantis & telegraphed news of the Minotaur from his own labyrinth? We Hellenists were, it may be, a people who sat in darkness but we had seen a great light. To live through a Renouveau is to be perforce reborn.[98]

Jane Harrison's reviews for the *Athenaeum* and other journals have, in spite of their obvious importance for her career, never been discussed before. From our analysis it appears that her reviews gave her the opportunity to articulate her own theories and convictions on the basis of the publications of

---

[97] *Athenaeum*, 23 April 1910.
[98] Unpublished letter, dated February 1923, in Cambridge University Library (U 95).

her peers. They undoubtedly contributed to her growing self-confidence as an author and an anthropologist. They were her *probatio pennae*, providing her with a theoretically safe way of publicly defending her ideas while at the same time bringing in some extra money at a period when she was most in need of it.

Chapter 5

Reviewing Fiction

I have been reading two books which, to say the least of them, are full of information and are often very suggestive, they are *French Women of Letters* and *English Women of Letters*, both by a Miss Julia Kavanagh. Herself a novelist, she treats exclusively of female writers of fiction, and only of those long dead. I looked into one of her novels, expecting something original, but as far as I could judge, it was a poor affair. *Good critics rarely make good authors.*[1]

Prose, and within that fiction, was one of the most important sections in the *Athenaeum* if one considers the sheer number of columns devoted to it. At the end of an article in which she presents a thorough comparison of the *Spectator*, the *Saturday Review* and the *Athenaeum* for the year 1883, Ellen Miller Casey confidently states that the *Athenaeum* is the first place to look 'for pithy, timely reviews of the most representative selection of fiction'.[2] The first Charles Dilke, the one associated with the journal's conception, meant the fiction section to provide an impartial judgement of the latest publications. In this way it was merely part of the ongoing battle which he waged against excessive puffery. He chose his fiction reviewers with care, as he did the reviewers for all the other subjects; their gender was immaterial. He met and promptly invited the popular novelist Maria Jane Jewsbury while she was one of Mrs S.C. Hall's principal guests at a literary soirée.[3] According to Norma Clarke, this new reviewer then went on to develop an authoritative-sounding but decidedly 'unfeminine' voice as the lead writer of the *Athenaeum*.[4] Clarke has no qualms about the combination of 'unfeminine' and 'feminist' when describing Jewsbury's contributions. With the former adjective she seems to refer to style and vocabulary, while she applies the latter to the ideas broached and the topics dealt with.

Unfortunately, Jewsbury disappeared to India and an early death in 1832, but not before having introduced Henry Fothergill Chorley as a potential

---

[1] *Lee's Letters*, p. 21; my emphasis.
[2] Ellen Miller Casey, 'Weekly Reviews of Fiction: The *Athenaeum* vs the *Spectator* and the *Saturday Review*', *Victorian Periodicals Review*, XXIII (Spring 1990), p. 11.
[3] Norma Clarke, Norma, *Ambitious Heights. Writing, Friendship, Love – The Jewsbury Sisters, Felicia Hemans, and Jane Welsh Carlyle*, London : Routledge, 1990, pp. 27 – 28.
[4] Ibid., p. 37.

reviewer.[5] Chorley was to contribute the principal critiques of art exhibitions as well as a great number of the reviews of newly published fiction for several decades. Even so, in spite of Chorley's long-standing connection with the weekly, it was to be T.K. Hervey who succeeded Dilke as editor in 1846. Disappointment may therefore well have prompted Chorley's complaint that he was assigned most of the literary chaff after that date. In reality he reviewed, beside 'chaff', the work of Charles Dickens, Thomas Macaulay, Benjamin Disraeli, Charlotte Brontë, Nathaniel Hawthorne, and other prominent writers.[6] To Hervey, apparently, we owe the recruitment of possibly the most prolific woman reviewer of the middle decades of the century: Geraldine Jewsbury, Maria Jane's sister. She, Chorley and the editor henceforth divided the fiction load, an arrangement which was continued after William Hepworth Dixon succeeded to the editor's chair in 1853. Jewsbury's importance as a prismatic filter between the production of fiction and its consumption by the public has been analysed at length in several of Monica Frykstedt's publications.

Frykstedt presents a largely appreciative picture of this reviewer, praising her as a middlebrow reader with an unusual expertise.[7] Jewsbury had had a remarkable career. She was a successful novelist and a reader for Bentley's and for Hurst & Blackett. John Sutherland even labels her 'the most accomplished all-round lady of letters of the nineteenth century'.[8] Yet her reviews reflect a very conservative, conventional viewpoint, advocating entertaining novels, which were true to life and yet did not embarrass the angels in the house by any allusion to the more intimate side of marriage. As for the women novelists, Jewsbury invariably compared them (only) to women novelists. They were kept, so to speak, within the bounds of their gender.

Jewsbury's work for the *Athenaeum* stopped with her death in 1880 but she had been assigned to the children's column in the last few years of her life because, Frykstedt argues, her eyesight had badly deteriorated and children's books were shorter and easier to read.[9] This explanation for her move towards the margins of the marketplace seems acceptable enough. Still, the advent of the new proprietor and the new editor may have been additional reasons for her being phased out.

Towards the last years of Jewsbury's life the 'New Novels' section was the field of a variety of reviewers. Some of them, such as Lewis Sergeant and George Saintsbury, were quite well known. Others, like Robert Collyer, E.T. Cook and A.J. Butler remain quite obscure. Helen Zimmern, too, put in the odd appearance to review a German or an Italian novel. In general the authors were given a fair chance in these assessments. In her analysis of the year 1883,

---

[5] Henry G. Hewlett, *Henry Fothergill Chorley. Autobiography, Memoir and Letters*, London: Bentley, 1873, vol. I, p. 88.

[6] Hewlett, *Chorley*, vol. II, p. 46.

[7] Frykstedt, *Geraldine Jewsbury's 'Athenaeum' Reviews*, p. 15.

[8] John Sutherland, *The Longman Companion to Victorian Fiction*, Burnt Mill: Longman, 1988, p. 335.

[9] Frykstedt, *Geraldine Jewsbury's 'Athenaeum' Reviews*, p. 14.

Ellen Miller Casey tries to find out why the *Athenaeum* was regarded as 'the first literary journal in the English language'.[10] One of the most signal differences was its emphasis on 'art': 'it was more eager to discuss the new American school or the new romance, more willing to give French authors some credit'.[11]

In spite of Casey's systematic and competent comparison between this journal and its most important rivals it is, apparently, all but impossible to rectify the persistent erroneous presentation of the *Athenaeum* as the 'unimaginative', periodical it had become under Dixon's editorship.[12] Even an eminent scholar like Ann Ardis relies on the *Athenaeum* to find some of her preconceptions on its aberrant criticism of the New Woman novel confirmed. She refers to the journal on several occasions, when, for instance, she wants to illustrate the introduction of the aesthetic criterion in the critics' denunciation of New Woman novels after 1895.[13] Before that year, according to Ardis, critics tended to dismiss New Woman fiction on account of the content or the form, that is, the 'generic impurity' of this type of novel, whereas the New Woman novel was simply labelled as aesthetically second-rate after 1895. Without wanting to diminish the value of Ardis's contribution to the debate on New Woman fiction, I should here like to present a more shaded picture. Thus, the quote from the *Athenaeum* which Ardis adduces with respect to May Crommelin's *Dust before the Wind*, saying 'it is not the kind of book that we desire to see multiplied', is not to be found in the relevant review (7 April 1894).[14] The 'marked file' reveals that that particular review of Crommelin's novel was written by 'Birchenough', probably Mabel Birchenough (1860–1936), a novelist and a frequent contributor of prose reviews.[15] This review is, indeed, rather dismissive, not in the words quoted but mainly because of its claim that the events and the characters in the book are outworn. Yet the reviewer declares that: 'the book is written with a care and skill worthy of better materials than those of which the story is composed'.

Contrary to the impression one might get from Ardis's analysis, many of the *Athenaeum* reviewers carefully read the books under review and tried to assess them objectively. Mabel Birchenough was a frequent reviewer of New Woman fiction and, though clearly not an adept herself, she seems to have appreciated (within bounds) some of the best-known representatives of that

---

[10] Malcolm Elwin, *Old Gods Falling*, New York: Macmillan, 1939, p. 83.

[11] Casey, 'Weekly Reviews of Fiction', p. 10.

[12] Alvar Ellegård, *The Readership of the Periodical Press*, p. 22.

[13] Ardis, *New Women*, p. 53.

[14] Unfortunately, the other extract chosen from a review by Williams is similarly flawed. B. Williams dislikes the log-rolling expressed in the novel – a familiar complaint at the time which has nothing to do with the New Woman novel. The review is, in fact, generally positive (3 February 1894).

[15] Mabel Charlotte Birchenough, née Bradley 1860–1936, novelist and critic was married to Henry Birchenough, a silk manufacturer and an unlikely candidate for the job of reviewer. The marked file, at times, fails to indicate the contributor's gender by means of the 'Miss' or 'Mrs' titles.

group. Her review of Ella Hepworth Dixon's book *The Story of a Modern Woman*, for instance, is most interesting because in it she voices her concerns about the representation of New Women in fiction as 'self-assertive, heartless, sexless thing[s]' which might tempt the public to regard those characters as typical modern women (16 June 1894). The modern woman in Dixon's tale, however, is shown to be a gentle and essentially feminine creature. Birchenough is at pains to point out that the heroine 'has no modernity' in her but was forced to earn a living by writing after the death of her father. It seems, therefore, that Birchenough shares the general disdainful attitude towards the New Woman novels, but she somehow distinguishes that objectionable category from fiction carrying the same label which she does find herself, sometimes quite unexpectedly, to appreciate. Another case in point is her discussion of Ella D'Arcy's short stories, *Modern Instances*, in the issue for 23 July 1898. Here she admits to being pleased with the careful and vivid portrayal of the characters in these stories, but she regrets the dreary subject matter. [16]

Mabel Birchenough stopped contributing to the *Athenaeum* in 1899, though she was only forty at the time and she went on to live thirty-six more years. She had by then contributed no fewer than 131 book reviews in the twelve years of her covert association with the journal. Yet her achievement disappears into nothingness when compared with the degree of involvement of the main fiction reviewer in those closing decades of the century.

Katharine de Mattos

From the second half of the 1880s onwards, Katharine de Mattos was added to the list of names for the 'New Novels' section. In the 'marked file' there is evidence that hers was not a familiar name. Her third contribution, a review of Henry Cresswell's *The Survivors*, is marked as by 'Mrs Mattock' (*Athenaeum*, 9 October 1886) indicating that the person noting down her name had not quite grown used to the un-English sound of 'De Mattos'. One wonders who introduced Katharine de Mattos to a place on the *Athenaeum* staff. She never acquired the fame which would explain her being given this influential and, indeed, remunerative job. There is no evidence that she frequented Lady Dilke's circles. The group with which she was associated before she filled the *Athenaeum* columns with her witty criticism was that of W.E. Henley and Robert Louis Stevenson.

---

[16] Another appreciative review by Mabel Birchenough of a New Woman Novel, Mary Gaunt's *Dave's Sweetheart*, reads: 'Even the "advanced women" of to-day would probably be prepared to admit that a story of wild and lawless mining life in Australia is an experiment which few feminine novelists could carry through with success. The necessary opportunities for rivalry with Mr. Bret Harte and his Californian dramas in miniature do not often present themselves to writers of the other sex. Miss (or Mrs) Gaunt has, nevertheless, acquitted herself very creditably in her tale of Sergeant Sells's mistaken marriage'. (7 April 1894)

Katharine Elizabeth Alan Stevenson (1851–1939) was the youngest of the three daughters and one son of Alan Stevenson (1807–1865), Edinburgh lighthouse engineer, and Margaret Scott Jones (1812–1895). Very little is known about her youth, except, perhaps, for the romantic story relating how she, her brother Bob and her cousin Robert Louis Stevenson roamed the hills on ponies, these ponies being called 'Heaven', 'Hell', and 'Purgatory'. According to Louis Stevenson's biographer Frank McLynn she was a charismatic and very intelligent woman whose adult life does not seem to have been a very happy one, that is if one relies on the scanty information about her life. She married the atheist William Sydney de Mattos (b. 1851) on 25 June 1874 to – in Stevenson's words – 'the great horror of her family'.[17] But the disappointment came almost immediately afterwards with her brother calling Sydney de Mattos 'a fool'.[18] De Mattos's sexual appetite is almost the only thing his contemporaries seem to remember of him although he had other achievements to his name, such as a BA from Trinity College, Cambridge and his position as lecture secretary of the Fabian Society.[19] In the correspondence of George Bernard Shaw, another Fabian, Sydney de Mattos is mentioned on several occasions and one of these allusions confirms the obvious explanation for the problems in the De Mattos marriage. In a letter of August 1892 Shaw calls him a 'satyromaniac' when reporting 'I hear from Oxford that de Mattos is ravishing every maiden in the country, and that even the tolerant Hines took umbrage when some seven or eight of his daughters had succumbed'.[20]

Katharine did not directly complain about that aspect of her husband's behaviour. She worried chiefly and continuously about her financial situation and asked for Stevenson's help in obtaining some well-paid work. His good intentions, spelled out in a letter to Frances Sitwell, sound rather spuriously self-sacrificial and patronizing :

> Surely if there is one thing pure and lovely and of good report, it is to give women work. I think I shall manage for her [Katharine]; but not without throwing a good deal on myself. I am going to take service with a daily paper here; I shall read the books and make my own notes, and then send them on to her; she can then write what she will, I can always straighten it up when it comes back ... [21]

The De Mattos couple separated after a few years with Robert Louis Stevenson assuming a large part of the financial responsibility for Katharine and her two children. William S. de Mattos later emigrated to Canada.

---

[17] Bradford A. Booth and Ernest Mehew, eds, *The Letters of Robert Louis Stevenson*, New Haven and London: Yale University Press, 1994, vol. II, p. 20.

[18] Booth and Mehew, *Letters of Robert Louis Stevenson*, vol. II, p. 65.

[19] See Dan H. Laurence, ed., *Bernard Shaw. Collected Letters 1874–1897*, London: Max Reinhardt, 1965, vol. I, p. 304.

[20] Ibid., p. 359.

[21] Booth and Mehew, eds, *Letters of Robert Louis Stevenson*, vol. II, p. 90. He repeated this in a letter to Bob, using somewhat different words though: 'she can send some rubbish about them easy enough' (ibid., p. 91).

Katharine de Mattos later survived by writing. It was in all likelihood her cousin, Robert Louis Stevenson, who introduced her to Henley's circle. Henley not only adopted her as a member of his circle but, according to Charles Baxter and Stevenson, also nourished a passion for her.[22] She wrote for Henley's *Magazine of Art* and the *Saturday Review*, and she contributed poems to such periodicals as *Sylvia's Journal*, the *Windsor Magazine*, the *Yellow Book*.[23]

If at all, De Mattos herself is now mainly remembered by Stevenson aficionados for her part in the Henley–Stevenson brawl; she is the one referred to in that one crucial sentence 'It's Katharine's; surely it's Katharine's?' which was the beginning of the end of the friendship between Stevenson and William Ernest Henley. The incident is well known to students of the period. Henley was accusing Fanny Stevenson, Stevenson's adored wife, of plagiarism. She, Henley claimed with some justification, had published one of Katharine's stories as her own. It led to the breach between those two friends but also to a much cooler relationship between Stevenson and Katharine de Mattos. At one time Stevenson considered paying an annuity to his cousin's daughter by way of compensation, but it is unclear whether that scheme ever came to anything at all and he certainly drastically reduced the amount of money he left to Katharine in spite of promises to his father.[24]

Katharine de Mattos at all events seems to have become one of the many professional women writers at the turn of the century. She wrote translations and published a few volumes of short stories under the pseudonym Theodor Hertz-Garten. The possibility of reviewing for the *Athenaeum* in the mid-1880s must have been more than welcome. To the *Athenaeum* Katharine de Mattos contributed on average seventy reviews a year during the peak of her involvement, in the late 1890s; she had started in 1886 and continued to write, though less intensively, until well into the twentieth century. All in all she contributed 1,300 book reviews over a period of twenty-two years. The frequency of her contributions nearly equals Geraldine Jewbury's, who wrote no less than 2,300 book reviews between 1849 and 1880.[25] After 1908, the name 'De Mattos', for some inexplicable reason, disappeared from the 'marked file'.

De Mattos was responsible for a great number of 'New Novels', also 'Novels of the Week', some of the 'Short Stories', and, exceptionally, a book in the 'Our Library Table' column.[26] Certain authors seemed destined to be discussed by 'the De Mattos', to use Henley's way of referring to her.[27] Seeing that she did not scruple to utterly condemn any work under review, they may have wished for another voice to judge their efforts.

---

[22] Booth and Mehew, eds, *The Letters of Robert Louis Stevenson*, vol. VI, p. 147.

[23] Linda K. Hughes, 'A Female Aesthete at the Helm: Sylvia's Journal and "Graham R. Tomson", 1893–1894', *Victorian Periodicals Review*, 29:2 (1996), pp. 173–92.

[24] Connell, *W.E. Henley*, London: Constable, 1949, p. 125.

[25] Frykstedt, *Geraldine Frykstedt's 'Athenaeum' Reviews*, p. 15.

[26] I have traced only one review of poetry, 'Recent Verse', in the *Athenaeum* issue of 8 March 1890.

[27] Connell, *W.E. Henley*, p. 246.

Rhoda Broughton was such an unfortunate one. She had been castigated by the *Athenaeum* – in fact by Geraldine Jewsbury – upon the appearance of her first successful publication, *Cometh up as a Flower*, in 1867.[28] Its anonymity, according to Jewsbury, was hiding a male author who was 'ignorant of all that women either are or ought to be', and one who believed women understand only two phases of existence, 'the delight of being kissed by a man they like, and the misery of being kissed by a man they don't like' (*Athenaeum*, April 1867). Katharine de Mattos continued in the same vein as Jewsbury. Of the Broughton novels which appeared in the 1890s she was to write nearly all the reviews and they, usually, had very little to say in the way of encouragement. *Alas* (1890) is discussed in a mildly sarcastic manner: 'Miss Broughton shows all, or nearly all, her usual facility and her easy command of the sort of material and motive which she has always chosen as her particular ground', she begins. This may seem quite harmless, but she becomes positively malicious when describing Broughton's hero: 'He, when crossed in a rash love affair, suddenly develops into a sort of human cyclone full of sound and fury, shedding torrents of tears and breathing forth volumes of sighs and yards of poetical quotation as he lies "prone" on the floor by the side of the unresponsive workbasket of the vanished fair' (*Athenaeum*, 1 November 1890). One must admit that De Mattos had the knack of turning a seemingly serious piece of work into an utterly ridiculous venture. In this she was anticipating another Katharine and more famous *Athenaeum* contributor, Katherine Mansfield.[29] In fact, Mansfield was to review Broughton's very last novel, *A Fool in her Folly*, published posthumously in 1920 in very much the same vein (*Athenaeum*, 20 August 1920).

De Mattos's utterances with regard to Rhoda Broughton's work seem, if possible, to grow even more condemnatory as the years wear on. Indeed, if Miss Broughton's *Alas* was still acceptable to her this can certainly not be said of *Mrs Bligh*, published in 1892. This review begins by remarking that Rhoda Broughton is still the 'Miss Broughton of old' though in this latest novel there is 'less sprightliness and less slang, and a smaller amount of rudeness from the "young person" to her admirers and (frequently) her betters. There are no clergymen set up for ridicule'. All things considered, there seems to be no reason why one should want to read a book like that, especially since the main character is clearly flawed. This story, she concludes, 'seems to have been hastily snatched in passing, and brightly, but not carefully, reproduced' (*Athenaeum*, 12 November 1892). Equally devastating is the discussion of Broughton's *A Beginner* which opens with the following words: '"A beginner" is devoid of anything approaching a plot. Were it not for the lightness, vivacity, and sense of movement inherent in Miss Broughton's touch, it would

---

[28] Jewsbury's criticism of Rhoda Broughton is discussed at length in Fryckstedt, *Geraldine Jewbury's 'Athenaeum' Reviews*, pp. 85–9.

[29] The practice is briefly discussed by Claire Hanson in her introduction to *The Critical Writings of Katherine Mansfield*, New York: St Martin's Press, 1987, p. 8.

hardly be even what is called "a story without a plot"' (*Athenaeum*, 5 May 1894).

But then, of course, one should know that *A Beginner* had been Broughton's deliberate attack on anonymous reviewers such as Jewsbury and De Mattos. Finally, it seems to me, Mrs de Mattos wanted to give the *coup de grâce* in her review of *Dear Faustina* in which, according to her, Broughton had tried to jump on the New Woman bandwagon but was too old to do so:

> Miss Broughton understood the young person of her epoch, and wrote of and for her – wrote of her language , manners, aspirations, with discrimination and daring ... Of the later growths of her garden of girls so much cannot be said. The sense of effort, the attempt to keep abreast with mental development and social progress (or the reverse), sit a little amiss on the brow of one whose function has been to provide not so much amusement combined with instruction as pure and simple amusement tinctured with sentimentalism. (*Athenaeum*, 12 June 1897)

De Mattos on Broughton gives an idea of the conscientiousness with which she attempted to annihilate or, at least, silence an importunate novelist. Of course it did not silence Rhoda Broughton, who was probably not amused but certainly continued to write.

And then there were the novelists whom De Mattos tended to like. If she believed the 'young girl' was to benefit from reading the novel she was inclined to bestow her blessing. Mrs L.B. Walford's many books, for instance, were nearly always greeted with a warm eulogy. Her *Sage of Sixteen* (1890) is said to be 'decidedly pleasant and healthful' (*Athenaeum*, 18 January 1890). The same goes for the stories by Stanley Weyman. For his historical romances she reserved her most superlative adjectives. *The House of the Wolf*, published in 1890, was hailed as a 'brilliant affair' (*Athenaeum*, 10 May 1890), three years later she is immensely pleased with the appearance of *A Gentleman of France*, a 'rattling good story' which, less than a year later, is followed by another of those excellent historical romances, *Under the Red Robe*.

Even so, it is difficult to generalise about De Mattos's views on, for instance, the adventure novel or the New Woman novel. Like other critics of the *Athenaeum* her views evolved with the times: she sometimes changed her opinion and, being human, her idea of what constituted good fiction was partly a subjective one. Besides, like the other *Athenaeum* critics she did not have the benefit of hindsight. She had to pronounce judgement there and then. Nor could she always immediately discern the formation of a new literary movement let alone delimit its membership. Unlike the scholar now, she could not use the list of New Woman novels drawn up by, for instance, Ann Ardis.

It is fair to say, however, that De Mattos tended to follow the prevailing moral guidelines: the anonymous author of *A Vicar's Wife* was presented with the rather discouraging verdict that it was an 'ill-considered and ill-advised sort of publication' (*Athenaeum*, 19 March 1892). Whether writers were still 'budding' or already 'blossoming' made no difference, nor did the author's gender. Authors who went 'too far' were dealt with in the same way. Grant

Allen's *The Woman Who Did*, for instance, was radically rejected. She was on the side of those who believed this novel might have a pernicious influence, rather than deter young women from having a sexual relationship outside of marriage. '*The Woman Who Did*', she argues, 'reads more like a somewhat broken-winged manifesto from a few extremists against marriage as an institution than a sensational work of fiction, a personal revelation, an intense conviction, or even a popular "cri de coeur"' (*Athenaeum*, 2 March 1895). *A Husband of no Importance* by 'Rita' is even less acceptable: 'A most mediocre affair, poor in conception and execution ... What effects there are are disagreeable' (*Athenaeum*, 20 October 1894).

But De Mattos was certainly not against all progressive writing, or New Woman fiction as such.[30] Nor did she, like Mabel Birchenough, have to resort to a rather contrived reason for her liking; she did not eschew the words 'modern' or 'new'. Mary Cholmondeley's *Red Pottage* she pronounced to be a 'clever, well-told story'. She appreciated its subtle depiction of modern life and manners. Nor does she seem to be offended by the negative presentation of the bigoted vicar and his wife. 'Never aggressively witty nor epigrammatic, she yet often says a good thing in a way that makes one wonder why it has not been said before, or not in the same fresh or whimsical fashion' (*Athenaeum*, 18 November 1899). De Mattos certainly closely followed what happened on the scene of the New Woman novel. Thus, she notices that male authors generally ridiculed them in their fiction. She was pleasantly surprised, therefore, to find that *The Career of Candida* by one George Paston was conducted along different lines. She could not know that George Paston was the pseudonym of Emily Morse Symonds.

Again, her stance towards such realists as George Gissing and Henry James depended on the book she was asked to review. She had the honour of reviewing *New Grub Street* when it appeared in 1891. Showing an awareness of Zola's theories about naturalism, she comments that Gissing 'sees life through the medium of a strong and keen individuality'. Compared to the earlier works this one shows 'a perceptible lightening of touch, a greater diffusiveness' but, she adds, no 'visible improvement of style' (*Athenaeum*, 9 May 1891). Two years later she is presented with another opportunity of discussing Gissing's work on the appearance of *The Odd Women* (1893), generally considered to be one of the most striking New Woman novels. Her judgement this time is clearly positive. She still believes the author might do something about his style, which she labels as 'journalese', but has to admit that this book is absorbing; indeed, she comes to the conclusion that 'Mr. Gissing has not, perhaps, on the whole, written anything stronger or more striking' (*Athenaeum*, 27 May 1893).

---

[30] I have checked her reviews against the list of New Woman novelists compiled by Ann Ardis.

PASSIONATE FEMALE LITERARY TYPES.
THE *NEW* SCHOOL.

Mrs. Blyth (newly married). "I WONDER YOU NEVER MARRIED, MISS QUILPSON!"
Miss Quilpson (Author of "Caliban Dethroned," &c., &c.). "WHAT? I MARRY! I BE A MAN'S PLAYTHING! NO, THANK YOU!"

Figure   5.1 'Passionate Female Literary Types. The *New* School',
             Punch, 2 June 1894.

Henry James was, at the time, of a different stature altogether. Towards the end of the decade his was a well-established name and he could count a great number of staunch supporters amongst the literary. In the early 1890s, however, it was less clear whether he was eventually to be counted among the great prose writers.[31] Thus, when De Mattos tackled *The Tragic Muse* in 1890 she started on a positive note, only to quickly dismiss the work under review:[32]

---

[31] Katharine de Mattos wrote reviews of the following works by Henry James: *The Tragic Muse* (26 July 1890), *The Lesson of the Master* (19 March 1892), *Terminations* (15 June 1895), *Embarrassments* (1 August 1896), *The Other House* (31 October 1896); Henry James, *What Maisie Knew* (6 November 1897), *The Awkward Age* (27 May 1899).

[32] Edmund Wilson had a similar experience: 'the first volume ... makes us think that it must be James's best novel, so solid and alive does it seem. [But] after the arrival of Miriam in London, *The Tragic Muse* is an almost total blank.' (see Wilson, 'The Ambiguity of Henry

'The Tragic Muse' has a good deal of the ingenuity and careful accomplishment which one expects from him, but little or none of the keenness of perception and discernment, the delicacy and distinction of touch, which marked 'Daisy Miller' and 'A Bundle of Letters', and made them famous. The handling is ill assured and tentative, as well as too heavily laboured for the issues and interests at stake (*Athenaeum*, 26 July 1890).

She also reviewed *An Awkward Age* when that novel appeared in 1899. The nine-year interlude had been a significant one in James's career. He had become the Master, the *eminence grise* with a small but devoted following. He had abandoned the theatre experiment and had come to terms with this then apparently unique position within the literary world of prestige without popularity. De Mattos's review articulates the views and tastes of the general educated reader. She manifestly weighed her words: 'with all respect for the sustained ability, adroitness, and suppleness of diction, moments of weariness and a sense of ineffectual striving with shadows do overcome one ... So much rarified psychology, paralysis of will, and general bloodlessness has, after a time, a stultifying effect on the mind' (*Athenaeum*, 27 May 1899).

This *Athenaeum* reviewer certainly preferred James's short stories to his more lengthy tales but she was to make an exception for *What Maisie Knew*. There is no doubt, according to De Mattos, that this shows the Master at his best: 'His treatment of the mind of Maisie itself is constantly beyond praise in spite of the circumstances in which he has set her ... he brings her forth unscathed and triumphantly through the ordeal'(*Athenaeum*, 6 November 1897). The treatment James could expect from Katharine de Mattos was, at all events, more soothing to his feelings than the curt dismissal which had been his lot at the hands of Norman MacColl in the short note on *The Reverberator* 'it is impossible to feel much interest in the rest of the tale' (June 1888).[33]

A detailed analysis of De Mattos's reviews is essential if one wants to reach a precise and correct picture of the *Athenaeum*'s views on current fiction. Most analyses of Victorian criticism which attempt to disclose the literary criteria in the *Athenaeum* have generally considered it as a monolithic institution with one single voice. The anonymous 'we' of whom they select a few pronouncements (according to the theory the respective authors want to propound) is confidently held to defend those same views in the other reviews as well. Yet, this was hardly ever the case. Looking at the *Athenaeum* 'Year in review' survey of 1893, any female author might rightfully take offence when reading:

James', 1934; repr. In *The Triple Thinkers* (1938), and in *The Question of Henry James*, ed. F.W. Duprez, London, 1957, pp. 172–201). With thanks to Derek Roper.
[33] Another denigratory remark on James's fiction is inserted in MacColl's review of Broughton's *Belinda* (20 October 1883): 'Miss Broughton has never been in the habit of using the tertiary tints affected by Mr. Henry James'.

> The year 1893, in its literary aspect, has been a year given over almost
> entirely to the younger writers, who have discovered one another
> throughout its course with unanimous and touching enthusiasm ... Along
> with the short story ('poisonous honey stol'n from France') has come a
> new licence in dealing imaginatively with life, almost permitting the
> Englishman to contend with the writers of other nations on their own
> ground; permitting him, that is to say, to represent life as it really is ...
> Not so very many years ago Mr. George Moore was the only novelist in
> England who insisted on the novelist's right to be true to life, even when
> life is unpleasant and immoral; and he was attacked on all sides. Now
> every literary lady is 'realistic,' and everybody says 'How clever! how
> charming!' (*Athenaeum*, 6 January 1894)

These denigrating remarks regarding women novelists, the short story, and
authors belonging to the realist tradition such as Moore and Gissing, have been
used to illustrate the *Athenaeum*'s views on Gissing's New Woman novel.[34]
The survey was anonymous but the 'marked file' reveals it to be by the hand of
Arthur Symons. The passage is a curious antipode to the above-quoted (but
less well-known) De Mattos review in which the short story and realistic
novelists are praised.

A more recent article by Ellen Miller Casey encounters similar
difficulties when wanting to draw general conclusions from a great number of
reviews of women novelists. Casey looks at the reviewers' judgements of
women writers, checks whether there was a double critical standard in place,
and analyses the reviewers' guesses as to the authors' gender. Naturally, she
had to draw her conclusions from a selection of reviews without knowing the
reviewers' identities.

Amongst other things, Casey argues there is a movement towards less
gender stereotyping after 1880, yet it is not so easy to find clearcut examples to
prove her case. Certain passages seem to point in that direction but other
reviews or articles, such as the year's survey of 1893 quoted earlier (which
obviously comes right in the middle of the period), seem to belittle women's
writings as such.

It is a fact, however, that most of Casey's quotes illustrative of a gender
bias were taken from reviews by male critics. In the criticism attributed to
Cook, for instance, there are numerous remarks which, if taken together, would
discourage the most spirited and dynamic of prospective women novelists.

> The author of 'The Unequal Marriage' has chosen a subject which has
> always been a favourite with writers of romance. It is most usual in
> modern arrangements of the theme for the outraged family whose scion
> marries into a lower rank to be represented by a haughty or harsh and
> unrelenting father ... Since most young ladies will write novels, it would
> be a wise thing if their teachers were to accept the inevitable, and, instead
> of throwing away time upon English grammar, which their pupils never
> learn, teach them how to work out sensibly a simple and commonplace
> plot like that ... (24 March 1879)

---

[34] See Ardis, *New Women*, pp. 87ff.

Cook wrote far less in the 1890s. Indeed, it is unsure whether the Cook contributing then was still the same person: was it Charles Archer (1849–1934) or Edward Tyas Cook (1857–1919)? The name is a very common one. The editor of the *Critical Heritage* volume devoted to R.L. Stevenson identified him as Edward Tyas Cook, but because of his age he could not have been the author of the reviews in the 1870s. And the name is entered as 'C.A. Cook' in the 'marked file' covering the early years of the twentieth century.[35]

Lewis Sergeant, on the other hand, another male colleague who shared the 'New Novels' column with De Mattos, was at times more lenient in his judgement of women writers. His was the welcoming voice behind the review of Iota's *A Yellow Aster* : 'The warmest of welcomes is due from the reading public to any new author who conspicuously unites the qualities of intuition, candour, respect for the human and the divine, and such a natural straightforwardness as, taken together ... a welcome of this kind is due to "Iota"' (*Athenaeum*, 17 February 1894). And he obviously could not help praising George Paston's *A Modern Amazon*: 'good novels, or novels conspicuous throughout for a general mediocrity of goodness, are so common in these days, and the essentials of human interest are so limited, that one cannot feel much surprise on coming across another well-written romance of a lovely wife ... Regina Haughton ... a lady journalist, up to date ... a little Ibsenite, a little "Woman's Rights", a little emancipationist, but as selfish in disposition and as *farouche* in manner as the most unlovely of her type'. (*Athenaeum*, 5 May 1894) But he, too, could be disheartened by faulty construction, stylistic infelicities or by the sheer lack of originality. Such disappointment was easily translated into stereotypical denunciations: '*A Daughter of a King* by "Alien"', is said to be 'another attempt by a woman to read the riddle of womanhood and of the universe' (13 October 1894). Even more distressing are the suggestions in his review of *The New Antigone*: 'the author ... is either a learned young lady or a fanciful man of letters', and, somewhat further, he has to admit the book 'is the work of a male intellect gone wrong' (15 October 1887).

Another attitude, a changed opinion, did not automatically mean the reviewer was a different one either. Discussing the reviews of Alan St Aubyn and their assumptions about the author's gender, Casey writes :

> Despite their interest, reviewers did not always identify gender, nor were their identifications always correct. This lack of consistency indicates that gender identification rested with a reviewer rather than with an editor. 'Alan St. Aubyn' epitomizes the reviewers' problems. The 1894 reviewer of *Orchard Damerel* identified St. Aubyn as 'her,' while two months later the reviewer of *In the Face of the World* referred to 'Mr. St. Aubyn.' The 1897 review of *A Proctor's Wooing* called the author 'him (or her)' while other reviews in 1898 and 1899 gave no indication of gender (reviews of *Fortune's Gate, Bonnie Maggie Lauder*, and *Mrs Dunbar's Secret*)

---

[35] One finds instances in the columns of 1904.

Interestingly, the author of four of these reviews was Lewis Sergeant. The second review was by Graves (*In the Face*), the fourth by J.M. Collyer (*Bonnie Maggie Lauder*). Sergeant had correctly established the author's gender as female in a review of 1894 but referred to a 'he or she', in a later review, perhaps after having read the interim note of his colleague Charles Larcom Graves. Then again, reviewers often referred to an author using a male pseudonym by 'him' or 'he' while knowing perfectly well that that pseudonym hid a female author. The male pronoun was simply the generic pronoun. Sergeant criticized the author for 'his or her' blatant ignorance about university life, so it would seem he was still convinced this was a woman writer. In his reviews of Alan St Aubyn he always makes the same judgement: the stories are readable and, sometimes, pleasing but he resents the deficiencies, the artlessness.

In Casey's article there is one longer excerpt taken from the August 1900 issue which serves to show the growing openness towards an author's gender. That review, not surprisingly, is from the pen of Katharine de Mattos. In a review of Jane Jones's *The Prison House* De Mattos observed that this novel 'does not suggest the handling of any female Jones. In the drawing of some of the situations and characters there is a hint of virility, and, as it were, the way of a man. Nowadays, when the feminine quality is to be found in unexpected places, and *vice versa*, this may be nothing'(*Athenaeum*, 4 August 1900). For De Mattos, so much is clear, the gender of the author is irrelevant to the quality of the novel. Unlike her male colleagues, she abstains from linking an author's assumed gender to some denigrating clichés about women.

Nevertheless, it would be simplistic to conclude that the alleged decline of the number of stereotypes about women writers in the reviews was the result of the greater number of reviews written by women reviewers. The female gender of the reviewer did not invariably guarantee such an 'neutral' approach. As shown above, Mabel Birchenough's reviews came perilously near to making sneering remarks about New Woman fiction. Moreover, in spite of her own gender and her aspirations as a fiction writer, Birchenough, like her male colleagues, indulges in making guesses about the author's gender on the basis of certain gender stereotypes. Witness her review of [Emma Frances Brooke's] *A Superfluous Woman*:

> A novelist whose most obvious purpose in writing a story is to proclaim to a corrupt generation his (or her) convictions about things in general is probably very young, and certainly very inexperienced, both with regard to society as it is and to novel-writing as it ought to be ... The author of 'A Superfluous Woman' has preached her sermon – it is too feminine a discourse to suggest the male pronoun. (3 February 1894)

Still, few if any of the women reviewers of the prose section fell into the trap of revealing their gender, as did some of their male colleagues. In the reviews contributed by De Mattos there was no intimation as to the 'sex' of the reviewer such as may be detected in Graves's review of Henry Erroll's *An*

Ugly Duckling: 'Mr. Erroll's name is unknown to us, and, unless we are much mistaken, is the pseudonym of *a writer of the other sex*, who shows considerable promise in a maiden effort'(*Athenaeum*, 23 July 1887; my italics). De Mattos might observe, at times, that 'no woman' would ever behave the way some of the fictional characters in the book under review did, but that was as far as she would go (*Athenaeum*, 6 August 1887).

The last prose reviewer who deserves at least a brief mentioning here is Emily Thursfield (née Herbert). In pure numerical terms, that is, counting the number of books rather than the number of lines, she reviewed more for the *Athenaeum* than Birchenough. In fact, after Geraldine Jewsbury's death, she dominated the children's fiction column (including the 'Christmas Books') for twenty-six years, thus contributing over 1,300 book reviews. Thursfield had married James R. Thursfield, a close friend of Sir Charles Dilke who was soon to become a well-known leader-writer for *The Times*, in 1880; she was engaged as a reviewer for the weekly that same year. Sir James himself contributed some of the 'Notes from Oxford' to the *Athenaeum* at the beginning of his career.

Emily Thursfield contributed no shocking viewpoints to the critical discourse of her age. Considering the kind of books she had to review that would have been a feat. She did, though, review some of the better boys' books; Rider Haggard's, Sir Arthur Conan Doyle, and Henty's adventure stories. Considering the editor's machinery behind the *Athenaeum* it is hard to see why she was specifically chosen to treat these kinds of novels, since she obviously had very little affinity with them. But she had obviously won the right to do so. Haggard's *She*, generally considered his best story, is dismissed because of the 'lamentable' treatment of the tale:

> Mr Haggard's language and dramatic force rarely rise to the level of a really great occasion; they often fall disappointingly below it. It would, in fact, seem that he has essayed a task beyond his natural powers. He can construct a thrilling story of adventure, he can describe with vigour and vividness, he can conceive a powerful, dramatic, and even tragic situation; but he cannot write an African 'Faust', he is not a Marlowe or a Goethe.

She admits, in short, the story's originality but she has to conclude it is "withal a disappointing work' (*Athenaeum*, 15 January 1887). Thursfield, in fact, makes it rather difficult for new 'romance' writers to come up to her standards since she used Robert Louis Stevenson's works as her touchstone. In a review that same year of Haggard's *Allan Quatermain*, she rejects all hasty comparisons with the author of *Treasure Island* because Stevenson is 'a literary artist of rare quality and a master of human character', while Haggard's art is of a 'coarser tissue, and his command of character and motive is not extensive' (*Athenaeum*, 16 July 1887). The accusations, especially with regard to Haggard's style and language, are not entirely without foundation. Again when 'Q', Sir Arthur Quiller-Couch, launches his first romance on the market,

Thursfield is there to evaluate him. She points out the similarities and the differences between Q's *Dead Man's Rock*, Stevenson's *Treasure Island* and Haggard's *King Solomon's Mines* and concludes: 'in point of goriness Q occupies a middle position between' the two (*Athenaeum*, 5 November 1887). These reviews come within the 'New Novels' section, indicating they are slightly better value than the children's books and thus giving Thursfield more room for discussion. Usually, however, in her regular column, she had to make do with two or three sentences to appraise a book. There was little opportunity for her to discuss matters of gender.

Coming back to Katharine de Mattos and her involvement with the *Athenaeum*, the 'marked file' reveals that her reviewing petered out in the early years of this century when she was assigned fewer and largely uninteresting books. She discussed thirty books in 1908 and then abruptly stopped. She lived until 1929, dying at the age of eighty-seven. According to the death certificate she was then earning her living as a tutor. The 'New Novels' section after her disappearance at the end of 1908 was slowly taken over by a new generation of reviewers, among whom were Camilla Jebb, W. H. Chesson, A. J. Dawson and the Marriott Watsons.

The greatest change, however, really came in 1910. The editor started that year with an assessment of 'the Publishing Season and the Book Trade' in which he gave vent to a general dissatisfaction with the way things were evolving. This is the age of 'the snippet and the paragraph' he began. The fierce competition amongst periodical publications led, according to him, to the disappearance of important journals. But things were turning for the worse in other branches as well. Authors of histories and memoirs had no scruples in copying – 'pillaging' – freely from existing sources. There was a wide production of the English classics, but annotated editions of the classics were missing in spite of the demand for them. And novels were spawned by the hundreds a month: 'This year we have received on one day more than thirty books in juvenile literature from a single house. How is it possible to deal with such a flood as this? and, even if criticism is regarded as worthless, does this superfluity of seasonal publications do anything but distract the buying public?' (*Athenaeum*, 1 January 1910). Drawing his conclusions from these observations Vernon Rendall was henceforth to reserve less space for the 'New Novels', while the list of 'New Books' (simply mentioning title, price and publisher) becomes longer. The reviewers, too, had to bear the consequences: their contributions became shorter and their pay was reduced to 5 shillings, 6 pence. Only some reviewers, representing the previous generation, such as H.B. Marriott Watson and his wife Rosamund (née Ball), still went on earning 10 shillings per review.

The fiction section only returned to its former prestigious place within the weekly after the First World War, with the start of John Middleton Murry's editorship, when the *Athenaeum*'s columns could boast the initials of Virginia Woolf, Katherine Mansfield, T.S. Eliot and E.M. Forster.

Chapter 6

Poets as Critics

> There is an imperial refusal in Victorian criticism to regard the poem as a
> self-contained, sealed-off entity on which moral and social questions
> external to it do not impinge.[1]

Poets had been welcome in the columns of the *Athenaeum* since the early days
of its existence. The journal published poems by recognized as well as
budding authors but, since it was the editor's policy to give priority to reviews,
only little space was reserved for original material.[2] According to Marchand
the *Athenaeum* mainly published mediocre or downright bad poetry during the
first decades of its running but he admits, indirectly, that judgements about the
value of these poems may be liable to changes of taste.[3] Besides, there were
also the occasional contributions by such poets as Matthew Arnold, Arthur
Clough, R.W. Emerson, H.W. Longfellow, George Meredith, Alfred Tennyson,
and William Wordsworth.[4]

The one eminent woman poet who made a regular appearance in those
early years was Elizabeth Barrett. Her poems adorned the *Athenaeum*'s pages
in the period 1836–1843.[5] It is significant, in the light of our research, that the
then editor, Charles Dilke (1789–1864), also commissioned her to write a
series of signed articles on 'The Greek Christian Poets' and a few reviews for
the journal.[6] Thus, in a way, Elizabeth Barrett Browning established the
tradition of women poets reviewing for the poetry section, a tradition which
was to languish somewhat during the editorial management of William
Hepworth Dixon (1821–1879) but which returned in full force during the last
decades of the century.[7]

---

[1] Armstrong, *Victorian Scrutinies*, p. 4.

[2] Marchand, *The Athenaeum*, p. 166.

[3] Ibid., p. 172.

[4] Ibid., p. 171.

[5] Margaret Forster, *Elizabeth Barrett Browning. A Biography*, New York: Doubleday,
1988, p. 109.

[6] In her article 'Poetry in the *Athenaeum*', Rosemary Scott refers to Barrett Browning
as being reviewed in the *Athenaeum* and as a contributor of some poems. For Scott, however,
the names, hence the identities of the reviewers are not always noteworthy (for example, the
reviewer 'Knight' is not given a first name), their gender must have seemed of even less
consequence. (see *VPR*, 29:1 (1996), pp. 19–32)

[7] As mentioned above, the main woman reviewer of the 1850s and 1860s was
Geraldine Jewsbury with 2,300 book reviews to her name. Jewsbury, however, was mainly
responsible for the 'New Novels' or 'Novels of the Week' section and only sporadically

Mathilde Blind

Mathilde Blind (1841–1896) fits in the category of poet reviewers who, to a certain degree, assumed responsibility for the poetry column of the weekly.[8] She was to review some twenty-six books in the 1870s and 1880s, and she had two of her poems published in the *Athenaeum*.[9] 'Miss Blind's introduction to the *Athenaeum* probably came through her stepfather, the German political refugee Karl Blind (1826–1907) whose house in Hampstead had become the meeting place of those politicians who had won Sir Charles Dilke's admiration; people such as Louis Blanc, Giuseppe Garibaldi, and Giuseppe Mazzini.

Mathilde Blind, born Cohen, had adopted her stepfather's name in her youth. She and her family had come to London in 1848 when she was only seven. Her brother, Ferdinand Cohen Blind, committed suicide in 1866 after having made an attempt on Bismarck's life. Her stepbrother, Karl Blind's son Rudolph,[10] followed an artistic career. The family was a colourful one to say the least.

Mathilde Blind's very first collection of poems was published under a male pseudonym: *Poems* by 'Claude Lake', 1867. Her first book, an *Ode to Schiller*, had appeared in 1859, when she was twenty-six. Vernon Lee was introduced to her in 1881 and left a characteristically lively description of the woman in her letters to her mother: 'Miss Mathilde Blind, the adopted daughter of Karl Blind ... is an ugly coarse, evidently amiable woman, extremely like Ouida. Mary [Robinson] says her poetry is just among the very best written at present'.[11] Vernon Lee had met Mathilde Blind at the house of Mrs W.K. Clifford where she was in the company of Helen Zimmern, another German expatriate. All four were to write for the *Athenaeum* at some stage in their careers but Blind was the first to become a fully-fledged member of the *Athenaeum* staff. Whether she acted as a negotiator between the *Athenaeum* and other female writers is hard to determine, but she seems to have known quite a number of its prospective contributors and she appears to have been a strong and influential figure. Leslie Stephen, another faithful visitor of the Clifford home, categorised Blind as one 'of Lucy [Clifford]'s freethinking friends'. He thought her a pernicious presence, however, because Blind wanted

---

reviewed poetry. Besides, unlike Barrett Browning and the women reviewers under discussion here, Jewsbury achieved fame as a novelist not a poet.

    [8] There is a long entry on Mathilde Blind by Richard Garnett in the *Dictionary of National Biography* (suppl. 1), and more recently by Rosemary T. Van Arsdel in *The 1890s*, George Cevasco, ed., New York and London: Garland, 1993.

    [9] Besides the entries and reviews ascribed to 'Miss Blind' a number of contributions are simply marked as by 'Blind'. Owing to the fact that the *Athenaeum* editor did not really consistently refer to ladies as 'Mrs' or 'Miss' – Geraldine Jewsbury, for example, was nearly always entered as 'Jewsbury' – and seeing that the subject matter reflects Mathilde Blind's pre-occupations, we may consider those reviews as hers.

    [10] Vernon Lee did not think very highly of this member of the Blind family either. She calls him 'an awful little snob'; see *Vernon Lee's Letters*, p. 66.

    [11] Ibid., p. 64.

Clifford to publish some of her late husband's writings on the institution of marriage.[12]

Another contemporary description of the poet came from her colleague Theodore Watts (later Watts-Dunton). He was responsible for the signed obituary which was published in the *Athenaeum* after the death of Mathilde Blind on 26 November 1896. Watts called her 'highly cultured and highly endowed' and compared her beauty to that of Scott's Rebecca. She was, in his words, a 'genius' and he went so far as to compare Blind's greatness of mind with George Eliot's but there, it seems, the comparison ended. The period was a difficult one for women such as Eliot and Blind, Watts averred, often forcing them into an unnatural isolation. Besides, and quite unforgivably, Mathilde Blind longed for fame: 'Just as the loveliest woman palls upon one the moment that she shows herself to be conscious of her beauty, so the finest poet will pall upon one the moment he exhibits an undue yearning for fame'.[13] Watts also thought her German background withstood her attempts to express feelings in poetry. According to him 'the verbal substance, lacking both exactitude and idiomatic spring, hung like a coloured curtain between the writer's conception and the reader's eyes'.

Later evaluations of Blind's poetry have been scarce, almost non-existent. Some of her work was reprinted in Elizabeth Sharp's anthology *Women's Voices. An Anthology of the most Characteristic Poems by English, Scotch and Irish Women* (1887) which was a deliberate – but unsuccessful – attempt on the part of the editor to rescue some poetry from oblivion. Vita Sackville-West was one of the few to recognize 'a woman of character' in this German *emigrée*, one whose poetry has been underrated and whose vision of nature 'esteemed not sufficiently'.[14] Recently, there has been a hesitant re-assessment with the brief entry in *The 1890s. An Encyclopedia of British Literature, Art and Culture* and, more importantly, with the appreciative inscribing in Isobel Armstrong's *Victorian Poetry. Poetry, Poetics and Politics*.[15] Armstrong, like Watts, is tempted to compare Blind and Eliot; she detects a shared determination to create 'new evolutionary and humanist myths'.[16]

Furthermore, she ends her chapter on women's poetry, significantly, with a brief harking back to Blind's poetry, adding that this poet 'represents what this tradition could do at its best: it could bring the resources of the affective state to social and political analysis and speculate on the constraints of the

---

[12] John W. Bicknell, ed, *Selected Letters of Leslie Stephen, 1882–1904*, Houndsmill, Basingstoke and London: Macmillan, 1996, pp. 344–5.

[13] *Athenaeum*, 5 December 1896.

[14] Vita Sackville-West, 'The Women Poets of the Seventies', *The Eighteen-Seventies. Essays by the Fellows of the Royal Society of Literature*, ed. Harley Granvile-Barker. Cambridge University Press, 1929, p. 129.

[15] And her work can now be found in Angela Leighton's anthology, and Joseph Bristow and Isobel Armstrong's anthology of Victorian women poets.

[16] Isobel Armstrong, *Victorian Poetry. Poetry, Poetics and Politics*, London: Routledge, 1993, p. 375.

definition of feminine subjectivity in an almost innumerable variety of contexts, indirectly and directly'. [17]

Mathilde Blind was to publish just two poems in the *Athenaeum*. The first one, 'The Dead', appeared on 2 April 1881, the second one, 'The Sakyeh', on 16 March 1895. In both, 'man's' place and function on earth is considered and weighed. The second poem, published the year before her own death is a dejected sigh coming from someone who has realised life is short and in many ways pointless:

> And men, who move in rhythm with moving stars,
> Should shrink to give the borrowed lives they hold:
> Bound blindfold to the groaning wheel of time.
>   (*Athenaeum*, 16 March 1895)

Blind's name first occurs in the 'marked file' of the *Athenaeum* in 1871 as a writer for the gossip column in which she announced or reported on very diverse matters such as new editions of poems, or German novelettes or the return to Italy of the remains of Gabriele Rossetti, father of the poets Dante Gabriel and Christina. And when she thought her own work worth mentioning she did so.[18]

Of Blind's twenty-six reviews, eighteen were poetry reviews. The other books for which she was consulted were mostly biographies (she reviewed one novel) which shows her to be recognised as a biographer as well. Her biography of *George Eliot*, the first in the Eminent Women Series (edited by John H. Ingram) was looked upon with a curious mixture of deference and scepticism in the *Athenaeum* review. Interestingly, it was her colleague Watts who had been asked to pronounce judgement. The review is a testimony to the bias which even such 'enlightened' critics as Watts held towards women professionals. Watts did not doubt the eminence of George Eliot nor, for that matter, that of her biographer, but he did regret the rise of the 'eminent woman'. For one thing he believed that eminence in women leads to bigger heads. And larger feminine 'crania', he imagined, might not be very flattering on women, 'an overworked reviewer' would probably prefer the 'smaller and better-proportioned heads which characterized the last generations', and, secondly, women were obviously meant for something else; in truth, they were only happy if that something else, in life, was fulfilled:

> Assuredly George Eliot was far from being a happy woman with all her fame and all her intellectual triumphs ... It is not literary fame that can satisfy the yearning in a woman's heart. 'Mais vous, de qui on m'assure que vous êtes une belle et agréable fille, n'avez-vous pas honte d'être si savante?' wrote Queen Christina to Mddle. Le Fêvre, when that learned Frenchwoman sent the queen a copy of her edition of Callimachus. And without saying that the final cause of the existence of a woman is that she should be loved by a man, this at least should be said, that to a woman the

[17] Ibid., p.377.
[18] See *Athenaeum*, 2 May 1874.

need of a man's love is so pressing a need that no success and no triumph will really bring satisfaction to her heart which do not minister, or seem to minister, to that need. (*Athenaeum*, 5 May 1883)

Watts is pleased, however, with this biography of George Eliot which he calls a picturesque as well as powerful narrative. One wonders whether Mathilde Blind knew who had been allocated her book. She was never to review any of Watts's books in return which, for him, was perhaps just as well.

Blind was not lenient when it came to assessing new publications. When discussing four minor poets in March 1874 she does not mince her words. Her verdicts, however, make pleasant reading because of the humour and the originality with which she phrases them. One Henry Malden, for instance, was to be dismissed as 'at his best ... diluted Tennyson; when at his worst, however, he can claim originality, for then he is unlike anyone but himself' (*Athenaeum*, 14 March 1874). And about the anonymous author of *Alfred: a Poem* she writes: 'execrable verse and tedious maundering are the only qualities characteristic of "Alfred"'.

In one of her very first reviews she is given the opportunity to judge William Morris's *Love's Enough*. Morris is one of the poets she does appreciate. *Love's Enough*, however, is not a subject which suits his poetic genius. He should have chosen a grander subject, one 'possessed of loftier proportions'. Why did he not return to the Arthurian legend, she wonders?

> we are inclined to think that, on the whole, it is rather a gain than a loss to Art that the same theme should be handled over and over again. If we had as many 'King Arthurs' as the Greeks possessed tragedies concerning the woes of the house of Agamemnon, or the Italians representations of the Madonna, we should probably find that in this way we could not fail to attain some culminating achievement ... like the block of marble under the sculptor's hands, he could mould, elaborate, and fashion forth into perfect loveliness, while, nevertheless, he would be bound down by the necessary conditions of his material. (*Athenaeum*, 23 November 1873)

She proved an extremely exacting critic in other cases as well. Three of Richard Watson Dixon's publications came into her hands and each time they were subjected to meticulous criticism.[19] *Mano: a Poetical History* was an interesting experiment in her eyes but nothing more (*Athenaeum*, 25 August 1883). Dixon had attempted to write this lengthy tale in *terza rima* using obsolete or archaic words. But Blind expected more than mere skilfulness in the handling of rhyme or metre. Dixon's verse is reproached with being cramped and mechanical, in no way approaching the melodious quality which *terza rima* normally achieves. The poet must have been near exasperation when reading these reviews in the *Athenaeum* for he could hardly ever find

---

[19] See the issues of 25 August 1883, on Richard Watson Dixon, *Mano: a Political History*; 11 October 1884 on Dixon's *Odes and Eclogues*; and 26 March 1887 on Dixon's *Lyrical Poems*.

favour in this anonymous reader's eyes.[20] Upon the publication of his *Lyrical Poems*, many years later, Blind admitted she appreciated these more. But she still regrets the use of the archaic vocabulary and far-fetched images. His use of the metaphor 'When leafy June has pinned on every hedgerow briar the frail wild rose' is ridiculed when Blind adds 'what a flight of the imagination does it not require to picture June going about from hedge to hedge on that interminable errand'.(*Athenaeum*, 26 March 1887). In order to be true poetry something special was needed, she explains yet elsewhere, 'a spark of vital fire', 'a harmonious inspiration', something which defies definition but which one recognizes when it is there (*Athenaeum*, 24 December 1881). Besides, contrary to her earlier argument, in Dixon's case she does not seem to think that good subjects can be used *ad infinitum*: 'The countless authors who are never weary of recasting Hellenic myths would almost seem to have a lingering belief that the stories have somehow the power of imparting to the products of their own brains some of the charm and beauties which have made the myths themselves imperishable' (26 March 1887).[21]

Unlike the critics, or the reviews, covered by Isobel Armstrong in *Victorian Scrutinies*, Blind's critical writings do include a vocabulary which allows for a description of the 'formal or aesthetic qualities' of a poem.[22] In her analysis Armstrong ascribed the typical absence of a technical assessment in the years 1830 to 1870 to 'the kind of men who reviewed literature'. She then proceeds to describe the journalists who reviewed poetry as: 'spacious all-round thinkers such as Bagehot, aspiring polymaths such as Lewes, men whose interests were never exclusively literary'.[23] Of course, the period covered in the present survey follows immediately upon the period Armstrong discusses so it is well-advised not to draw too many conclusions from these comparisons. But it remains a fact that little thought has so far been given to the possibility of women reviewers of poetry, let alone women poets as reviewers. Blind's expertise when it comes to rhyme, metre and other aspects of poetry lore is displayed at length in the above mentioned review of Dixon's *Mano*:

> Shelley and Mr Browning are nearly our only poets who have made use of the *terza rima*, with the exception, of course, of those writers who have translated the 'Divine Comedy' into English. Shelley was evidently fond

---

[20] His friend and correspondent Gerard Manley Hopkins had sent him the announcement of the publication in the *Athenaeum* on 9 June 1883 (C.C. Abbott, ed., *The Letters of Gerard Manley Hopkins to Richard Watson Dixon*, London: Oxford University Press, 1935, pp. 109–10).

[21] This is also her line of thought in her review of 24 December 1884, reviewing Thomas Woolner's *Pygmalion* : ' it is a dangerous thing to dress the clearly wrought classical myths in a modern garb, and to make them the vehicle of thoughts and sentiments not only foreign but often repugnant to their nature ... The reason of this probably is that the genius of Greece has already embodied its own conceptions with such supreme plastic power as to render all after attempts feeble by comparison'.

[22] Armstrong, *Victorian Scrutinies*, p. 5.

[23] Ibid., p. 5.

of this metre, in which the flow and rush of interwoven lines and rhymes have something of the continuous rolling of the waves running and fusing one into the other ... The 'Ode to the West Wind' is the only complete poem which Shelley has left us in the *terza rima*. He has, however, somewhat modified the metre by dividing a certain number of lines into stanzas, each ending with a couplet.

Mathilde Blind's eminence as a reviewer is confirmed when we find her as the author of the long introductory review of 30 April 1887 in which she debates the qualities of Lewis Morris's *Songs of Britain*. In these songs Morris aspires to retell a selection of ancient Welsh legends. The first one, relating the marriage of the nymph of the lake and an ordinary human, leads her to make this pointed comment: 'the elemental wife, in spite of having entered the marriage state, which, according to Goethe, is the grave of woman's genius, has still occasional visitings of her immortal nature'. Blind appreciates Morris's efforts but gives the distinct impression that the result is not always up to the mark especially in those passages where he wants to digress on modern philosophy and politics : 'The enumeration of our many blessings, and of the gradual improvement of the lot of the poor in factories and mines, reads too much like a pamphlet written for electioneering purposes'. She believes only the 'great' poets can poeticise the present. Victor Hugo and Tennyson successfully transfigured what appears common but Morris does not possess that gift.

Blind was to die in 1896 but by then she had stopped contributing to the *Athenaeum*. The review of Lewis Morris's volume had been the very last she was to write. Mathilde Blind may possibly be seen as the example *par excellence* of a new generation of women poets who stood out on account of their unconventional ideas. She was a professional writer, a freethinker and a professed feminist. It was this kind of mixture which, it seems, the editor of the *Athenaeum* was looking for when he engaged the woman poet who was to write most poetry reviews between 1885 and 1895.

Augusta Webster

> ... the great & dreaded Theodore Watts. Everyone seemed much awed by
> him, & Mary & Miss Blind were evidently much honoured by his notice.
> He is a litle scrubby, eyeglassy, caddish, imitation of Giminez.[24]

Before her *Athenaeum* involvement came to a halt in 1887, Mathilde Blind had been joined by one of the most formidable women writers of the late nineteenth century. Augusta Webster (1837–1894) was certainly one of the most vociferous amongst the *Athenaeum* feminists though she – by and large – refrained from making these concerns public in her anonymous writings for the journal.

---

[24] *Lee's Letters*, p. 74.

Webster was the daughter of Vice-Admiral George Davies who settled in Cambridge in 1851 after having been appointed Chief Constable of Cambridgeshire. Augusta's youth was special in the sense that she spent a lot of time on board her father's ship when she was a little girl. But later she had to settle for the school life of any middle-class girl, finishing her education eventually by attending the Cambridge School of Art.[25] Augusta, however, was interested in acquiring languages. She learned Greek – significantly – while helping a younger brother with his studies and she later was to learn French, Italian and Spanish.[26] But it was her mother Julia Davies, née Hume, who must have had the literary connections (and perhaps writing talent) as the daughter of Joseph Hume, a friend of Lamb, Hazlitt and Godwin.

Miss Davies married Thomas Webster, a Fellow and later law lecturer, of Trinity College, Cambridge, in 1863 and she was the mother of one daughter. This – to Victorian standards – exceptionally small family was later celebrated in the sonnet sequence *Mother and Daughter*. Interestingly, one of her first publications was a classical translation, *The Prometheus Bound of Aeschylus* (1866), which she produced hesitantly, hiding behind an apologetic preface written by her husband: 'The reason why the title-page of this book bears the name of an Editor as well as that of the translator is, that my wife wished for some better guarantee of accuracy than a lady's name could give, and so, rightly or wrongly, looked to me for what she wanted'. [27]

This publication and its foreword merely confirm the claim that talented women in the nineteenth century still had to conquer that innate fear of trespassing when using the printed word in order to enter the public sphere. Translation was, for Webster, as for the reviewer–translators discussed in an earlier chapter, the first step towards overcoming that anxiety. Her three previous publications (two volumes of poetry and one novel) betray a similar reluctance to step into the public limelight, which was possibly exacerbated by a distrust of the 'double critical standard'.[28] She published those under the male pseudonym: 'Cecil Home'. After having gone through that rite of passage she became more assertive and stuck to her own name: Augusta Webster.

Webster's move from Cambridge to London has been explained as the fulfilment of her girlhood dream. She wanted to mix in literary circles and develop her literary talents in a place which was more congenial to them. Hake and Compton-Rickett point to Watts as the person who nursed her genius 'with unremitting zeal' and who praised her publications in the *Athenaeum*.[29] Again,

---

[25] Her episode at South Kensington Art School is not mentioned in the *Dictionary National Biography* entry.

[26] As Victorianists will know, young women were not supposed to study the classics at the time. George Eliot's *Mill on the Floss* gives a good idea of what was generally thought to be suitable or unsuitable for a young woman's mind.

[27] Augusta Webster, *The Prometheus Bound of Aeschylus*, London: 1866, preface.

[28] Showalter, *A Literature of their Own from Charlotte Brontë to Doris Lessing*, London: Virago, 1978, p. 73.

[29] Thomas Hake and Arthur Compton-Rickett, *The Life and Letters of Theodore Watts-Dunton*, 2 vols. London: Jack, 1916, p. 16.

there is no mention of Webster's own reviews in the *Athenaeum* but if we may follow Hake and Compton-Rickett's train of thought, then Watts may well have been instrumental in helping her to secure a foothold on the *Athenaeum* staff. Other elements, however, may have been weightier.

Another picturesque description in Vernon Lee's correspondence shows Webster as the hostess of a house-warming party to which both MacColl and Watts had been invited:

> Wednesday evg. Mabel [Robinson] & I went to a housewarming party at Mrs. Augusta Webster's at Hammersmith. The lady is more like Mme Hellibrand [Hildebrand?] than Sappho. An enormous crush, of ill-dressed, eccentric literary frumps. I spoke to Wm Rossetti, Watts, [William] Sharp & MacColl. (Entry for Friday 13 June 1884)[30]

The entry is an interesting one because it shows Norman MacColl surrounded by a selection of his reviewers or prospective reviewers: there was Mathilde Blind, Vernon Lee, Mabel Robinson and Augusta Webster who was soon to join their ranks, her first review appearing in August of that year.[31]

Webster, it appears, joined the staff a few months before the Dilke marriage. She and Emilia Dilke may well have been acquainted, considering the fact that both had been students of the South Kensington Art School in the late 1850s. Also, of course, Augusta Webster was a militant feminist and would therefore quite naturally belong to Emilia's circle of acquaintances. She fought with zeal and perseverance for women's suffrage, the campaign which split the female intelligentsia of the time into two separate groups. The Dilkes, Norman MacColl and, by the same token, their weekly were propitious to the pro-suffrage crusade.

Augusta Webster's attitude towards suffrage was absolutely clear. Her angry response to John Bright's anti-suffrage speech in 1876 was *ad rem* though it verged on the personal.[32]

> I watched you, and I watched the faces on our side of the house. If you looked ill at ease in your novel *rôle*, the liberal benches contained anxious and constrained countenances ...
> You say women are not a class. Let us not quarrel about words ... Women are more than half the nation, and when they tell you in a gentle and dignified language that they are treated as a class,[33] that they are

---

[30] *Lee's Letters*, p. 145.

[31] Within the context of the current interest in such 'forgotten' women, Augusta Webster's case has been eloquently put forward by Angela Leighton in part of her excellent study *Victorian Women Poets. Writing Against the Heart*, Hemel Hempstead: Harvester Wheatsheaf, 1992.

[32] Curiously enough this letter was reprinted in Jane Lewis's *Before the Vote was Won. Arguments for and against women's suffrage*, New York and London: Routledge, 1987, pp. 257–63, but left unidentified.

[33] A point amply proven by E.A. Bennett's unequivocal views in E.A. Bennett, *Journalism for Women: A Practical Guide*, London: John Lane, 1898, p. 12.

legislated for as a class, that the delicate instincts and feelings you are so anxious to shield are daily outraged by the Acts of a Parliament of which you were a Member ...

Another inconsistency strikes me – but your speech is so full of them that if it had been spoken by a woman it would have been used by our opponents as a perpetual peg on which to hang the charge of the logical incapacity of the sex.

Yet, in spite of this and other well-argued exposés there is hardly any mention of Augusta Webster's role in the women's movement in recent feminist histories. The reason may lie in the anonymity of much of what she wrote. She hid behind the male pseudonym of 'Cecil Home' for her first two works and published the open letter to John Bright anonymously. All credit to Angela Leighton, therefore, for having rescued Webster's life and work from oblivion in her recent analysis of Victorian women poets.[34] Webster's pro-suffrage views clearly did nothing towards helping her gain a place on the canon yet they probably did help when it came to being offered the well-paid job of reviewer for the *Athenaeum*.

To be sure, Webster may have drawn the attention of Sir Charles himself. In 1879 and again in 1885 Webster was elected on the London school board. Sir Charles had been instrumental in the establishment of school boards when Forster's Education Law was passed in 1870.[35] He must soon have recognized Webster as a kindred soul. Elizabeth Lee, her biographer for the *Dictionary of National Biography*, characterises her as a working rather than a talking member and explains that her plans for elementary schools were of a democratic nature and, therefore, very much in the line of Sir Charles's thinking.[36] Besides, Dilke became president of the local government board in 1882 and is sure to have met this striking woman then.

It is equally clear that, by the mid-1880s, Webster had become a highly respected reviewer and woman of letters. William Minto (1845–1893), editor of the *Examiner*, another paper to which she contributed regularly, was to remark upon her death that: 'she had no superior, scarcely an equal'.[37] William Rossetti, the poets' (D.G. and Christina's) brother (1829–1919), predicted rather optimistically after her death that: 'Mrs Webster's reputation rests securely upon several volumes of verse – highly remarkable verse, at once feminine and in a right sense masculine – including four dramas' .[38] Indeed, her life and work was judged significant enough to deserve a long entry in the *Dictionary of National Biography*.

---

[34] Webster is also among those women poets whom Elizabeth Sharp hoped to have rescued by publishing her anthology.

[35] Gwynn and Tuckwell, *Sir Charles Dilke*, pp. 94–100.

[36] See Rubinstein, *A Different World for Women*, p. 30.

[37] Quoted in the *Athenaeum* of 15 September 1894.

[38] W. Rossetti, 'Introductory Note', to Webster, *Mother and Daughter*, London: Macmillan, 1895, p. 12.

Webster's poetry stands out as belonging to the most powerful writings of her age, that is, the last quarter of the century. She had chosen forceful forms: the dramatic monologue and the short, incisive sonnet. She adapted the dramatic monologue entirely to her own ends, giving it a distinctly feminist mission. In a poem such as 'Circe', for instance, she has attempted what would now be labelled as a postmodern, feminist revision of the tale of Ulysses.[39] The distrust of man's nature as revealed in 'Circe' is put across even more vigorously in another of Webster's monologues, 'The Castaway', which voices the thoughts of a prostitute. The dramatic monologue here is a long interior monologue spoken by a lonely talented woman who had expected much of her life but was betrayed both by her lover and her brother and thus was coerced into making a living as a prostitute.

Webster reserved her prose for her anonymous reviews in the *Athenaeum*, her articles in the *Examiner* and her political writings. The forty-eight *Examiner* essays were collected in a volume tellingly entitled *A Housewife's Opinions*. They discuss matters such as 'servants', and 'gossip', but equally the more 'serious', more threatening subjects such as women's education and votes for women. It would be foolish to underestimate the strategic importance of such a reprint in the process of immortalising a writer's name. Most 'men of letters' had selections of their writings reprinted for the benefit of their readers, future generations and their own purse. Yet, the publication of *A Housewife's Opinions* was not received warmly. The anonymous *Athenaeum* reviewer, A.T. Cook, even proclaimed she had made two great mistakes in publishing it: 'first, in reprinting her essays ... at all, and, secondly, in writing a preface' in which she claimed the essays had a lasting value.

But he has to admit that her essays on women's education are 'better' and her review of two translations of the *Agamemnon* is worthwhile reprinting. Cook is clearly not interested in a housewife's opinions or the topics which interest her and believes the reading public should not be presented with such a volume:

> her essays stand condemned. Light essays meant to be read and forgotten are not worth republishing in a permanent form, and it is a waste of power for an able writer to give them all the care and thought which she might have bestowed on a work which was intended to last (*Athenaeum*, 4 January 1879).

The question of whether or not there was a female reading public which wanted to read about those subjects rather than others does not occur to him. Woolf's celebrated lines come to mind: 'it is the masculine values that prevail. Speaking crudely, football and sport are "important"; the worship of fashion, the buying of clothes "trivial" and these values are invariably transferred from

---

[39] Webster, 'Circe', 1887; rptd. *Victorian Women Poets. An Anthology*, Angela Leighton and Margaret Reynolds, eds, pp. 428–33.

life to fiction' and to essays such as these.[40] Both in the choice of her subjects and in the treatment of her notably feminist issues of suffrage and education, Webster shows herself to be an active campaigner in the women's movement. In their attempt to convince and convert, these essays therefore follow another strategy than her poems, working on a different level of the reader's psyche yet essentially striving to achieve the same goals. The polemical essays in the collection, which I would like to set on a par with political pamphlets, are signed or, in the case of the one open letter which survived, signed as 'By a Lady'. These writings, therefore, are clearly gendered.

Webster began to write for the *Athenaeum* in 1884 when she reviewed four books. She took care of the same number of books in 1885 and 1886, and reviewed three volumes in 1887. Then, suddenly, the number rose to twenty-four books in 1888. Her main colleagues in the poetry section in the late 1880s seem to have been H.F. Wilson and Mary Robinson. In some issues she was reviewing alongside Arthur Symons and Watts. But she was soon playing first fiddle. It was Webster who reviewed Robert Bridges, J.R. Lowell, O.W. Holmes, and several of her colleagues' writings: Arthur Symons, Mary Robinson and Edith Nesbit.

Augusta Webster died in 1894, her last ghostly appearance in the *Athenaeum* is dated August 1895. She had become the voice of the poetical department in the late 1880s and early 1890s with no fewer than 228 book reviews in the one decade of her *Athenaeum* career. By way of comparison one can look at the year 1877, which according to Watts's biographers was the most intensive period of his involvement with the *Athenaeum*. Hake and Compton-Rickett claim Watts published one lengthy article a week in that year but the 'marked file' only reveals thirteen reviews by Watts in the two volumes for 1877.[41] Webster, on the other hand, reviewed more than forty books a year in the early 1890s.[42]

Webster's review essays on poetry often assumed just as prominent a place in the weekly as the reviews written by her male colleagues. She, too, was given the opportunity to open the issue, filling several columns with her views on a recent publication; and we may assume that such leading articles were markedly better paid than the other reviews.[43] She mostly reviewed poetry but was occasionally asked to discuss biographies and translations as well. According to Laurel Brake these subjects 'pertain to areas associated with men'.[44] A close look at the reviews reveals the (not so surprising) fact that

---

[40] Woolf, *Professions*, p. 735.

[41] Thomas Hake and Arthur Compton-Rickett, *The Life and Letters of Theodore Watts-Dunton*, 2 vols, London: Jack, 1916, p. 238.

[42] The reviewer who took over the bulk of the poetry reviews immediately after Webster's death was Arthur Symons (1865–1945). He, curiously enough, is also absent from Marchand's overview. Symons's most intensive period of involvement with the *Athenaeum* were the years 1895 and 1897, that is, after Webster's death. He stopped reviewing for the journal in 1900.

[43] The editor entered the sum of money next to the contributor's name in the 'marked file' from 1906 onwards.

[44] Brake, *Subjugated Knowledges*, p. 30.

the persona behind the writing was constructed as male, in the sense of neuter.[45] Considering the general dissatisfaction with the current feminisation of poetry and of culture Webster would have been unwise to change the convention.[46]

With her poetry reviews Webster joined the ongoing critical debate on such issues as Truth, and the 'essence' of the poet. She believes in Truth, in 'the' Truth; which must be a poet's concern. More importantly, in view of post-modernist reflections, she believes in 'the Poet'. The central question of her reviews is whether the person producing the verses is a poet or not, whether what lies before her is genuine poetry or not. She talks about the 'instinct of the poet' (*Athenaeum*, 22 June 1995). And she can usually answer that question unhesitatingly. Here is a sample:

> It is not often the reviewer meets with anything so amusingly bad. J.E.D.G. is ambitious, and attempts many things, only to fail in all ...
> As a rule Mr Sladen's poems do not rise above the level of uninteresting mediocrity ...
> The doctrines contained in Mr Stubbs's verses are unimpeachable. So much unfortunately, cannot be said of their poetic quality ...
> (*Athenaeum*, 23 August 1884)

But there are a few difficult cases. There is Robert Bridges, for instance, whose *Eros and Psyche* is far less remarkable according to her than his *Prometheus the Firegiver* since there are, she says, no indications of power and individual thought. But he gets the benefit of the doubt and is given the advice to throw aside all imitation of Greek drama and give free scope to his own poetic impulses (*Athenaeum*, 3 April 1886). This claim places Webster, as a critic, directly opposite such an influential critical voice as Matthew Arnold. She wants spontaneity, not imitation of the Greek.[47] And this is in line with the distinction she makes between what she calls a 'literary artist' and a 'poet', as in the following excerpt: 'How far Mr. Waddington is a poet is more difficult for a critic to decide than how far he is an excellent literary artist' (*Athenaeum*, 5 April 1890).

Quite predictably, she also expressed her views on polemical verse: 'We can call to mind no verse directly dealing with any question agitating the public mind, calling for any wrong to be righted, urging any great measure, which has had it in it to survive as poetry the success of its cause except [and this is possibly one of the few slippages indicating her gender] Mrs Browning's "Song of the Children"' (*Athenaeum*, 12 October 1889). She is not, however, rejecting her own poetic efforts here. The polemical or political writings which she fails to appreciate are those which deal with controversial matters in an

---

[45] As in all *Athenaeum* reviews, pronouns referring to the reader, and the critic are always masculine. Webster will not have done so deliberately. Woolf in *A Room of One's Own* still refers to 'man', 'he' and 'his' when referring to the human being in general. The fact remains that this so-called neutral stance helps to hide the writer's gender.

[46] See also chapter 1.

[47] *Athenaeum*, 24 March 1888, 12 May 1888.

abstract, direct way. They are too 'argumentative', she writes, and therefore lose their power and their charm once the controversy is over.

The critical opinions and judgements put forth in Webster's *Athenaeum* reviews testify to her general dissatisfaction with the poetic production of the 1880s. A review of George Barlow's *The Pageant of Life* in 1889, begins with the remark that according to the title page the book is an epic poem but, when one glances through it, the collection is no more than a series of unconnected lyrics.[48] William Allingham is rebuked for always serving the same poems in a different combination. But she does consider him to be a true poet and devotes four columns to his *Flower Pieces, and other Poems*.[49]

Another drawback for the poetry reviewer at the time seems to have been the interminable flow of sonnet collections which she was asked to review. It is hard, she admits, to write something new in that field. And yet this is exactly what Wilfrid Scawen Blunt thinks he has achieved. Her patience is sorely tried when reading that poet's introduction. Blunt believes the form so difficult that great authors like Tennyson, Browning, Morris and Lowell produced only a few good ones. Webster takes a deep breath before venturing this reply:

> Fancy the Laureate wistfully resigning the sonnet because blank verse, although less to his mind was easier ! Fancy Robert Browning pining for the Petrarchan symmetry and restraint, but afraid he could never do with only one rhyme for four lines! ... fancy the author of the Bigelow papers giving up anxious efforts as a sonneteer because words would not rhyme in as he wanted!

Blunt's looking for a solution in a redefinition of the sonnet sounds ridiculous to her: 'a sonnet is a sonnet and not some other, perhaps preferable, verse' (*Athenaeum*, 1 March 1890).

Webster's book notices in the 1890s, of which the previous extract gave a taste, tend to reveal more of the anonymous reviewer's personality than she had hitherto done. As time elapses she grows somewhat more hopeful: there were signs of a new generation of poets whom she could appreciate. There was Michael Field, for instance, a good 'modern' poet, whose poetry she reviewed for the first time in January 1893, upon the appearance of *Sight and Song*. Webster was disappointed when she read that volume of poems because those were such skilfully vivid and richly detailed descriptions of paintings, yet they were never 'in any true sense' poems.[50] In short, she detected a talent there which had not yet achieved its full potential. No wonder she is relieved to find the poet returns soon afterwards with *Underneath the Bough*, four books of lyrics on which Webster has only praise to bestow though she admits that the poet's subject matter is a bit too morbid. Webster's review of 9 September 1893 assumes a central place in the career of Michaeld Field, the

---

[48] *Athenaeum*, 13 April 1889.
[49] *Athenaeum*, 18 May 1889.
[50] *Athenaeum*, 7 January 1893.

pseudonym used by Katherine Harris Bradley (1846–1914) and her niece, Edith Emma Cooper (1862–1913). For one thing, it came several years after their identities (and their gender) had allegedly been revealed by Robert Browning to the *Athenaeum*, after which they had expected to be 'dwarfed' and 'enfeebled' because critics were bound to 'stifle' them in 'drawing room conventionalities'. [51] Secondly, this *Athenaeum* review (as well as the previous one) appeared at a time when the two poets felt neglected by both their publisher and the critics. [52] Their pleasure at being finally and unexpectedly acclaimed by an empathic critic was glaringly obvious in their journal entry the next day: 'A day of perfect autumn. The Athenaeum Review of *Underneath the Bough* is taken up to a high knoll top, encircled with bushes of oak. We read, rejoice, dance madly, pluck the oak apples'. [53]

In most of her reviews, Webster loved to use the striking metaphor. Her images, in a way, were gendered and often suffused with a lot of humour. In a review of a joint publication with *Love's Looking Glass* as its connective theme[54] she compares the interspersing of the contents to 'the layers of a striped jelly'. In a generally depreciative review of John Davidson's *In a Music Hall, and Other Poems* she observes with regard to one particular passage that it 'detaches itself from its surroundings like a jessamine flower in a nosegay of cabbage blossoms'. [55] But she could be very serious as well, especially, it seems, when she was genuinely moved by what she had read. W.B. Yeats was clearly one of her favourites. Upon the publication of *The Countess Kathleen, and Various Legends and Lyrics* she expressed her admiration in the following terms:

> The poem which gives its name to the collection is described as 'an Irish Drama', and though loosely constructed and quite unsuitable for stage representation, arrests attention alike by the beauty of the subject, the charm of the imagery, and the force and melody of the diction ... and Mr Yeats handles the blank-verse metre with freedom and skill. (*Athenaeum*, 7 January 1893)

---

[51] 'The report of lady authorship will dwarf and enfeeble our work at every turn – you are robbing us of real criticism, such as man give man', was what they wrote to Robert Browning in November 1884. The poet knew the identities behind 'Michael Field' and was thought to have betrayed them (*Works and Days: from the Journal of Michael Field*, 1922, London: Harrap, pp. 6–7). But there are nine years between those letters and the following entry in their journal for 23 August 1893: 'So at last it is all out. The date is a consecration' next to a cutting from an undated and unidentified newspaper in which Michael Field's true personality is revealed (British Library, Add Ms 46781). Not one of Michael Field's recent critics comments on the lapse of time between the two events. See for instance Robert P. Fletcher, '"I leave a page half-writ" Narrative Discoherence in Michael Field's *Underneath the Bough*', Isobel Armstrong and Virginia Blain, eds, Houndmills: Macmillan, 1999, p. 166.

[52] Leighton, *Victorian Women Poets*, p. 227.

[53] Journal entry for 10 September 1893, in the British Library, Add. Ms. 46781.

[54] *Athenaeum*, 8 June 1892.

[55] *Athenaeum*, 6 August 1892.

There is here, and elsewhere, a pronounced interest in poetic imagery. A year before her death she took the opportunity to discuss the felicitous use of imagery in a review of Arthur Symons's *Silhouettes*:

> It were to be wished that Mr. Symons did not sometimes fall into the sin of vain metaphor ... Metaphor and simile are worse than useless if they do not seem to be the natural, spontaneous impression that has sprung to the poet's mind, and do not, as handed on by him, carry that impression to his readers with the immediateness and certainty of a revealing light. But such forced and invalid comparisons as those just quoted, instead of revealing anything, instead of bestowing any illuminated conception, any freshly vivid idealization, only hinder the flow of meaning in the stanza and set the baulked reader the troublesome task of research into the how and wherefore of the supposed likeness. (*Athenaeum*, 4 March 1892)

In one instance Webster seizes the occasion to go into one of her favourite subjects: women's education. *Susan*, the anonymous tale of a humbly-bred young woman who marries a wealthy country gentleman, yet chooses to remain one of his servants as well was, unsurprisingly, a revolting idea to the reviewer. She even goes so far as to call the author of this poem a Frankenstein since he created this 'impossible' being (*Athenaeum*, 9 September 1893). She could have no idea that the author, in this case, was describing a situation in which he lived, since this poem was the work of Arthur Munby whose unusual alliance with his servant, Hannah, has since been the subject of quite a number of academic publications.[56]

Poetry was clearly Webster's special subject but she was assigned a few translations as well. It was she, not as one might have expected Helen Zimmern, who had to evaluate one of the many Faust translations: 'Sir Theodore Martin has been well aware of the difficulties he was encountering, and has for the most part faced them manfully . Yet not always'. Webster can hardly resist the temptation of making fun of Sir Theodore. That inclination is present in the entire review, as, for instance, in the diverting examples which she has chosen:

> At intervals he has yielded to obstacles and drifted away into expansions – as ... when he spreads the ejaculation of the Homunculus, aware of what Faust sees in his sleep, 'Beautifully surrounded!' (*i.e.*, by the scene he is dreaming) into 'What a gorgeous garniture of dreams!' and when the Sirens' song of four short lines in praise of the Kabiri, –
> > Great in might,
> > Small of make,
> > Saviours of the shipwrecked,
> > Primevally honoured gods, –

---

[56] See Arthur Munby, *Man of two worlds. The Life and Diaries of Arthur J. Munby 1828–1910*. London: Murray, 1972. Munby reacted anonymously to the review on 30 September 1893. He countered that *Susan* was based on real life.

Is eked out into
>   Great in might, though small in form,
>   Such as shipwrecked are ye save,
>   When in thunder and in storm
>   Ships go down beneath the wave;
>   Gods in deepest reverence held
>   From the days of primefield !
>   (*Athenaeum*, 29 May 1886).

The *Athenaeum*'s faithful public will have smiled and assented when reading these lines, thus she established the connivance necessary to keep her in her position of critic and conferrer of artistic value. Her discussion of Douglas Ainsley's translation of Goethe's *Reineke Fuchs* is less good-humoured. This time she seems to resent the translator's lack of respect for the aesthetic quality of the original. Surely, she believed, the contemporary reader chiefly appreciated the literary quality of this piece of literature, its satirical aspect was only an additional charm. As it was, Douglas Ainsley's translation was a sad failure because he had transposed the original into 'dispiriting' verse:

>   The lion Noble held a court,
>   His trusty vassals all
>   From every side and quarter came
>   To meet their leader's call;
>   The crane called Litky, hawk Markárt,
>   His trusty barons bold ...

'This jaunty jog-trot wearies the reader early, and carried on through 338 pages becomes irritating or stupifying', she concludes. The translator should merely have tried to convey Goethe's 'touch and tone', not go in for self-devised digression (*Athenaeum*, 7 August 1886). In her review Webster seemed to advocate the old, familiar precept of literal translation: no one could improve the source text.[57]

In the last analysis, it is fair to say that Webster openly confronted the reading public, as a woman, in her signed essays in the *Examiner* and in her political pamphlets, presenting them with her straightforward feminist views. Before these publications she had written highly subversive poetry in which she had deconstructed the usual female stereotypes (such as that of the prostitute and that of the *femme fatale*), pointing at society's neglect of a large number of its population and man's inveterate egoism, thus preparing the ground for her own polemical essays. As a professional critic, however, she assumes a gender-neutral position which will automatically, because of her anonymity, be characterised as male. Here it seems she preferred to disguise her gender in order to safeguard her position of 'objectivity' and – dare one say

---

[57] See, for instance, Ezra Pound's translation theory as set forth in, among others, Theo Hermans, 'Breekpunt, Breuklijn, Breukvlak', *Vertaalwetenschap*, André Lefevere and Rita Vanderauwera, eds, Leuven: Acco, 1979, pp. 107–11.

it – of power. This at first sight inexplicable stance for such a vociferous feminist was justified (or at least understandable) considering the sharp condemnation by her male colleagues of the feminisation of the press, with authors going so far as to write: 'the monthly magazines are getting so lady-like that naturally they will soon menstruate'.[58] The subject position constructed in Webster's reviews is precise as to its views on poetry but blurred when it comes to gender.

Webster was aware of the growing importance of women in London's expansive cultural life. She wanted to stimulate that evolution and avert the reactionary backlash. Her writings all worked towards granting women the same chances as men, the same professional possibilities and the same (political) power. Her own job as a well-paid reviewer of the *Athenaeum* gave her the independence she wished and let her taste some of that power. She could not afford to jeopardise this.

Augusta Webster died at the age of fifty-seven on 5 September 1894. She had suffered from poor health in the 1880s and had spent some time in the south of Europe convalescing. But there is little to document the circumstances of her untimely death.

Edith Nesbit

After an interim period in which Arthur Symons dominated the poetry department, Webster's place in the poetry section was first filled to a large extent by Edith Nesbit. Nesbit is best remembered as a writer of children's books and perhaps she does not seem such an obvious choice in the light of the two women poets who had preceded her.[59]

Edith Nesbit was born the youngest of four on 15 August 1858. Her father, a talented scientist and teacher, died when Edith was a toddler of four. A few years later Mrs Nesbit moved first to the south of England later to southern France in an effort to save the life of her eldest daughter, Mary, who was dying from leukaemia. It gave Edith, or Daisy, a unique experience of life abroad, of other languages and of other peoples which she would turn to good use in her later stories.

Edith married Hubert Bland in 1880, two months before the birth of their son. They had three children in rapid succession but Edith was also to raise the two children whom Hubert had fathered on Alice Hoatson, her best friend. About the two main actors in this *ménage à trois* Bernard Shaw had this to say: 'Edith was an audaciously unconventional lady and Hubert an exceedingly

---

[58] Quoted in Ernest Earnest, *Silas Weir Mitchell*, University of Pennsylvania Press, 1950, p. 174.

[59] Margaret Stetz has recently protested that Nesbit was more than just a children's author. Stetz was thinking of Nesbit's short stories which she finds to be 'filled with humor, but never unmixedly comic' as they also integrate poverty and death into the laughter. (See Stetz, 'Turning Points: E. Nesbit', *Turn-of-the-Century*, 6 (1987), p. 2.)

unfaithful husband'.[60] Edith Nesbit began her writing career with the publication of *The Prophet's Mantle* (1885), a tale she had written together with her husband and published under the pseudonym 'Fabian Bland'. She had by then been introduced to a new class of people, a new circle of acquaintances who together were to establish the Fabian Society. It would lead Edith to a new way of living: she had her hair cut short, adopted loose clothing and started to smoke. Edith Nesbit had become an advanced or 'New' woman.

Possibly it was her newly-found feminism which brought her in touch with the *Athenaeum* management, but this remains a hypothesis. She started writing for the weekly in 1895 and would continue to do so up to 1901, authoring 108 book reviews and contributing seven signed poems. [61]

Nesbit effectively started her *Athenaeum* career where Webster left off. Whether she continued to review in line with the hesitant modernism which Webster seemed to have embraced is another question. Her modernism was a lifestyle rather than a literary attitude. That she stepped into the place which Webster had involuntarily vacated is equally proven by the fact that she was assigned the second edition of Arthur Symons's *Silhouettes*. It would have been interesting to read Webster's comments on a second edition of a volume which she did not seem to appreciate. Nesbit, on the other hand, is in this case irresistibly drawn towards Symons's poetry since she calls the author 'a true poet, if not a great one' (*Athenaeum*, 12 September 1896). She advises him to start looking for other materials, though, urges him to forget about ephemeral emotions and to deal with themes that will ensure his place among the immortal writers. Then, in 1897, she has the opportunity to write about his *Amoris Victima* and is disappointed not to find any change there:

> Mr Symons's poems will, we fear, always lack the breadth of treatment and the variety of theme which distinguish the work of the great poet. But the charm of his great graceful and tender verse is not to be destroyed even by the persistence of its subjective note; and, indeed, to a certain class of readers the very intensity and dominance of this note will prove an additional attraction. (*Athenaeum*, 2 October 1897)

Symons, then, writes well, is a poet, yet chooses the wrong topics, while someone like Annie Matheson chooses glorious, exalted topics but cannot write poetry. On the whole, Nesbit, like Webster, dislikes much of the new poetic production. She wonders how it is possible for so much trash to be published; after all, why do people not realise that 'poets are born, not made' (7 January 1899). Occasionally a poet rises above 'the depressing average of

---

[60] Julia Briggs, *Edith Nesbit, A Woman of Passion. The Life of E. Nesbit 1858–1924*, London: Hutchinson, 1987, p. xiv. Briggs mentions unsigned poetry criticism in the *Athenaeum* for 1896 only.

[61] See the *Athenaeum*, 2 December 1893: 'In the Temple of Wisdom'; 22 September 1894: 'At Century's End'; 1 September 1894: 'The Pool to Narcissus'; 19 September 1896: 'A Dirge'; 12 September 1896: 'New College Gardens'; 24 July 1897: 'A Last Appeal'; 17 September 1898: 'Via Amoris: a Sequence'.

modern minor poetry'; A.B. Miall does just that (12 September 1896), and Emile Verhaeren. But then, Verhaeren should have put somewhat more effort into his verses so that he is able to present a finished product.

Nesbit also deplores the new tendency of poets praising other literary people who might 'be of use'. Mr Reynolds Anderson, for instance, is such a fawner in verse: 'His book contains verses to every one in the world of letters who can possibly be of use to him'. The impudence reaches its climax at the very end when he writes that he 'stoops and strokes his cat, as God may stroke the soul of Mrs Graham Tomson' (19 October 1895). Nesbit could not know that Graham Tomson was to join the *Athenaeum* staff a few years later.

Like her predecessor, Nesbit readily reviewed the work of former, current or future colleagues on the *Athenaeum* staff. Arthur Symons's edition of Mathilde Blind's poems, for instance, was discussed in great detail. Her appreciation of Symons's editorial work was evident and as an admirer of Blind's poetry she could only applaud such an initiative, but she stopped well short of including Blind among the great poets. The breadth and the variety of her poetry resulted, according to Nesbit, in weakness rather than strength. Unlike Christina Rossetti, Blind had still to prove that she could leave a mark on the English language: 'She had intellect, Christina Rossetti temperament; both were poets, but the difference in their poetry which will send one down to posterity and may relegate the other to the shelves of the collector is mainly this of inspiration' (*Athenaeum*, 3 December 1898).

Nesbit does not seem to think of Blind as one of the great women poets, then, or does she? When reviewing Rosamund Marriott Watson's collection of poems *Vespertilia, and other Verses* she begins by remarking that now that 'Christina Rossetti has left us, there remain to us but three women poets, and of these Mrs Marriott-Watson is one' (*Athenaeum*, 4 April 1896). One is left to wonder who, according to her, were the other two?

She seems entirely out of tune with Webster and Blind's convictions when generalising on women's poetry. In a review of Sophie Jewett's *The Pilgrim, and other Poems* she obviously considers the 'woman poet' as a 'species' with its own problems. Writing ill-constructed verse is one of them:

> Inaccuracy of rhyme and of rhythm is, alas! so common a fault ... It would seem that women are especially prone to such errors, possibly from lack of early training in classical verse-forms. But even a woman need not stoop to the slovenliness of unrhymed alternates. It is a hard saying, but one that our women-versifiers would do well to lay to heart, that the effort for finished form makes also for finished thought, and the slipshod verse often enshrines the slipshod idea. (*Athenaeum*, 12 September 1894)

These views may seem unduly harsh, coming as they do from a woman writer. Yet her motives may have sprung from a true concern for the place of the woman writer in the literary world rather than from the bias typically associated with the 'critical double standard'.[62] Or, indeed, this may have been a conscious attempt at adapting her critical disposition to her idea of the *Athenaeum*'s readership. Even so, the sentiments revealed in this short extract at least appear to be a step backwards from Webster's rather than otherwise. Nesbit does to some extent follow Webster in her love of Yeats's poetry when reviewing *The Wind Among the Reeds* (1899): 'Mr Yeats's sketches are full of charm; his poems are full of lyric sentiment; a slight voice sings, but it sings truly, sweetly, and with a clean and fresh sincerity'. [63]

Nesbit contributed 125 reviews during the seven years of her *Athenaeum* career, the frequency with which she reviewed for the journal therefore nearly equals that attained by her predecessor Augusta Webster. Her direct colleagues again seem to have been Watts and Symons, with Watts's reviews being few and far between and generally restricted to canonised, that is, dead poets. Nesbit also had some of her own poems published in the weekly. They all exhale a certain wistfulness, a sad remembrance of things past. Unrequited or past love seems to be the dominating theme. In 'A Dirge', for instance, the narrator stands by Love's grave and does not mourn 'him':

> A little joy he gave, and much of pain,
>> A little pleasure, and enduring grief,
>> One flower of joy, and pain piled sheaf on sheaf,
> Harvests of loss, for every bud of gain.
>> (*Athenaeum*, 19 September 1896)

To all appearances Nesbit stopped contributing reviews when Norman MacColl vacated the *Athenaeum* offices to be succeeded by Vernon Rendall in 1901. After an interim period of two years her place was partly filled by yet another woman poet of some renown. From the turn of the century, however, and up to the First World War, poetry (like fiction) was treated rather ungenerously in the *Athenaeum*.

Rosamund Marriott Watson

a certain degree of feminism must be latent in all women, however reasonable[64]

Rosamund Marriott Watson was possibly even more 'audaciously unconventional' than Nesbit had ever been. Watson was born as Rosamund Ball on 6 October 1860 and only acquired the name Marriott Watson in 1895 after two marriages and three children. In the meantime she had led an active

---

[62] Elaine Showalter, *A Literature of their Own*, p. 73.
[63] *Athenaeum*, 15 July 1899.
[64] Vita Sackville-West, 'The Women Poets of the Seventies', p. 111.

life as a poet as well, achieving especial fame under the name Graham Tomson.

It is a curious fact that Vernon Lee had already described Watson as being '*Athenaeumy*' several years before she actually worked for the weekly.[65] Apparently the journal, and hence the adjective Lee derived from it, denoted certain characteristics in people of which Marriott Watson was a prime example. Both Rosamund and her husband Henry Brereton Marriott Watson were to contribute at fairly regular intervals. They obviously moved in the same circles as many of the *Athenaeum* staff. Henley was a close friend and Andrew Lang, an early admirer of Rosamund, was a friend of the new editor.[66]

Rosamund Watson joined the *Athenaeum* staff in 1903 as a reviewer of an odd mixture of books. As a new recruit she was asked to discuss second-rate novels, children's books including one of Beatrix Potter's tales, and she was given the first of a series of books focusing on the home and its interior decoration. This last assignment was not such an odd request if one realises that some of her verses described paintings or furniture in an attempt to make the arts fuse.[67] She was not to contribute anything in 1905 but returned in full force with many more contributions in 1906. After that she contributed non-stop, though less frequently, until the last year of her life.

Poetry reviews definitely constitute a minority within Watson's more than 150 book reviews. After the disappearance of MacColl, followed in 1904 by the death of Lady Dilke, books assigned to women were manifestly of a lesser calibre. Paradoxically, this may serve to explain why Watson was asked to discuss Emily Dickinson's collection of poetry when Higginson's edition was published by Methuen in 1905. Admitting that the English public will have no great liking of this idiosyncratic poet, the reviewer keeps herself on the safe side when evaluating that American mystery, but the scales undoubtedly tip in favour of Dickinson: 'those who are genuinely interested in poetry will like to possess this specimen of the genuine thing.' And she proceeds to quote a couple of 'lyrical gems'. Then again she feels on unsafe ground with poems such as 'I died for beauty ...' and she feels the necessity to observe that 'as often as not, her wild career merely issues in vagueness, in helplessness, in a mist in which she gropes hopelessly after a lost and intangible significance' (*Athenaeum*, 4 March 1905).

If metaphorical language is conspicuously absent in Watson's reviews, an exception must be made for the metaphor of jewels. In a review of Dora Wilcox's *Verses from Maoriland* she elaborated this imagery when writing that:

---

[65] *Vernon Lee's Letters*, p. 340.

[66] In the introduction to his life of *Alfred Tennyson* (1891) Lang thanks both Edmund Gosse and Vernon Rendall for having read the proofs of his book.

[67] See Linda K. Hughes, 'Rosamund Marriott Watson', *The 1890s. An Encyclopedia of British Literature, Art, and Culture*, ed. George Cevasco, New York and London: Garland, 1993, p. 627.

Amid the perennial output of more or less mellifluous verse it is by no means unusual to find here and there not only promise, but also a certain measure of performance that rises distinctly above the average tide-mark of metrical expression. It is ... a lucky bag into which you dip, finding as a rule dull pebbles or bit of common glass worn smooth by the waves, but occasionally a cornelian, an iridescent shell, or even a piece of amber. (*Athenaeum*, 20 May 1905)

No poetry came her way during the remainder of that year. Publications within the genre were assigned to more prestigious reviewers such as Arthur Symons, F. Thompson (1859–1907) and H. Buxton Forman (1842–1917).[68]

Watson's place on the *Athenaeum* staff has to be distinguished from Webster's or Nesbit's in the sense that poetry was only a small part of her usual fare and that it was only her subject in the early years. Indeed, in the years leading up to her early death in December 1911 most of the books she reviewed were children's books – both tales and poems – books on gardening and on interior decoration. Poetry seems to have passed into other critics' hands such as the Reverend Dr Figgis (1866–1919), and especially the prolific but for the rest unknown R.G. Pickthall.

Rosamund Watson was kept on as a regular contributor with up to twenty-nine books reviewed in 1909. The exact number of her reviews is hard to determine, an additional difficulty lying in the possible confusion with reviews by her husband who was also on the staff and who, if we rely on the 'marked file', wrote on much the same subjects. And, to make matters even more confusing, another 'Mrs Watson', a Lily Watson, was assigned similar books at about the same time. There is no easy way out here and I have considered as hers only the reviews marked as being by Mrs Marriott Watson.

Fortunately, the poems Watson published in the *Athenaeum* were signed. There were sixteen of them. Linda K. Hughes has fairly recently discussed Rosamund Marriott Watson's poetry within the pages of *Victorian Poetry*.[69] She has convincingly foregrounded the bird imagery in Watson's poetry, relating that to myth and classical legend. The *Athenaeum* poems, too, display a rich variety of birds which the reader has to associate with specific feelings, thoughts and moods of the author and, perhaps less evidently in these cases, autobiographical situations. The last poems in the series seem to contain a conscious foreboding of her own death. Here, too, birds are manifestly present. In 'Omnia Somnia', for instance, the birds, all kinds of birds, welcome the narrator on a 'bare hill side' in the middle of the winter. But this is a dream leaving her to wish 'the heart may keep its songs of spring/ Even through the wintry dream of life's December' (*Athenaeum*, 10 April 1909).

---

[68] '*Demeter: a Mask* by Robert Bridges', 1 July 1905; '*Minor Poets of the Caroline Period*, ed. George Saintsbury', 5 August 1905; '*The Poems of John Keats*, ed. E. de Sélincourt', 21 October 1905.

[69] Linda K. Hughes, '"Fair Hymen holdeth hid a world of woes": Myth and Marriage in Poems by "Graham R.Tomson" (Rosamund Marriott Watson)', *Victorian Poetry*, 32:2 (Summer 1994), pp. 97–120.

One of the few poems which eludes the general pattern is 'The Lost Leader'. These lines precede the William Ernest Henley obituary written by her husband Henry Brereton Marriott Watson. The poem was meant to stand as a final tribute to one who had obviously meant a lot to her. Though the subject is left unnamed there is no doubt as to the identity of this 'lost leader' since Watson chose to play upon what were probably Henley's most famous words: 'I am the master of my fate / I am the captain of my soul'.

> Hail and farewell ! Through gold of sunset glowing,
> Brave as of old your ship puts forth to sea;
> We stand upon the shore to watch your going,
> Dreaming of years long gone, of years to be.
>
> The ship sails forth, but not from our remembrance,
> We who were once of your ship's company :
> Master of many a strong and splendid semblance,
> Where shall we find another like to thee?
>
> Your ship sets sail. What'er the end restore you,
> Or golden Isles, or Night without a star,
> Never, Great-Heart, has braver barque before you
> Or sailed, or fought, or crossed the soundless bar.
> (*Athenaeum*, 18 July 1903)

As indicated earlier there was a steady decline of the poetry column after the appointment of Vernon Rendall as new editor of the *Athenaeum* in 1901. Poetry receded into the background, with fewer books reviewed and those given less space within the weekly's pages and, anyway, women reviewers no longer stood out as reviewers of poetry.

Considering the large number of poetry reviews ascribed to Webster and Nesbit in the 1880s and 1890s, however, it seems more than appropriate to inscribe these two women poets as poetry critics, or better 'the' critics of the 'Recent Verse' column in the *Athenaeum*. For Blind and Watson it is equally important to acknowledge these poets' critical exertions next to their purely poetic productions. Their *Athenaeum* reviews as well as their other regular critical writings show women poets negotiating their position in the literary world in very much the same way as their male colleagues did. In order to sustain and develop their literary careers they had to be professionally occupied with reviewing as well as writing poetry. Reviewing meant immediate and, in the case of the *Athenaeum*, satisfactory remuneration as well as keeping in touch with the newest tendencies within 'rival' publications.

Perhaps even more important to note is the fact that, unlike their colleagues in the prose department, the poetry reviewers of the *Athenaeum* were quite successful writers in their own right. This entitled them to that very special position of being both judges and judged. In Bourdieu's terms this made them dependent on the dominant, on – in our case – the editorial management as well as the readers of the *Athenaeum*:

> The specific, and therefore autonomous power which writers and artists possess *qua* writers and artists must be distinguished from the alienated, heteronomous power they wield *qua* experts or cadres – a share in domination, but with the status of dominated mandatories, granted to them by the dominant.[70]

For Bourdieu the women reviewers had, perhaps, no reason to be exultant about their newly-acquired influential position. Indeed, one might further argue that when (or perhaps because) women moved in, poetry lost some of its former prestige and was following the downward trend associated with the feminisation of culture.[71] Only modernism and the reviewers it spawned could, if one subscribes to the latter interpretation, help return poetry to its previous seat of superiority.

But there are other lines of reasoning to follow. The women who had won the seat of the poetry reviewer may quite simply have been chosen because of their intrinsic qualities. Looking at the women discussed in the previous pages, they all seem to have been especially well equipped since they had won the admiration of their male colleagues and the public before their recruitment by the *Athenaeum* editor. Norman MacColl and Sir Charles Dilke certainly chose competent women reviewers for the poetry section, just as they had done for the other subjects in which they had shown themselves to be 'men's equals'.

---

[70] Bourdieu, *Field of Cultural Production*, p. 273.
[71] Joseph Bristow, ed., *The Victorian Poet: Poetics and Persona*, Beckenham: Croom Helm, 1987, pp. 8–9.

Chapter 7

The *Athenaeum* : Gender, Criticism and the Anticipation of Modernism?

Women there are who say the world is slow
To recognize their scientific power;
Wherefore they fill with heat the flying hour,
And let the beauty of their sweet life go
Like water thro' a child's frail fingers. So
Might the tree murmur not to be a tower,
Might envy of the strong storm vex the shower
That wakes sweet blossoms and makes brooklets flow.
The lady whom I love has no such thought;
No stolid strength of mind shall make her weak,
No folly sink her in the sad abyss
Where these same scientific souls are caught.
She knows a kiss befits a lovely cheek,
Ay, and that rosy lips were made to kiss.[1]

This book is about criticism. It deals with criticism and the gender of the critics; but it is also about structures of power influencing the changes in the cultural production. Through their reviews, the women reviewers of the *Athenaeum* made their bid for some of that power but, as appears from this study, they only sporadically inscribed their gender into their reviews in a clearly recognizable way. Their reviews, unlike the ones produced by many of their male colleagues, were by and large ungendered or gender-neutral, as if the author had no gender. If we may rely on the few testimonies by women reviewers about their professional practice, disguising their gender seemed the right (and only) course to adopt. Elizabeth Barrett Browning probably modelled Aurora Leigh's situation to some extent on her own when she wrote: ' I learnt the use /Of the editorial "we" in a review/ As courtly ladies the fine trick of trains,/ And swept it grandly through the open doors/ As if one could not pass through doors at all/ Save so encumbered'.[2] As reviewers, these professional women enjoyed a certain economic freedom: their regular contributions gave them financial security as well as the liberty to write less remunerative stuff: '...what you do/ For bread, will taste of common grain,/ Not grapes,.../ To work with one hand for the booksellers/ While working with

---

[1] Mortimer Collins, *Athenaeum*, 9 September 1876.
[2] Elizabeth Barrett Browning, *Aurora Leigh*, 1856; rpt. *The Works of Elizabeth Barrett Browning*, Karen Hill, ed., Ware: Wordsworth, 1994, p. 414.

the other for myself'. One of the most powerful accounts of a woman reviewer's need to shed her gender when writing reviews comes in the form of a well-known review by Virginia Woolf. In her essay 'Professions for Women' Woolf explains how she had to kill the Angel in the House before being able to write her first review: 'I discovered that if I were going to review books I should need to do battle with a certain phantom ... It was she who used to come between me and my paper when I was writing reviews. It was she who bothered me and wasted my time and so tormented me that at last I killed her'.[3]

In the lives they led beyond the printed page, however, the *Athenaeum* women belonged to the assertive class, several of them even being militant feminists. All of them, in one way or another, resisted or transcended against the traditional role-patterns of the Victorian women, yet on the page they refrained from offending, carefully protecting the position they had acquired. The label 'feminist' is here used in the sense Philippa Levine gave to the term, as 'describing the lifestyles and activities of women activists pursuing various changes in law'.[4] Levine, however, entirely excluded men from her study, claiming that 'women permitted men only partial admittance as helpers'. But within the context of this study, male feminists could not be left out of the picture, as will appear even more clearly from what follows.

The *Athenaeum* management of Sir Charles Dilke and Norman MacColl proceeded to attract what one can fairly call ambitious women from the moment the *Athenaeum* came into their hands in 1870–71. Yet the number of those women's contributions still remained quite minimal when compared to the degree to which women were involved from 1885 on. It would undoubtedly be naïve to disregard the socio-historical circumstances of such a development. As the century progressed towards its end, more women received a proper, indeed classical, education; and more women deliberately opted for a professional career. According to Martha Vicinus, 'by the end of the century public opinion had begun to support middle class women's work'.[5] The facts and figures, both in terms of payment and in terms of involvement, seem to show the *Athenaeum* as particularly well-disposed towards women contributors, and that was even more true for the period from the middle of the 1880s onwards. After 1885 the *Athenaeum* published many more reviews by women and, interestingly, quite a number of these women represented another, socially less established or financially less secure class. The one event which may have been responsible for this more radical course is Dilke's marriage to Emilia Pattison in October 1885.

One can, by way of comparison, compare the figures for the years 1881 and 1891. In 1881 eight women contributed a total of thirty-two reviews: Mathilde Blind, Millicent G. Fawcett, Elizabeth Hasell, Margaret Hunt, Louise Chandler Moulton, Emilia Pattison, Emily Thursfield and Helen Zimmern. The number of their contributions was actually lower than the number of

---

[3] Woolf, 'Professions', p. 1,345.
[4] Levine, *Feminist Lives*, p. 2.
[5] Vicinus, *Independent Women*, p. 28.

reviews by women in the 1860s and 1870s because Geraldine Jewsbury, who had been contributing some seventy reviews annually since 1849, died of cancer in September 1880.[6] In 1891, however, there were 209 reviews by twelve women writers. The number of reviews apportioned to women was to rise steadily until the turn of the century, with 293 books being reviewed in 1900. This, on a total number of some 1,400 reviews for that year, constitutes about 12 per cent of that year's criticism in the *Athenaeum*. Then, the figure declined again to 188 in 1902, a number maintained with no great fluctuation until the end of the decade (195 in 1909).

There are, when one looks at the figures, two facts which form something of a paradox. There can be no doubt as to the steep rise in contributions by women in the years immediately following the Dilke marriage, but these contributions must be ascribed to a handful of women, in fact not that many more than before 1885. A partial explanation may be found in the taint of scandal surrounding the Dilkes. Millicent Garrett Fawcett, for instance, Dilke's one-time close friend and correspondent, could not let herself be associated with Dilke's compromised character after the trial and withdrew from his company and his journal.[7] Similarly, Mary Ward, another eminent reviewer, disappears from the pages of the 'marked file' in 1886. In her case, too, Dilke's reputation may have been a good reason for doing so, but it was certainly not the only one. Fawcett and Ward joined opposite camps in the suffrage debate. Mary Ward later even became the leader of the anti-suffrage league and her convictions would have been a good enough reason for her to distance herself from the pro-suffrage proprietors of the *Athenaeum*, in spite of her having contributed fairly regularly from 1882 onwards. There had, after all, been serious clashes between Ward on the one side and Millicent Fawcett and Mrs Ashton Dilke, Emilia Dilke's sister-in-law, on the other. Also, Ward may not have needed to write reviews for the *Athenaeum* after the glorious success of her *Robert Elsmere* (1888). Finally, after a painful experience with a case of plagiarism, she may have thought it wiser not to get involved as a reviewer any more. Norman MacColl had in that instance not proven himself a trustworthy ally.[8]

---

[6] She was almost immediately replaced for the children's literature department by Mrs J.R. Thursfield.

[7] Rubinstein, *A Different World*, p. 89.

[8] Vernon Lee's letters home alluded to yet another painful incident which may have been the cause for Mary Ward's withdrawal. In March 1883 Ward had accused Mrs Middlemore of plagiarism in her volume *Round a Posada Fire*. Soon after that publication, however, she had, *dixit* Lee, been frightened by Henry Fawcett and Sir Charles Dilke, to whom Mrs S.G.C. Middlemore applied threatening a law suit. The *Athenaeum* was to print two apologies. But no one believed those, Lee continued, and as 'Middlemore is frantic to be reinstated (I hear that he has got even Gosse & Lang against him) he made his wife write a letter to Mrs. W[ard], the most grotesque & impudent mixture of English browbeating and Spanish sasiego, "we in Spain think" etc. conceivable, telling Mrs. W. that if she comes to Chelsea she shall be fully forgiven. Of course Mrs. W. cannot go. But I think that Middlemore's dodge was to get a letter of hers refusing, & then to hand it about saying "You see – she is afraid to face us."' Vernon Lee thereupon advised Mrs. W. to: 'carry war into the enemy's country by replying that she was too busy to go to Chelsea, but would be delighted to

Many of the turn-of-the-century women who used the weekly to articulate their critical views are not listed in the *Wellesley Index to Victorian Periodicals*. Others are represented in that admirable overview by a very limited number of contributions. It seems evident that the periodicals covered by the *Wellesley Index* were not as welcoming towards certain professional women writers as the *Athenaeum*; yet it remains difficult to compare the *Athenaeum*, in this respect, with other journals of note with a similar broad readership and a policy of anonymous contributions. A comparison with the *Saturday Review*, for instance, might have been extremely interesting. In the absence of a 'marked file' for the *Saturday Review* we can only look at the one available for the *Spectator*, and that starts as late as 1880. The *Spectator*, too made ample use of female pen power when it came to reviewing, especially when it came to reviewing literature. But the 'power' here was wielded by an entirely different type of intellectual woman with writers like Julia Wedgwood (d. 1913), Mrs Cashel Hoey (1830–1908) and E.A. Dillwyn contributing many of the cultural entries in the 1880s and 1890s.[9] Only the occasional contribution or letter by Frances Power Cobbe injected that worthy weekly with a bit of controversial, feminist blood.

If the *Athenaeum* was different when it came to its reviewers' social profile one wonders why these women were given the opportunity to do the job and do it so frequently. We have already touched upon Sir Charles Dilke's personal ties with women contributors such as Millicent Garrett Fawcett, Kate Field and Emilia Dilke and the effect his turbulent life may have had on the composition of the *Athenaeum* staff. The *Athenaeum*'s editor, Norman MacColl, who was to serve honourably from 1871 to 1901, may have had even more of an impact on this woman-friendly policy.

It has been noted in passing how under MacColl's successor, Vernon Rendall, some long-standing contributors stopped writing for the journal altogether. Rendall's views on women's writings or women journalists were anything but encouraging. He saw women writers in terms of stereotypes: 'Women have recently won a big place in the papers dilating with ecstasy on the dictates of fashion, and for the most part hopeless slaves to the cliché' (*Athenaeum*, 7 May 1910). To be sure, he chivalrously admitted that MacColl's attitude contrasted strongly with his own. Rendall's obituary of his predecessor is most revelatory in this respect. He remembers how 'MacColl was one of the young men who offered themselves as tutors for the first English women students at Hitchin in 1869, before Girton was built; and on the occasion of the famous division of Cambridge concerning the admission of women to degree, he [MacColl] went down, at some inconvenience, to record his vote in their favour'. This testimony strongly endorses the hypothesis that

---

see Mrs. Middlemore in Russell Square, if Mrs. M. wished to bring before her those convincing proofs which, she says, satisfied MacColl. Of course Mrs. M. would refuse, & Mrs. W. would thus have the game in her hands'(*Lee's Letters*, p. 119).

[9] There are concise, informative entries on both Mrs Cashel Hoey and Julia Wedgwood in John Sutherland's excellent *Longman Companion to Victorian Fiction*.

MacColl, like Dilke, was a male feminist. Worth quoting, too, is Rendall's description of MacColl's working method as an editor:

> Maccoll wrote less himself, and brought in a host of new and valuable contributors. His independence was remarkable ... He chose his men, and chose usually with unerring judgment, often without regard for current reputations. Once chosen they had a free hand and his full confidence, though they knew that their reviews were subject to correction if they were inaccurate or unfair. And dealing largely with specialists, he knew the specialist's vices.

From the sheer number of books he assigned to women reviewers it appears that MacColl did not share the current view of women's writings as being invariable slovenly and inaccurate. Yet he was an exacting editor according to Rendall:

> Of English he was an excellent judge; a slow writer, as an artist must be, he would not tolerate slang or slackness in grammar ... He preferred not to alter other people's writings ... He would never send a book for review to an intimate friend of the author if he knew it, most certainly never to an enemy. He tried as far as he could to use the competent and dispassionate stranger. (*Athenaeum*, 24 December 1904)

That last remark does not exclude his own acquaintances or that of the proprietor. As has been shown above, a close analysis of the contributors to the *Athenaeum* seems to point to the reverse. Even so, one might still question whether there was anything like a 'Dilke' or a 'MacColl' network. The most obvious way to find out is by looking at the women's names in the 'marked file' and investigating their possible links with the Dilke family, with MacColl, and/or with feminism.

Several of the women reviewers discussed above have been described or saw themselves as actively engaged in the women's movement. In the 1890s their ranks were strengthened by women with very much the same convictions, striking women such as Charlotte Carmichael Stopes, another manifest champion of women's rights and the rational dress movement,[10] and her famous daughter Marie Stopes. Charlotte Stopes joined the *Athenaeum* team in 1896 as the specialist on Shakespeare. Her daughter was assigned scientific works from 1904 up to the First World War. In this case it was probably Charlotte Stopes's husband Henry, a scientist and a friend of Norman MacColl, who functioned as the link with the weekly's management.[11] An equally

---

[10] Charlotte Carmichael Stopes was the anonymous reviewer of more than thirty books on Shakespeare's life, works, mystery, religion, and so on, but she also authored several signed articles. Her feminist views, however, were with a few exceptions reserved for some items in the equally anonymous gossip column. In the early 1880s she founded a discussion group for ladies and a Shakespeare Reading Society and in 1894 she published *British Freewomen and their Historical Perspectives* which marked her as a prominent member of the women's movement.

[11] June Rose, *Marie Stopes and the Sexual Revolution*, London: Faber, 1992, p. 16.

interesting acquisition for the weekly was May Abraham. This impecunious young Irish woman came to London at the age of eighteen after the death of her father and the collapse of the family fortunes. Fortunately, she had brought with her a letter of recommendation to Lady Dilke and in due course became her private secretary. Shortly afterwards May Abraham was to share lodgings with Gertrude Tuckwell, Lady Dilke's favourite niece, who was just as actively engaged in the women's trade unions. In 1893 Abraham was appointed as one of the two first women Factory Inspectors, a post she relinquished reluctantly when she married H.J. Tennant in 1896.[12] It is this 'Miss Abraham' who reviewed cookery books in the early 1890s, a subject which, it was assumed, any woman could tackle at the time. It was easy to pass this particular subject to a young woman whose chances in life one wanted to promote and who was in need of some financial remuneration. Abraham stopped contributing in 1895.

Unlike May Abraham Tennant, most of the women contributing to the *Athenaeum* remained single and deliberately opted for a career rather than a family. Kate Field, Jane Ellen Harrison, Helen and Alice Zimmern, Mabel Robinson, Vernon Lee, Mathilde Blind and Alice Werner have been mentioned earlier. Others, like Louise Chandler Moulton, Mary Robinson, Augusta Webster and Emilia Dilke, were married but had no children or only one. And then there were the very unusual cases like Katharine de Mattos and Rosamund Marriott Watson, who were divorced.

Philippa Levine, following Barbara Caine's argument, has suggested in her study of Victorian feminists that there was a direct correlation between activism and childlessness (or few children). This 'life style', according to Levine, indicates a feminist ideology. Spinsterhood, for instance, may have been an active choice, allowing a woman to concentrate on her career rather than on the family. Besides, she adds, not every woman enjoyed male company. Gillian Hanscombe and Virginia Smyers, on the other hand, interpreted the same lifestyle, in the early decades of the twentieth century, not such much as an indication of a woman's political conviction as of her modernism. The modernist women's network of writers and editors which Hanscombe and Smyers chose to discuss is said to have challenged social conventions at a time when 'the overwhelming social expectation was that a woman should marry, bear children, and remain both married and monogamous'.[13] Yet women like H.D., Dorothy Richardson, Gertrude Stein, Mina Loy, Djuna Barnes and others were, it is argued, not politicised: 'it is hardly surprising to find these women absent from the ferment for female suffrage which it seems to us now must have been boiling all around them'. The women contributors of the *Athenaeum* constitute an overlap between these two groups and other, more traditional 'categories', thereby resisting classification. Unconventional and sometimes blatantly anti-conventional,

---

[12] Violet R. Markham, *May Tennant. A Portrait*, London: Falcon Press, 1949, pp. 10ff.

[13] Gillian Hanscombe and Virginia L. Smyers, *Writing for their Lives. The Modernist Women 1910–1940*. London: The Women's Press, 1987, p. 12.

these women opted for a lifestyle which allowed them to pursue a professional career. At the same time, however, many of them were ardent feminists who equally used their pens in the service of the cause.   Were they the New Women, the fictional heroines of their own lives? Did they constitute the threat against which some of their colleagues, also writing for the *Athenaeum*, inveighed?

THE LATEST LITERARY SUCCESS.
" The Woman who wanted to."

Figure   7.1. 'The Latest Literary Success: The woman who wanted to', *Punch*, 26 October 1895.

The New Woman in New Grub Street

> Literature nowadays is a trade. Putting aside men of genius, who may
> succeed by mere cosmic force, your successful man of letters is your skilful
> tradesman. He thinks first and foremost of the markets; when one kind of
> goods begins to go off slackly, he is ready with something new and
> appetising. He knows perfectly all the possible sources of income. Whatever
> he has to sell he'll get payment for it from all sorts of various quarters; none
> of your unpractical selling for a lump sum to a middleman who will make
> six distinct profits.[14]

George Gissing was one of the late-nineteenth century authors who, it appears
from his work, was riveted by the New Woman phenomenon. His novel *The Odd
Women* is usually mentioned in this context and the book was, interestingly,
hailed by Katharine de Mattos as 'intensely modern, actual in theme as well as
treatment' (27 May 1893). But for our analysis his previous novel *New Grub
Street*, more hesitantly welcomed by the same reviewer in the same journal a few
years earlier, is of greater interest. The realistic setting of the novel mirrors the
lives of authors like Gissing, editors like MacColl or Dixon, reviewers like
Theodore Watts-Dunton and anonymous female drudges. Of course, the
presentation is Gissing's and, as a creative writer, his view of the reviewer or
even the hack writer was warped. Still, certain aspects are quite obviously
modelled on life's experiences. When Alfred Yule, one of Gissing's sad
characters in *New Grub Street* (1891), sees the prospect of becoming the new
editor of the weekly the *Study* looming before him, this naturally morose and
irritable man becomes positively cheerful. An editorship of the *Study* would give
him the power to which he has always aspired:

> The *Study* was a weekly paper of fair repute. Fadge had harmed it, no doubt
> of that, by giving it a tone which did not suit the majority of its readers –
> serious people, who thought that the criticism of contemporary writing
> offered an opportunity for something better than a display of malevolent
> wit. But a return to the old earnestness would doubtless set all right again.
> And the joy of sitting in that dictatorial chair! The delight of having his own
> organ once more, of making himself a power in the world of letters, of
> emphasising to a large audience his developed methods of criticism! (p.
> 127)

The *Study* is not unlike the *Athenaeum*, indeed, Gissing may have intended it to
refer to the real weekly, since it too has a gossip column, the distinctive feature of
the *Athenaeum*. Yule's daughter, the fair Marian, however, is far worse off than
the female *Athenaeum* critics. She is a real female drudge of the kind described by
Nigel Cross in *The Common Writer*: 'The two major obstacles to a successful
career in authorship were lack of education and lack of motivation – the latter

---

[14] George Gissing, *New Grub Street*, 1891, Harmondsworth: Penguin, 1968, pp. 38–9.

attributable to the meek acceptance of paternal authority'.[15] She writes her father's articles which he then publishes anonymously. But Gissing is aware of the potential which a young woman like Marian represents, both in terms of writing talent and in terms of economy:

> Her task at present was to collect materials for a paper on 'French Authoresses of the Seventeenth Century', the kind of thing which her father supplied on stipulated terms for anonymous publication. Marian was by this time almost able to complete such a piece of manufacture herself and her father's share in it was limited to a few hints and corrections. The greater part of the work by which Yule earned his moderate income was anonymous: volumes and articles which bore his signature dealt with much the same subjects as his unsigned matter, but the writing was laboured with a conscientiousness unusual in men of his position. The result, unhappily, was not correspondent with the efforts. Alfred Yule had made a recognisable name among the critical writers of the day; seeing him in the title-lists of a periodical, most people knew what to expect, but not a few forbore the cutting open of the pages he occupied. He was learned, copious, occasionally mordant in style; but grace had been denied to him. He had of late begun to perceive the fact that those passages of Marian's writing which were printed just as they came from her pen had merit of a kind quite distinct from anything of which he himself was capable, and it began to be a question with him whether it would not be advantageous to let the girl sign these compositions. A matter of business, to be sure – at all events in the first instance. (p. 111)

There is no evidence to suggest that any of the *Athenaeum* reviewers were exploited by their relatives like this, quite the contrary. So far as it has been possible to find out, the reviewers were very much their own women, the wages they earned by writing were their own.

Another fictional portrayal of the professional reviewer's life came from the pen of Rhoda Broughton. Broughton was aware of the gender of some of her reviewers and ascribed their at times acerbic reviews to some deep frustration as a result of their own failure at publishing popular fiction. In Broughton's *A Beginner*, Miss Grimstone is said to 'tomahawk' the books she has to review for her uncle's journal *The Porch*: 'Slaves always make the worst slave-drivers'. The name 'Grimstone' itself has the most unsavoury associations. Eventually, however, it will turn out that it is not Miss Grimstone who is responsible for the slashing review of the young woman novelist's first book in the *Porch*, but Edgar Hatcheson (an equally telling name), who thereby forfeits all chances of ever winning her hand. Hatcheson, typically, goes in for all the clichés which one finds in so many *Athenaeum* reviews by male reviewers, including the guesses about the gender of the anonymous novelist: 'we can predict with complete certainty four things concerning the author of "Miching Mallecho": that she is young, female, foolish, and innocent of any personal acquaintance with the lofty society to which, with such generosity, she introduces us'.[16]

---

[15] Cross, *The Common Writer*, pp. 166–7.
[16] Rhoda Broughton, *A Beginner*, London: Bentley, 1894, p.172.

What these two novels have in common is that they present the bright New Woman writers as being attractive as well as clever. Still, the reviewers in both are doomed to remain spinsters. There is no personal choice involved. Marian Yule is pronounced to be a 'A good example of the modern literary girl'. Her poverty, however, makes her unattractive to the ambitious Milvain. The 'beginner' of Rhoda Broughton's book, Emma Jocelyn, opts for married life rather than a writing career in which the reviewer and failed novelist Miss Grimstone seems to have got stuck.[17] Women reviewers, then, are not presented as successful people, are not looked upon with admiration but rather the reverse: they are either frustrated because they have been unsuccessfully trying for a share in popular acclaim, or they are an unhappy, downtrodden bunch.

In reality, there were advantages to being a professional writer – if, that is, one was successful at it. Harriet Martineau experienced and expressed this earlier in the century. When her family suddenly lost its fortune she experienced a sense of liberation: 'we had lost our gentility. By being thrown, while it was yet time, on our own resources, we have worked hard and usefully, won friends, reputation and independence, seen the world abundantly, abroad and at home, and, in short, have truly lived instead of vegetated'.[18] This sense of financial independence and the broadening of the intellectual horizons was undoubtedly a shared experience for all the *Athenaeum* reviewers. Unlike the Miss Grimstones and the Marian Yules, the unmarried *Athenaeum* reviewers had consciously opted for a professional career, often combining the steady income of the reviewer with the uncertain prospects of the creative writer. As contributors to the *Athenaeum* they received the same wages as their male colleagues for the same kind of work, an unusual situation at the time.[19] Similarly, in the *Spectator*, payments were based on the length of the contribution. The gender of the author played no role, but very few women contributed lengthier (more remunerative) pieces, leaders or sub-leaders, to that weekly.[20]

The liberating and empowering effect of enjoying financial independence, even though it meant 'grinding articles', was a reward in itself for the *Athenaeum* reviewers. A point of view articulated even more eloquently by Virginia Woolf, a century after Martineau :

> One does *not* want an established reputation, such as I think I was getting, as one of our leading female novelists. I have still, of course, to gather in all the private criticism, which is the real test. When I have weighed this I shall

---

[17] I have not considered Henry James's creation, Henrietta Stacpole (*The Portrait of a Lady*), because she is an American woman reporter, not a reviewer, although she is said to have been an art critic for a very brief time.

[18] Martineau , *Autobiography*, vol. I, p. 142.

[19] Vicinus, *Independent Women*, pp. 25–6.

[20] With poems, however, it was the poet's fame that mattered: Henry Newbolt was paid £10·10 for a poem of 6 inches long which appeared in the *Spectator* in October 1899, whereas A.J. Butler only received half that sum for a poem of 9 inches published that same month.

be able to say whether I am 'interesting' or obsolete. Anyhow, I feel quite alert enough to stop, if I'm obsolete. I shan't become a machine, unless a machine for grinding articles. As I write, there rises somewhere in my head that queer, & very pleasant sense, of something which I want to write; my own point of view. [21]

Woolf, too, as Bridget Elliott and Jo-Ann Wallace remarked in *Women Artists and Writers*, preferred to write for the journal which paid well rather than for the 'little magazines' in spite of those quite often being edited by women. Elliott and Wallace also point to the paradox which makes Woolf associate '"popularity" both with the feminine and the market place; it is only outside of market considerations, with the help of her own press and the "private criticism" of friends, that she can aspire to genuine literary substance'. [22]

Seeing that the New Woman reviewers were in a position to praise New Woman novels and, it seems, effectively did so, one is left to wonder why their at times positive reviews, written from an ungendered critical stance, were not more influential. Conversely, the damning survey in Arthur Symons's 'English Literature in 1893', has even been 'recuperated' by feminist criticism: it is mentioned by Ann Ardis[23] and later by Elaine Showalter[24] as a result of (and in spite of) its derogatory remarks. Symons's destructive anonymous critique thus belatedly gained much attention. Unfortunately, the rule which equates unpopularity with artistic merit does not seem to work for the New Woman novelists either. 'Most critics have excluded New Woman novels from genealogies of modernism', Ann Ardis has remarked.[25] The same is true of New Woman poetry and drama. Only now, slowly and not always eagerly, are literary critics under the impulse of feminist research rediscovering the plays of Elizabeth Robins and the poetry of Augusta Webster.

From the New Woman to the Modern and Modernist Woman

What kind of a platform was the *Athenaeum* at the turn of the century? Was it potentially a platform for modernist writers in spite of its age and its halo of respectability and money? Was it, in other words, the nature of the *Athenaeum* which allowed it to be taken over by a modernist generation after the First World War? Were the women critics writing for the *Athenaeum* at the turn of the century more than New Women come true. Indeed, were they harbingers of a modernist lifestyle and a modernist culture? Did they prepare the way for the likes of

---

[21] Anne Olivier Bell and Andrew McNeillie, eds, *The Diary of Virginia Woolf*, New York: Harcourt Brace Jovanovich, 1978, vol. II, pp. 106–7.
[22] Bridget Elliott and Jo-Ann Wallace, *Women Artists and Writers. Modernist (im)positionings*, London and New York: Routledge, 1994, p. 72.
[23] Ardis, *New Women*, pp. 86–7, 98.
[24] Elaine Showalter, *Daughters of Decadence. Women Writers of the Fin-de Siècle*, London: Virago, 1993, p. xii.
[25] Ardis, *New Women*, p. 2.

Katherine Mansfield and Virginia Woolf? Or were the opportunities which the *Athenaeum* obviously offered to career-minded women in those last decades of the nineteenth century the logical consequence of the woman-friendly policy implemented by a feminist editor? Each of these questions is a complex one which may elicit many different answers.

What, to start with, is a modernist periodical? Considering the difficulties associated with the term 'modernism' as such, and the changeable nature of periodical literature, it will come as no surprise that a standard reference work like Alvin Sullivan's, which attempted to map the modernist journals of the twentieth century, at times resorted to such tentative phrasings as 'vaguely modernist in flavour', 'an English modernism', or a 'more mature modernism',[26] words which remind one of some refined characterizations of cheeses or wines, products which even connoisseurs find hard to describe precisely. Michael Levenson begins his genealogy of modernism with the remark: 'vague terms still signify'. A more precise term would, he believes, 'exclude too much and too soon'.[27] He also refuses to quibble over dates, yet admits that dating is a 'preliminary convenience'.   Sullivan, for instance, explains the start of modernism in the preface to his book as 'a reaction to the social and economic realities brought about by the first world war'. According to him this led to the marriage of politics, literature and economics.[28]   The definition is exact if, like him, one chooses 1914 as the starting point of modernism.   Still, some periodicals and some writers had flaunted a modernist spirit well before the First World War. An analysis of pre-war cultural Europe caused critics like Michael Levenson and, more recently, Bruce Clarke, to make a distinction between an early and a late modernism, with the early phase being almost diametrically opposed to its later form: 'modernism was individualist before it was anti-individualist, anti-traditional before it was traditional, inclined to anarchism before it was inclined to authoritarianism'.[29] Clarke suggests '1923' as the crucial date in the change from 'early' to 'late' with Eliot's launching of the *Criterion* as its most manifest sign.[30] He also seems to agree with Marjorie Perloff in considering the period between 1910 and 1914 as the zenith of early modernism.[31] It seems perfectly warranted then cautiously to consider an overlap period between the modernist period and the Victorian era when it comes to analysing periodicals.

As a rule, 'modernist periodicals' suggest the 'little magazines', those idealistic enterprises launched at the end of the nineteenth or at the beginning of the twentieth century with the specific purpose of giving modernist writers a

---

[26] Alvin Sullivan, ed., *British Literary Magazines. The Modern Age, 1914–1984*, Westport: Greenwood Press, 1986, pp. 115, 31, 33.

[27] Michael H. Levenson, *A Genealogy of Modernism. A Study of English Literary Doctrine 1908–1922*, Cambridge: Cambridge University Press, 1984.

[28] Ibid., p. vii.

[29] Levenson, *A Genealogy*, p. 79

[30] Bruce Clarke, *Dora Marsden and Early Modernism. Gender, Individualism, Science*, University of Michigan, 1996, p. 4.

[31] Marjorie Perloff, *The Futurist Moment: Avant-Garde, Avant Guerre, and the Language of Rupture*, Chicago: University of Chicago Press, 1986.

platform, 'a local habitation and a name'. Yet it would be unjust to deny the mainstream papers the role they played in the careers of modernist artists. Virginia Woolf, quoted earlier, freely admitted that she needed to write for a well-established and well-paying journal in order to be economically unfettered and free to produce fiction which was likely to be unpopular. Apart from that, we must remember that the 'little magazines' were magazines, that is, they published reviews as well as original work and therefore differed in nature from a weekly such as the *Athenaeum* which, with the exception of the 1917 to 1918 period, was mainly devoted to cultural criticism.[32]

It is well known that Woolf, Mansfield, Eliot, Huxley and Pound wrote reviews for the *Athenaeum* from 1919 on, but the weekly could, by then, boast a long connection with modernist artists and thinkers. The painter Clive Bell, Woolf's own brother-in-law, wrote regularly from 1909 onwards. Roger Fry, another Bloomsbury artist and friend of the Woolfs, had started to contribute reviews as early as 1901. Yet his authorship was revealed only after the First World War when John Middleton Murry, persuaded by his wife and valuable contributor Katherine Mansfield, introduced initials (and an explanatory list of the initials).

If the *Athenaeum* had slowly been transforming itself into a journal with a modernist inclination at the end of the nineteenth century and in the early years of the twentieth century it had, with the succession of the new editor in 1901, also in a sense become more conservative in its editorial policies. Rendall's views on women, looked at earlier, were a considerable step backwards and his letters reveal a strong reactionary stance towards Jews as well. In a letter of 22 November 1924, he observed: 'It would be a terrible prospect if the world did away with nationalism & decided to be ruled by the Jews instead'.[33]

Sir Charles Dilke's views on women and on the Jewish question[34] were clearly at odds with those of his editor but, as a subsequent editor was to write, although Sir Charles kept a vigilant eye on the journal he was reluctant to interfere with the policy of his editor.[35] Rendall remained the editor of the

---

[32] Some of Virginia Woolf's reviews and articles were collected in *Contemporary Writers*, published by the Hogarth Press in 1965. Her essays and reviews were the subject of a recent anthology of critical articles edited by Beth Carole Rosenberg and Jeanne Dubino (*Virginia Woolf and the Essay*, London: Macmillan, 1997).

[33] Unpublished letter, British Library, Add. Ms 59669, f. 90. The letter continues with some pretty gross remarks at the address of a female actress: ' I have been to the Tivoli to see a much advertised film play, which was no great shakes. Also, I saw May Murray, a pretty, stupid vamp of a blonde, whose only action is to purse up her mouth scornfully. She plays Circe, & is hopelessly inadequate, as she appears to have no brains, & I always supposed C. had some. She might make pigs of men, but not in Circe's way.'

[34] Dilke was a close friend of Joseph Reinach, secretary to the politician Gambetta and a passionate Dreyfusard.

[35] This was attested by one of the subsequent editors, Arthur Greenwood, in an article on Dilke and the *Athenaeum* published in November 1917. There is one letter from Rendall to Dilke, written in April 1908, which indicates that the relationship between them was rather tense at one time, though the letter hints at problems of a financial nature and Dilke's impatience with an editor who lacks a certain decorum: 'I understand that you are gravely dissatisfied, & am surprised that, if so, you did not write to me directly. I have been sounded as to "retrospective" proposals, which I gather to mean that you expect me to pay back money

Athenaeum until 1916; as Peter Brooker has eloquently argued, modernism and reactionary politics were not incompatible for certain modernist representatives.[36] Besides, quite a number of *Athenaeum* reviews were still being written by women up to and including the first two years of the war, only one notices that the subjects they now tackled seldom fell outside the range of soft subjects and very few of the familiar names were still there. Charlotte Stopes and her daughter Marie, for instance, still had their say now and then. Among the contributors listed in the 'marked file' after 1911, one frequently notices the names of Camilla Black, Miss Hayllar and Mrs J.E. Francis (the new proprietor's wife). These were 'maids of all work', apparently capable of reviewing almost everything.

The face of the weekly also changed in those pre-war years. Columns, headings became less fixed. The regular items formerly found in the 'New Novels' column were now dispersed over columns entitled 'This Week's Books', or 'Fiction', or 'Novels and Short Stories', or 'Books and their Makers', or even, very briefly, in the 'List of New Books'. Rendall also liked to give prominence to his personal views on journalism and the art of criticism. An editorial of 1 January 1910 announced his intention to devote from time to time 'our first article to themes of literary interest'. This was, perhaps somewhat paradoxically, in line with his conviction that politics could not be entirely eschewed. He firmly believed that the weekly had to be the forum of a wide spectrum of voices and viewpoints. When a review of two books on war and peace provoked an angry response from one of the readers because of its alleged hidden socialist message, Rendall pounced on it to express his own views on the matter: the *Athenaeum* preserves an 'independent' standpoint, but in criticism a bias is 'inevitable'. Therefore, the editor is sure to choose reviewers who are in sympathy with the

---

already received for N & Q. This is after a definite settlement by Hudson (representing you), J.E. Francis, and myself that my offer of reduction of my own pay for Randall was not at present to be accepted. To go back on such a settlement seems to me amazing. I regard it as quite impossible, & I am so indignant that a repetition of the suggestion will lead at once to my looking for work   elsewhere ... It has been a great discouragement to me that you have apparently taken as a matter of course a great amount of my gratis work for the paper, which though anonymous, has been repeatedly praised by others. On the strength of one article on Dickens I was asked to edit the millionaire's edition at 300 £ or 400 £ a year – I forget which. There is hardly ever a special number which secures an increase of advertisements which does not contain work done by me at high pressure which there is no time for anyone else to do. I am not aware that you know this. I resented & still resent, the ignorance or misjudgment that kept me idling away much of my time as subeditor when you might have had an opinion worth 2 guineas to a publisher on any amount of novels ... My room is always untidy for the simple reason that I am always attempting to squeeze in a few more notices of books which would not be noticed at all, unless I did them. If, after all this work, you are greatly dissatisfied, it becomes a question with me whether I should not go elsewhere, where recognition is assured, & where I might, perhaps, hope to be a moderate success ... I have frequently preferred to tackle myself than see blundered & delayed. I really think that no one else would do half so much as I do in some ways, though they might be far more competent in others. But in the present state of affairs I do not know where I am, and am rapidly losing all confidence in being able to do anything. There are several things here I might criticize, but I have never made difficulties. Now, I am obliged to ask for a clearing up of a position which I have hardly realized, it seems, as I should have' (Add Ms 43 920, ff. 77–86). In the absence of Dilke's reply one has to assume that Rendall's protests, voiced in the letter, settled the matter.

[36] Peter Brooker, ed., *Modernism/Postmodernism*, London: Longman, 1992, pp. 6ff.

books they are meant to review. He also admits here to holding a very broad interpretation of the term 'literature', and to having paid increased attention to issues dealing with social reform (30 March 1912).

During the war years, the *Athenaeum* was confronted with an acute 'scarcity of paper', a 'labour shortage'[37] and a need for capital which made the management first decide to establish a co-operative scheme.[38] Later they were forced to opt for a monthly publication instead of a weekly one. Edmund Gosse was given the honour to introduce the new policy in a signed, semi-autobiographical leader in January 1916:[39]

> If it were the practice of a journal, while dealing briefly, as must be done, with the mass of ephemeral production, to set aside books of high permanent importance for lengthy and responsible examination, the unrelated reader would have a guide to follow. But for this innovation, or rather renovation courage is needed. I know *The Athenaeum* has never lacked courage ... The change now proposed by its proprietors is certainly a proof of courage in that they prefer to forego their weekly number in favour of a monthly publication which shall be more in accordance with these ideals, and also a return to a greater consideration of the interest of the reader and buyer.

A more thorough change was announced at the end of 1916 which may or may not have been unconnected with the death of John Collins Francis in December of that year. John Francis and his cousin J. Edward Francis had inherited the journal after the death of Sir Charles Dilke in 1911. The editorial of December 1916 promised that the *Athenaeum* was henceforth to be 'an organ for the expression and criticism of ideas of Reconstruction'. Its subtitle changed from 'Journals of Literature, science; the fine arts, music, and the drama' to 'Journal of Politics, Literature, Science and the Arts'. The new editor was Arthur Greenwood (1880–1954), a young and promising Labour politician who combined the responsibilities of his editorship with a job as a civil servant at the Ministry of

---

[37] These were the conditions which, according to the then editor Arthur Greenwood, led to the shortcomings of the paper in the period between 1917 and 1919.

[38] See *Athenaeum*, 13 March 1915.

[39] His exposé actually starts with an interesting paragraph on the influence the *Athenaeum* exerted on his own life: 'In the morning-room of the little house in Devonshire where my childhood was passed, a strange collection of volumes languished behind a protective screen of scolloped leather. Here were Books of Beauty, travels in Mesopotamia, Pope's "Homer", and several treatises on prophecy. But among these, heavily bound in calf, were three odd sets of *The Athenaeum*; if my memory serves me, they were those for the years 1829, 1831, and 1832. How they got there I know not, and as they have ceased for thirty years to be in the family possession it is too late for me to make any investigation. It was not until after being baffled by the vacuity of several books, irritatingly entitled "Amulets" or "Keepsakes", that I dragged one of *The Athenaeums* out from behind the leather pinking and suddenly found, what I had not expected, that there was mixed reading exactly to my taste. What bias this discovery may have given to my life's plan, I will not be so tiresome as to inquire; but certainly this was my earliest introduction to a class of writing which afterwards became excessively familiar to me, the review or literary estimate'.

Reconstruction.[40] Henceforth the main theme was to be the war. Many of the reviews published during the Greenwood era were left unidentified in the 'marked file'. From the few columns that were marked it appears that not one of the former reviewers was kept on. Greenwood surrounded himself with a new generation of writers who shared his progressive attitude towards the future, the post-war period.

The journal changed hands again in 1919 when it was bought by Arnold Rowntree,[41] a wealthy chocolate manufacturer and philantropist who appointed John Middleton Murry (1889–1959) as its new editor. Murry was an Oxford graduate with some editorial experience: he and his wife Katherine Mansfield (1888–1923) had edited the short-lived *Rhythm*. It is not my intention to analyse Mansfield's criticism here, nor that of that other famous woman critic, Virginia Woolf. Their reviews have been reprinted, quoted from and discussed at length in several other studies.[42] What I want to do is look at the way the change of editor affected the nature of the *Athenaeum*, possibly hastening its disappearance. And naturally, since the journal had had this history of openness towards women reviewers I shall evaluate the policy of the editor *vis-à-vis* the gender of its reviewers mainly by focusing on the part played by his wife.

With Murry literature was immediately reintroduced. In a farewell note Greenwood explains that the weekly's reverting to its former self, that is as a largely literary publication, was in the best interest of the paper since it is 'the form with which it is most closely associated in the public mind' (March 1919).

The handing over of the editorship to John Middleton Murry instilled the new editor and the people immediately surrounding him with a feeling bordering on euphoria.[43] For Murry it meant financial security as he was first offered a salary of £800 and, from 1 January 1920 onwards, that was raised to £1,000.[44] T.S. Eliot was invited to become the second assistant editor but he decided to stay on at the bank when his bosses promised him 'some new work ... of an interesting and important kind' and a salary rise.[45] Besides, he argued, 'in writing

---

[40] His editorship of the *Athenaeum* is not mentioned in the *DNB*-entry devoted to his life.

[41] See Cherry A. Hankin, ed., *Letters Between Katherine Mansfield and John Middleton Murry*, London: Virago, 1988, p. 413. See also Valerie Eliot, ed., *The Letters of T.S. Eliot, 1898–1922*, vol. I, London: Faber & Faber, p. 276, though she identified the 'rich man' as Arthur Rowntree.

[42] Murry himself edited his wife's reviews posthumously in 1930 as *Novels and Novelists*, London: Constable, 1930; Clare Hanson edited *The Critical Writings of Katherine Mansfield*, New York: St Martin's Press, 1987. Leila Borsnan wrote extensively on Virginia Woolf's journalism in *Reading Virginia Woolf's Essays and Journalism*, Edinburgh: Edinburgh University Press, 1997.

[43] Middleton reported on the enthusiasm shown by Sidney Waterlow, Bertrand Russell and E.M. Forster in his letters to Mansfield (see for example Hankin, ed., *Letters Between*, p.210)

[44] Hankin, ed., *Letters Between*, p. 241.

[45] Eliot, ed., *The Letters of T.S. Eliot*, vol. I, pp. 279–80. This was Eliot's account of the facts. Goldie, quite correctly, juxtaposes this to Murry's explanation which stresses his unsuccessful attempts to get a salary raise of £500 for Eliot; see David Goldie, *A Critical Difference. T.S. Eliot and John Middleton Murry in English Literary Criticism*, Oxford: Clarendon Press, 1998, p. 39.

for a paper one is writing for a public, and the best work, the only work that in the end counts, is written for oneself'.[46] Instead, therefore, Aldous Huxley was offered the job. Yet Eliot valued the connection with the *Athenaeum*; he certainly appreciated this more than, for instance, the three-year tutorial class in Modern English Literature which he gave at Southhall starting in 1916.[47] In a letter to his mother he commented: 'I can make more money as well as more reputation from the *Athenaeum*'. Eliot was to do a great amount of writing for the *Athenaeum*: he contributed 'a longish critical review about three weeks out of four'[48] and many shorter notices. One such short notice remained anonymous, perhaps because it partly referred to his own poetry.[49] But he stopped writing for the weekly after the publication of the second part of his paper 'The Perfect Critic' in July 1920, possibly because of the tension which had arisen between him and Murry after the publication of that paper.[50]

Murry seems to have surrounded himself with a select group of male contributors. Indeed, the number of women writing for the *Athenaeum* in the Murry period is amazingly small when one compares that to the pre-war period. The list of contributors for the first half of 1919 mentions thirty-one names, two of which refer to women: Virginia Woolf and Katherine Mansfield. The second half lists sixty-two names, four of which belonged to women. The two new names, Sylvia Lynd and Mrs H.T. Smith, however, have very few reviews to their names. There were more contributions by women in 1920, when Camilla Jebb joined the team to deal with the short notes on fiction.

Katherine Mansfield, wrote profusely for the *Athenaeum*. In fact she devoted the larger part of the little time she had left to live to raising the quality of the journal which, she thought, would establish her husband's *renommée* as an editor and a literary critic. From the beginning, Murry also thought of inviting Virginia Woolf to contribute, though we may gather from Mansfield's letters that it was she who first broached the subject with Woolf.[51] The contributions by other women are negligible. The group which now controlled the *Athenaeum* was essentially a literary and a male one. This naturally narrowed the scope of the paper. If, before the war, the *Athenaeum* was known for the enormous diversity of its subjects covered by an equally diverse group of experts, that situation had now changed entirely. David Goldie calls the weekly 'a hybrid': 'on the surface it maintains the form and the comprehensiveness of the Victorian Review, but in its contents it displays the radical uncertainty of the

---

[46] Eliot, ed., *The Letters of T.S. Eliot*, vol. I, p. 285.
[47] See Ronald Schuchard on the Extension lectures, 'T.S. Eliot as an Extension Lecturer, 1916–19', *Review of English Studies*, New Series, xxv, 98 (May 1974), pp. 163–73.
[48] Eliot, ed., *The Letters of T.S. Eliot*, vol. I, p. 315.
[49] I am referring to his review of *Coterie* (3 October 1919) where he mentions 'the curious shapes of Mr. Eliot and Mr. Pound'.
[50] There is very little to clarify what happened between the two. David Goldie refers to strained relationships in his book on the two men (see Goldie, *A Critical Difference*, p. 89).
[51] Vincent O'Sullivan and Margaret Scott, ed., *The Collected Letters of Katherine Mansfield*, Oxford: Clarendon Press, 1987, vol. II, p. 302.

post-war world'.[52] But it was different in other fundamental respects as well. Firstly, literature became a much more narrowly defined category and one that needed special treatment. The literary critics who now wrote for the *Athenaeum* did not think of literature as a 'soft' subject easily relegated to women with time on their hands but no academic background.[53] They were on a mission which was to change the face of English literary criticism. This was obvious from the choice of reviewers, the tone of the reviews and the disappearance of the amateur literary critic from the pages of the *Athenaeum*.[54] Secondly, the editor abandoned all attempts at presenting his reading public with unbiased criticism. Whereas it used to be the editor who decided who was going to review which book under MacColl and Greenwood, it now appeared that authors, often friends of the editor, felt free to suggest a suitable reviewer for their own publications. Thus, T.S. Eliot asked Murry to send his *The Sacred Wood* to Leonard Woolf for review, immediately afterwards notifying Woolf of the fact so as to make sure Woolf knew he was in control.[55] A favourable review duly appeared in the *Athenaeum* of 17 December 1920. And Eliot was not the only one to follow this procedure. Katherine Mansfield did the same thing in at least one case, when she absolutely forbade that Virginia Woolf should write on her work.[56]

Mansfield's strong emotions evoked by the paper and everything that appeared in it are quite unique. In those last years of her life she lived a fairly lonely life. Ill with tuberculosis and often separated from her adored husband, she seems to have considered the *Athenaeum* as their child, the fruit of their love,[57] which she, too, could nurse and cherish even from a distance. She devoted all her time and attention to the weekly as if it were the most precious thing on earth: 'this makes me keener than ever on our paper (*our* in humility, love – its your hat – yes I know) ... Oh, I feel our responsibility is so tremendous'.[58] She worked incessantly trying to get the reviews ready in time: '[t]omorrow I am buried alive under the Athenaeum' she wrote to her friend Violet Schiff on 28 June 1920.[59] And she wanted those contributons to be top quality: 'If you knew how I have this paper at heart! Turn down anything of mine you dont care for'.[60] Yet she received little in return. The editors of Mansfield's letters rightly noticed how Murry sometimes even flagrantly ignored his wife's expertise. Thus, he would for instance 'ask Sydney Waterlow to write on the centenary of George Eliot when his wife had been discussing the same subject with Virginia Woolf for *her* essay in the *Times Literary Supplement*', and it was Murry who reviewed Chekhov's

---

[52] Goldie, *A Critical Difference*, p. 37.

[53] This, according to Vincent O'Sullivan might explain why Murry sent his own wife such dull fiction *Collected Letters*, vol. III, p. 8.

[54] Dr Marie Stopes could still write a review now and then, but Murry not Charlotte Stopes dealt with Shakespeare.

[55] Eliot, ed., *The Letters of T.S. Eliot*, vol. I, p. 415.

[56] O'Sullivan and Scott, *Collected Letters*, vol. IV, p. 124.

[57] She also named one of the new kittens Athenaeum (later abbreviated as Athy) in April 1919 (See O'Sullivan and Scott, *Collected Letters*, vol. II, p. 310.

[58] O'Sullivan and Scott, *Collected Letters*, vol. III, p. 84.

[59] O'Sullivan and Scott, *Collected Letters, 1920–1921*, vol. IV, p. 17.

[60] Ibid., 1919–1920, vol. III, p. 55.

novels while she frequently had to comment 'on ephemeral novels'.[61] There is no evidence, the editors continue, that these decisions irritated her.[62] This, however, is not entirely true. She was seriously disappointed by Waterlow's article on George Eliot even claiming that she felt 'she must stand up for [her] SEX': 'he is ungenerous. She was a deal more than that. Her English, warm, ruddy quality is hardly mentioned. She was *big*, even though she was "heavy" too.'[63] Also, Mansfield's attitude to writing reviews as opposed to concentrating on her creative writing very much echoes Eliot's opinion quoted above. Yet, she was and certainly felt bound, as the wife of the editor, to write for the *Athenaeum* in spite of her misgivings. Mansfield discussed 129 novelists (sometimes twice) in the 1919–1920 period, ending, if one lists the names alphabetically, with the totally unknown Patience Worth. But was it worth her patience? In her letter to Murry of December 1920 she clearly recorded her feelings with regard to the sacrifices she felt she had to make:

> Reviewing is on my chest – AND a sense of GUILT the whole week! However it can't be helped. I'll win out and then don't want to read another novel for – But isn't it grim to be reviewing Benson when one might be writing one's own stories which one will never have time to write on the best showing! [64]

He, for his part, tried to keep her on the job by pointing out how much he needed her. In his letter of 13 November 1920, Murry had told her that 'What I feel, and what a great many other people feel, is that as long as your novel page is there, there can't be a really bad number of the *Athenaeum*'.[65]

And then she suffered from the friction and the strained relationships her reviews often caused. Mansfield's reviews contain an honest and personal evaluation of the fiction she was asked to discuss. As a result she often exposed herself to the rancour of her friends and colleagues. When she reviewed Virginia Woolf's *Night and Day*, for instance, Murry had to explain the review to the author who obviously resented the way Mansfield had discussed her novel. It soured the relationship between the two women: 'I know just how angry Virginia et cie are with me. They ought not to be for indeed I tried my best to be friendly & erred on the side of kindness'. [66]

Reviewing, therefore, not only encroached upon her time, it also added more worry to her already strained nerves. It should be noted, however, that Mansfield could also truly enjoy a well-written review whether this was her own or someone else's. In November 1919 she wrote to Murry: 'V.W[oolf] does it

---

[61] Ibid., vol. II, p. xiii.
[62] Ibid.
[63] Ibid., vol. III, p. 110.
[64] Hankin, ed., *Letters Between*, p. 328.
[65] Ibid., p. 210.
[66] *Collected Letters*, vol. III, p. 122. A more detailed analysis of the relationship between these two writers is presented in Angela Smith's recent publication *Katherine Mansfield & Virginia Woolf. A Public of Two*, Oxford: Clarendon, 1999. One of her reviews also upset May Sinclair (Hankin, ed., *Letters Between*, p. 286)

very well. Aint she a snob? But she does it very well in her intellectual snobbish way'.[67] The profession or the art of the reviewer was one she, like her colleagues on the *Athenaeum* staff, liked to comment on. Clive Bell, Murry, T.S. Eliot and other male colleagues had set forth their views in signed essays.[68] Mansfield for her part had the editorial at her disposal, and used its anonymity to assume the male point of view of the reviewer and to reprimand critics who praised too easily and too lavishly: 'we venture, with an esquire's modesty, to offer them a stout resolution to buckle on ... a little less charity, a little less tenderness and sympathy and desire to help the weak' (*Athenaeum*, 27 August 1920).

By the end of 1920 the *Athenaeum* had probably achieved what, according to Goldie, its new crew had wanted it to do: 'orienting modernist ideas in the mainstream of literary culture'. It had changed, too, from a paper which aimed for objectivity and impartiality to what was effectively a critical review in which writers discussed each other's work in public, a luxury position financially supported by a reading public which was, by and large, left out of the picture. The *Athenaeum* had thereby acquired some of the characteristics of the little reviews. Financial difficulties were bound to pursue its editor.[69] His position became untenable when exacerbated by the disappearance of his prize contributors, Katherine Mansfield and T.S. Eliot.

It seems fair to conclude, therefore, that Mansfield herself valued the art of reviewing and was convinced that 'writing a good review' needed an intelligent, perspicacious critic but that there were pitfalls to the job: it produced enemies, appreciation of the critic's work by the general public was non-existent, and even her colleagues were chary with their praise. She was also realistic enough to know that reviewing had never yet made a writer famous, hence her frustration when she had to neglect her own story-writing as a result of her involvement with the *Athenaeum*.

Once she gave up reviewing at the end of 1920 everything went downhill for the *Athenaeum*. She stopped her contributions on account of her declining health and Murry, when he joined her in Menton for Christmas later that year, decided to give up the editorship of the *Athenaeum* so as to be able to stay

---

[67] *Collected Letters*, vol. III, p. 118.

[68] See for instance Clive Bell, 'Criticism', 26 September 1919 and J.M. Murry, 'The Social Duty of the Critic', 7 November 1919. T.S. Eliot's two-tiered article 'The Perfect Critic', (9 July and 23 July 1920) is discussed at length by Goldie (*A Critical Difference*, pp. 60ff.).

[69] He had already been left a bankrupt after the débâcle of *Rhythm* and, as his biographer remarked, Murry was not the man to compromise with Fleet Street methods in order to compete with other periodical publications (F.A. Lea, *The Life of John Middleton Murry*, London: Methuen, 1959, pp. 65ff.)

with his wife. The impression one is left with, when juxtaposing these facts, is that the post-war success and the survival of the *Athenaeum* was, to a certain extent, dependent on Katherine Mansfield's commitment to this weekly. She had invested a huge amount of energy into this venture which she obviously believed would further her husband's career and establish his reputation as an editor. Her capitulation sounded the death-knell of the weekly.

Selected Bibliography

Abbot, C.C., ed., *The Letters of Gerard Manley Hopkins to Richard Watson Dixon*, London: Oxford University Press, 1935.

Aldington, Richard, *Life for Life's Sake. A Book of Reminiscences*, London: Cassell, 1968.

Altick, Richard D., *The English Common Reader*, Chicago and London: University of Chicago Press, 1957.

Andersen, Bonnie and Judith P. Zinsser, *A History of their Own*, vol. II. Harmondsworth: Penguin, 1988.

Ardis, Ann, *New Women, New Novels. Feminism and Early Modernism*, New Brunswick and London: Rutgers University Press, 1990.

Arlen, Shelley, "'For Love of an Idea": Jane Ellen Harrison, heretic and humanist', *Women's History Review*, 5:2 (1996), pp. 165–90.

Armstrong, Isobel, *Victorian Scrutinies. Reviews of Poetry 1830–1870*, London: Athlone Press, 1972.

———, *Victorian Poetry. Poetry, Poetics and Politics*, London: Routledge, 1993.

Asquith, Betty, *Lady Dilke. A Biography*, London: Chatto & Windus, 1969.

Bainton, George, *The Art of Authorship. Literary Reminiscences, Methods of work, and advice to Young beginners, Personally contributed by leading authors of the day*, London: Clarke, 1890.

Baring, Anne and Jules Cashford, *The Myth of the Goddess. Evolution of an image*, London: BCA, 1991.

Barrett Browning, Elizabeth, *Aurora Leigh*, 1856; rpt. *The Works of Elizabeth Barrett Browning*, Karen Hill, ed., Ware: Wordsworth, 1994, pp. 374–539.

Beckson, Karl, Ian Fletcher, Lawrence W. Markert and John Stokes, *Arthur Symons: A Bibliography*, Greensboro, NC: ELT-Press, 1990.

Beetham, Margaret, *A Magazine of her Own? Domesticity and Desire in the Woman's Magazine, 1800–1914*, London and New York, 1996.

Bennett, E.A., *Journalism for Women, A practical guide*, London & New York: John Lane, 1898.

Benstock, Shari, *Women of the Left Bank. Paris, 1900–1940*, Austin: University of Texas Press, 1986.

Bicknell, John W., ed., *Selected Letters of Leslie Stephen*, vol. II, 1882–1904, Basingstoke and London: Macmillan, 1996.

Björnhovde, Gerd, *Rebellious Structures. Women Writers and the Crisis of the Novel 1880–1900*, Oslo: Norwegian University Press, 1987.

Booth, Bradford A. and Ernest Mehew, eds, *The Letters of Robert Louis Stevenson*, 8 vols, New Haven and London: Yale University Press, 1994–1995.

Boumelha, Penny, 'The Woman of Genius and the Woman of Grub Street: Figures of the Female Writer in British *Fin-de-siècle* Fiction', *ELT*, 40:2 (1997), pp. 164–80.

Bourdieu, Pierre, *The Field of Cultural Production. Essays on Art and Literature*, Randal Johnson, ed., Cambridge: Polity Press, 1993.

Bradbury, Malcolm and James McFarlane, eds, *Modernism. A Guide to European Literature 1890–1930*, Harmondsworth: Penguin, 1976.

Brake, Laurel, *Subjugated Knowledges. Journalism, Gender & Literature in the Nineteenth Century*, Basingstoke: Macmillan, 1994.

Brandon, Ruth, *The New Women and Old Men. Love, Sex and the Woman Question*, London: Secker & Warburg, 1990.

Briggs, Julia, *A Woman of Passion. The Life of E. Nesbit 1858–1924*, London: Hutchinson, 1987.

Brooker, Peter, ed., *Modernism/Postmodernism*, London: Longman, 1992.

Caine, Barbara, *Victorian Feminists*, Oxford: Oxford University Press, 1992.

Casey, Ellen Miller, 'Weekly Reviews of Fiction: The *Athenaeum* vs the *Spectator* and the *Saturday Review*', *Victorian Periodicals Review*, 23:1 (Spring 1990), pp. 8–12.

———, 'Edging Women Out', *Victorian Studies*, 39:2 (Winter 1996) , pp. 151–71.

Cevasco, George, ed., *The 1890s. An Encyclopedia of British Literature, Art, and Culture*, New York and London: Garland, 1993.

Chodorov, Nancy, *The Reproduction of Mothering. Psychoanalysis and the Sociology of Gender*, Berkeley: University of California Press, 1978.

Clarke, Bruce, *Dora Marsden and Early Modernism. Gender, Individualism, Science*, Ann Arbor: University of Michigan, 1996.

Clarke, Norma, *Ambitious Heights. Writing, Friendship, Love – The Jewsbury Sisters, Felicia Hemans, and Jane Welsh Carlyle*, London: Routledge, 1990.

Clifford, Lucy, *Mrs. Keith's Crime. A Record*, London: R. Bentley, 1885.

———, *Love-Letters from a Worldly Woman*, London: Arnold, 1891.

Cohen, Morton, ed., *Rudyard Kipling to Rider Haggard. The Record of a Friendship*, Rutherford: Fairleigh Dickinson University Press, 1965.

Comyns-Carr, Alice, *Reminiscences*, London: Hutchinson, n.d.

Connell, John, *W.E. Henley*, London: Constable, 1949.

Coppens, E.C., *Paul Fredericq*, Gent: Liberaal Archief, 1990.

Cornford, F.M., 'Jane Ellen Harrison', *Dictionary of National Biography*.

Creighton, Louise, *Life and Letters of Mandell Creighton*, 2 vols, London: Longmans, 1904.

Cross, Nigel, *The Common Writer. Life in Nineteenth-Century Grub Street*, Cambridge: Cambridge University Press, 1985.

Demoor, Marysa, ed., *Friends over the Ocean. Andrew Lang's Letters to his American Friends*, Gent: Universa, 1989.

———, ed., *Dear Stevenson. Letters from Andrew Lang to Robert Louis Stevenson with Five Letters from Stevenson to Lang*, Louvain: Peeters, 1990.

Derrida, Jacques, *L'Oreille de l'autre*, Montmagny: VLB Editeur, 1984.

Dixon, Ella Hepworth, *As I Knew Them*, London: Hutchinson, 1930.

Duby, Georges and Michelle Perrot, Michelle, eds, *A History of Women*, part IV, Geneviève Fraisse and Michelle Perrot, eds, *Emerging Feminism from Revolution to World War*, Belknap: Harvard, 1993.

Earnest, Ernest, *Silas Weir Mitchell*, Philadelphia: University of Pennsylvania Press, 1950.

Edel, Leon, *Henry James. The Master 1901–1916*, London: Hart-Davis, 1972.

———, ed., *Henry James Letters*, 4 vols, Cambridge, Mass.: Harvard University Press, 1974–1984.

Eliot, T.S., ed., *Literary Essays of Ezra Pound*, London: Faber & Faber, 1960.

Eliot, Valerie, ed., *The Letters of T.S. Eliot*, London: Faber & Faber, 1988.

Ellegård, Alvar, *The Readership of the Periodical Press in Mid-Victorian Britain*, Göteborg: Göteborgs univetsitets årsskrify, 1957.

Elwin, Malcolm, *Old Gods Falling*, New York: Macmillan, 1939.

Ferguson, Marjorie, *Forever Feminine: Women's Magazines and the Cult of Femininity*, Aldershot: Gower, 1983.

Flint, Kate, *The Woman Reader 1837–1914*, Oxford: Oxford University Press, 1993,

Forster, Margaret, *Elizabeth Barrett Browning. A Biography*, New York: Doubleday, 1988.

Frykstedt, Monica Correa, *Geraldine Jewsbury's 'Athenaeum' Reviews*, Uppsala: Uppsala University Press, 1986.

————, 'Geraldine Jewsbury's *Athenaeum* Reviews: A Mirror of Mid-Victorian Attitudes to Fiction', *Victorian Periodicals Review*, 23:1 (Spring 1990), pp. 13–25.

————, 'Retrieving a Synchronic Perspective of Victorian Culture: The *Athenaeum* as a Research Tool', *Victorian Periodicals Review*, 25:2 (Summer 1993), pp. 87–92.

Gilbert, Susan and Sandra Gubar, *The Madwoman in the Attic. The Woman Writer and the Nineteenth Century Literary Imagination*, New Haven and London: Yale University Press, 1979.

————, *No Man's Land. The Place of the Woman Writer in the Twentieth Century*, volume I, *The War of the Words*, New Haven and London: Yale University Press, 1988, volume II, *Sexchanges*. New Haven and London: Yale University Press, 1989.

————, *The Norton Anthology of Literature by Women. The Traditions in English*, New York: Norton, 1996.

Goldie, David, *A Critical Difference. T.S. Eliot and John Middleton Murry in English Literary Criticism 1919–1928*, Oxford: Clarendon Press, 1998.

Gross, John, *The Rise and Fall of the Man of Letters. Aspects of Literary Life since 1800*, Penguin: Harmondsworth, 1991.

Gunn, Peter, *Vernon Lee. Violet Paget, 1855–1935*, London: Oxford University Press, 1964.

Gwynn, Stephen and Gertrude Tuckwell, *The Life of the Rt. Hon. Sir Charles W. Dilke*, 2 vols, London: Murray, 1917.

Haight, Gordon, ed., *The George Eliot Letters*, 9 vols, London: Oxford University Press, 1954.

Hake, Thomas and Arthur Compton-Rickett, *The Life and Letters of Theodore Watts-Dunton*, 2 vols, London: Jack, 1916.

Hankin, Cherry A., ed., *The Letters of John Middleton Murry to Katherine Mansfield*, London: Constable, 1983.

————, ed., *Letters between Katherine Mansfield and John Middleton Murry*, London: Virago, 1988.

Hanscombe, Gillian and Virginia L. Smyers, *Writing for their Lives. The Modernist Women 1910–1940*, London: The Women's Press, 1987.

Hanson, Clare, ed., *The Critical Writings of Katherine Mansfield*, New York: St Martin's Press, 1987.

Harrison, Jane Ellen, *Ancient Art and Ritual*, New York: Holt, 1913.

————, 'Homo Sum', *Alpha and Omega*, London: Sidgwick, 1915.

————, *Reminiscences of a Student's Life*, London: Hogarth Press, 1925.

Hermans, Theo, 'Breekpunt, Breuklijn, Breukvlak', *Vertaalwetenschap*, André Lefevere and Rita Vanderauwera, eds, Leuven: Acco, 1979, pp. 107–11.

Hewlett, Henry G., *Henry Fothergill Chorley. Autobiography, Memoir and Letters*, 2 vols, London: Bentley, 2 vols, 1873.

Hiller, Mary Ruth, 'The Identification of Authors: The Great Victorian Enigma', J. Don Vann and R.T. VanArsdel, eds, *Victorian Periodicals. A Guide to Research*, New York: Modern Language Association, 1978, pp. 123–148.

Horstman, Allen, *Victorian Divorce*, London and Sydney: Croom Helm, 1985.

Hughes, Linda, '"Fair Hymen holdeth hid a world of woes": Myth and Marriage in Poems by "Graham R.Tomson" (Rosamund Marriott Watson)', *Victorian Poetry*, 32:2 (Summer 1994), pp. 97–120.

————, 'Rosamund Marriott Watson', *The 1890s. An Encyclopedia of British Literature, Art, and Culture*, George Cevasco, ed., New York and London: Garland, 1993.

————, 'A Female Aesthete at the Helm: *Sylvia's Journal* and "Graham R. Tomson", 1893–1894', *Victorian Periodicals Review*, 29:2 (Summer 1996), pp.173–87.

Humphry, Mrs, *Manners for Women*, London: Ward, n.d.

Israel, Kali, 'Writing Inside the Kaleidoscope: Re-Representing Victorian Women Public Figures', *Gender & History*, 2:1 (Spring 1990), pp. 40–8.

Jenkins, Roy, *Sir Charles Dilke. A Victorian Tragedy*, London: Collins, 1958.

Jerome, Jerome K., *My Life and Times*, Bungay: Richard Clay, 1926.

Krontiris, Tina, *Oppositional Voices. Women as Writers and Translators of Literature in the English Renaissance*, London and New York: Routledge, 1992.

Lang, Andrew, *Old Friends. Essays in Epistolary Parody*, London: Longman, 1892.

Laurence, Dan H., ed., *Collected Letters of G.B. Shaw*, 2 vols, London: Max Reinhardt, 1965–1970.

Lea, F.A., *The Life of John Middleton Murry*, London: Methuen, 1959.

Ledger, Sally, 'The New Woman, *The Bostonians* and the Gender of Modernity', *Essays from ESSE, Barcelona English Language and Literature Studies*, Marysa Demoor and Jane Moore, eds, 3:3 (1996), pp. 55–62.

————, *The New Woman. Fiction and feminism at the fin de siècle*, Manchester and New York: Manchester University Press, 1997.

Lee, Vernon, *Miss Brown*, London: Blackwood, 1884.

————, *Vernon Lee's Letters with a Preface by her executor*, L. Cooper-Willis, ed., priv. printed, 1937.

Leighton, Angela, *Victorian Women Poets. Writing Against the Heart*, Hemel Hempstead: Harvester Wheatsheaf, 1992.

Levenson, Michael, *A Genealogy of Modernism A Study of Literary Doctrine 1908–1922*, Cambridge: Cambridge University Press, 1984.

Levine, Philippa, *Feminist Lives in Victorian England. Private Roles and Public Commitment*, Cambridge: Blackwell, 1990.

Lewis, Jane, *Before the Vote Was Won. Arguments for and against women's suffrage*, New York and London: Routledge, 1987.

Liddle, Dallas, 'Salesmen, Sportsmen, Mentors: Anonymity and Mid-Victorian Theories of Journalism', *Victorian Studies*, 41:1 (Autumn 1997), pp. 31–68.

Low, Frances, *Press Work for Women. A Textbook for the Young Woman Journalist*, London: Upcott, 1904.

McAleer, Edward C., *Learned Lady. Letters from Robert Browning to Mrs. Thomas Fitzgerald 1876–1889*, Cambridge, Mass.: Harvard University Press, 1966.

McKenzie, D.F, 'Bibliography and the Sociology of Texts', *The Panizzi Lectures*, London: 1986.

McLynn, Frank, *Robert Louis Stevenson. A Biography*, London: Hutchinson, 1993.

Mansfield, Katherine, *Novels and Novelists*, John Middleton Murry, ed., London: Constable, 1930.

Manton, Jo, *Elizabeth Garrett Anderson*, London: Methuen, 1965.

Marandon, Sylvaine, *L'oeuvre poétique de Mary Robinson*, Bordeaux: priv. printed, 1967.

Marchand, Leslie, *The Athenaeum. A Mirror of Victorian Society*, Chapel Hill: North Carolina University Press, 1941.

Markham, Violet R., *May Tennant. A Portrait*, London: Falcon Press, 1949.

Mattheisen, Paul F., Arthur C. Young and Pierre Coustillas, eds, *The Collected letters of George Gissing*, 1863–1880, vol. I, Athens, Ohio: Ohio University Press, 1990.

Meynell, Viola, *Alice Meynell. A Memoir*, 1929, London: Jonathan Cape, 1947.

Michie, Helena, *The Flesh Made Word*, Oxford: Oxford University Press, 1987.

Mitchell, Sally, 'Careers for Girls: Writing Trash', *Victorian Periodicals Review*, 15:3 (Fall 1992), pp. 109–13.

Morgan, Charles, *The House of Macmillan, 1843–1943*, London: Macmillan, 1943.

Munby, Arthur, *Man of two worlds. The Life and Diaries of Arthur J. Munby 1828–1910*, London: Murray, 1972.

Nevill, Ralph, *London Clubs. Their History and Treasures*, London: Chatto & Windus, 1911.

Newton, Judith, *Starting Over. Feminism and the Politics of Cultural Critique*, Ann Arbor: University of Michigan Press, 1997.

Nicholls, David, *The Lost Prime Minister. A Life of Sir Charles Dilke*, London and Rio Grande: The Hambledon Press, 1995.

Nunn, Pamela Gerrish, *Victorian Women Artists*, London: Women's Press, 1987.

Orr, Clarissa Campbell, *Women in the Victorian Art World*, Manchester and New York: Manchester University Press, 1995.

O'Sullivan, Vincent and Margaret Scott, *The Collected Letters of Katherine Mansfield*, 4 vols, Oxford: Clarendon Press, 1987–1996.

Paglia, Camila, *Sexual Personae. Art and Decadence from Nefertiti to Emily Dickinson*, New Haven: Yale University Press, 1990.

Peacock, Sandra J., *Jane Ellen Harrison. The Mask and the Self*, New Haven and London: Yale University Press, 1988.

Perloff, Marjorie, *The Futurist Moment: Avant-Garde, Avant Guerre, and the Language of Rupture*, Chicago: University of Chicago Press, 1986.

Phillips, K.J., 'Jane Harrison and Modernism', *Journal of Modern Literature*, 17:4 (Spring 1991), pp. 465–76.

Prettejohn, Elizabeth, 'Aesthetic Value and the Professionalization of Victorian Art Criticism', *Journal of Victorian Culture*, 2:1 (Spring 1997), pp. 71–94.

Robbins, Ruth, 'Vernon Lee: Decadent woman?', in Stokes, ed., *Fin de Siècle/ Fin du Globe*, pp. 139–61.

Rose, June, *Marie Stopes and the Sexual Revolution*, London: Faber, 1992.

Rosenberg, Beth Carole and Jeanne Dubino, eds, *Virginia Woolf and the Essay*, Basingstoke: Macmillan, 1997.

Rubinstein, *Before the Suffragettes: Women's emancipation in the 1890s*, Hemel Hempstead: Harvester Weatsheaf, 1986.

————, *A Different World for Women. The Life of Millicent Garrett Fawcett*, Hemel Hempstead: Harvester 1991.

Sackville-West, Vita, 'The Women Poets of the Seventies', *The Eighteen-Seventies. Essays by the Fellows of the Royal Society of Literature*, Harley Granvile-Barker, ed., Cambridge University Press, 1929.

Schuchard, Ronald, 'T.S. Eliot as an Extension Lecturer, 1916–1919', *Review of English Studies*, New Series, 25:98 (May 1974), pp. 163–73.

Scott, J.W. Robertson, *The Life and Death of a Newspaper*, London: Methuen, 1952.

Scott, Rosemary, 'Poetry in the *Athenaeum*: 1851 and 1881', *Victorian Periodicals Review*, vol. XXIX (Spring 1996), pp. 19–32.

Shackleton, John Richard, *Two Early Female Economists: Jane Marcet and Harriet Martineau*, London: Polytechnic of Central London, Faculty of Social Sciences and Business Studies, 1988.

Sharp, Elizabeth A., ed., *Women's Voices. An Anthology of the Most Characteristic Poems by English, Scotch, and Irish Women*, London: Walter Scott, 1887.

Shattock, Joanne and Michael Wolff, eds, *The Victorian Periodical Press: Samplings and Soundings*, Leicester University Press, 1982.

Showalter, Elaine, *A Literature of Their Own. From Charlotte Brontë to Doris Lessing*, London: Virago, 1979.

Sieburth, Richard, *Instigations. Ezra Pound and Remy de Gourmont*, Cambridge, Mass.: Harvard University Press, 1978.

Simon, Sherry, *Gender in Translation. Cultural Identity and the Politics of Transmission*, London: Routledge, 1996.

Small, Ian, 'The Economies of Taste: Literary Markets and Literary Value in the Late Nineteenth Century', *English Literature in Transition*, 39:1 (1996), pp. 7–18.

Smith, Angela, *Katherine Mansfield & Virginia Woolf. A Public of Two*, Oxford: Clarendon, 1999.

Spender, Dale, *Living by the Pen. Early British Women Writers*, New York and London: Teachers College Press, 1992, p.12.

Stark, Susanne, 'Women and Translation in the Nineteenth Century', *New Comparison*, no. 15 (Spring 1993), pp. 34–44.

Stetz, Margaret D., 'Turning Points : E. Nesbit', *Turn-of-the-Century Women*, 6 (1987), pp. 2–10.

Stewart, Jessie, *Jane Ellen Harrison. A Portrait from Letters*, London: Merlin Press, 1959.

Stokes, John, ed., *Find de Siècle/ Fin du Globe*, London: Macmillan, 1992.

Sutherland, John, *The Longman Companion to Victorian Fiction*, Burnt Mill: Longman, 1988.

Swindells, Julia, *Victorian Writing & Working Women*, Cambridge: Polity Press, 1985.

Tener, Robert and Malcolm Woodfield, eds, *A Victorian Spectator. Uncollected Writings of R.H. Hutton*, Bedminster: Bristol Press, 1989.

Thomas, William Beech, *The Story of the Spectator 1828–1928*, London: Methuen, 1928.

Thompson, Nicola Diane, *Reviewing Sex. Gender and the Reception of Victorian Novels*, Houndmills: Macmillan, 1996.

Trollope, Anthony, *An Autobiography*, Oxford: Blackwell, 1929.

Tuchman, Gaye with Nina Fortin, *Edging Women Out. Victorian Novelists, publishers, and Social Change*, London: Routledge, 1989.

Van den Broeck, Raymond, ed., *Literatuur van Elders. Over het vertalen en de studie van vertaalde literatuur in het Nederlands*, Leuven: Acco, 1988.

Vann, J. Don and Rosemary T. VanArsdel, *Victorian Periodicals. A Guide to Research*, New York: Modern Language Association, 1978.

Venuti, Lawrence, ed., *Rethinking Translation. Discourse, Subjectivity, Ideology*, London: Routledge, 1992.

Vicinus, Martha, *Independent Women. Work & Community for Single Women 1850–1920*, London: Virago, 1985.

Webster, Augusta, *The Prometheus Bound of Aeschylus, Literally translated into English Verse*, Thomas Webster, ed., London and Cambridge: Macmillan, 1866.

———, 'A Castaway', *Portraits*, 1870; rptd *Victorian Women Poets. An Anthology*, Angela Leighton and Margaret Reynolds, eds, Oxford: Blackwell, 1995, pp. 417–50.

———, *A Letter to the Rt. Hon. John Bright, M.P. from A Lady in 'The Gallery'*, London: Matthews, 1876.

———, *Parliamentary Franchise for Women rate payers*, London, 1878

———, *A Housewife's Opinion*, London, 1879.

———, *Mother and Daughter*, London: Macmillan, 1895.

Whiting, Lilian, *Kate Field. A Record*, London: Sampson Low, Marston & Co. Ltd, 1899.

———, *Louise Chandler Moulton: Poet and Friend*, London: Hodder & Stoughton, 1910.

Willis, Irene Cooper, ed., *Vernon Lee's Letters*, privately printed, 1937.

Wilson, Edmund, 'The Ambiguity of Henry James', 1934; rptd In *The Triple Thinkers* (1938), and in *The Question of Henry James*, F.W. Duprez, ed., London, 1957, pp. 172–201

Wingerd, Kathy, *New Voices in Victorian Criticism: Five Unrecognized Contributors in Victorian Periodicals*, Kent State University: UMI Dissertation Services, 1987.

Woolf, Virginia, 'Professions for Women', 1942, *Norton Anthology of Literature by Women*, Sandra Gilbert and Susan Gubar, eds, New York, London: Norton, 1996, pp. 1345–8.

———, *A Room of One's Own*, London: Hogarth Press, 1959.

———, *The Diary of Virginia Woolf*, Anne Olivier Bell and Andrew McNeillie, eds, New York: Harcourt Brace Jovanovich, 1978, vol. II, pp. 106–7.

Woolford, John, 'Periodicals and the practice of literary criticism, 1855–64', *The Victorian Periodical Press*, Joanne Shattock and Michael Wolff, eds, pp. 109–142.

Zach, Natan, 'Imagism and Vorticism', Bradbury and McFarlane, eds, *Modernism*, pp. 228–2.

Index